Improving Leadership Performance

SECOND EDITION

Improving Leadership Performance

Interpersonal skills for effective leadership

SECOND EDITION

Peter L. Wright and David S. Taylor

University of Bradford Management Centre

Prentice Hall
NEW YORK   LONDON   TORONTO   SYDNEY   TOKYO   SINGAPORE

First published 1984
This edition published 1994 by
Prentice Hall International (UK) Ltd
Campus 400, Maylands Avenue
Hemel Hempstead
Hertfordshire, HP2 7EZ
A division of
Simon & Schuster International Group

Typeset in 10/12pt Century Old Style
by Keyset Composition, Colchester, Essex

Printed and bound in Great Britain by
T. J. Press (Padstow) Ltd, Cornwall

Library of Congress Cataloging-in-Publication Data

Wright, Peter L.
    Improving leadership performance : Interpersonal skills for
effective leadership / Peter L. Wright
and David S. Taylor. -- 2nd ed.
        p.   cm.
    Includes bibliographical references and index.
    ISBN 0-13-043779-4
    1. Leadership.   2. Interpersonal skills.   I. Taylor, David S.   II. Title.
HD57.7.W75   1994
658.4'092--dc20   93-34929
                                                                   CIP

British Library Cataloguing in Publication Data

A catalogue record for this book is available from
the British Library

ISBN 0-13-043779-4

1 2 3 4 5   98 97 96 95 94

Contents

Preface to the second edition

Since the publication of *Improving Leadership Performance* ten years ago, interest in the field of managerial interpersonal skills training has continued to grow.[1] The Bradford Approach to interpersonal skills training has been applied in several new areas, including lateral communication within organisations, managing group meetings,[2] training interpersonal skills tutors,[3] and, most recently, handling negative emotions in interviews.[4] Research on interpersonal communication at the microskills level continues to be heavily weighted in favour of nonverbal as opposed to verbal communication, partly perhaps because nonverbal behaviour is much easier to study.[5] Nevertheless, there are signs that attempts are being made to redress this balance in recent research studies.[6]

The second edition of *Improving Leadership Performance* has been revised and updated on the basis of such developments. Chapter 1 includes a much wider review of current developments in leadership research and theory. In Chapter 2, the checklist for improving work performance has been extended and the guidelines for its use expanded on the basis of recent research, while Chapter 3 has been updated and a new exercise included at the end of the chapter. A new section on giving information has been included in Chapter 4 and the section on handling emotion has been greatly expanded. In Chapter 5, the section on nonverbal cues of emotion has also been expanded, there are new sections on the nonverbal cues of deception and confidence and on variations in nonverbal cues, and a new exercise on the identification of nonverbal cues at the end of the chapter. Additional methods of structuring interactions are identified in Chapter 6 and a short answer test completes the chapter. Finally, a new integrative exercise is included at the end of Chapter 7 which is designed to provide an opportunity to review the material on verbal leader behaviour from Chapters 4, 6 and 7.

However, the underlying philosophy of the book remains the same. We believe that there are a number of core interpersonal skills which can be used in a wide variety of different types of interaction with other people. Not all of them are likely to be needed in any one situation and some may be counterproductive for some purposes. Nevertheless, each type of interaction will require different combinations or subsets of these skills if they are to be handled well. Thus, managing such interactions effectively requires the ability to perform a wide variety of the core skills and the ability to select from these the particular skills which are most likely to steer the interaction towards a successful conclusion. Our aim in this book is to help managers both to expand the range of interpersonal skills which they can perform well and to increase their ability to identify at any point in an interaction the skills that are most likely to help them to achieve their objectives.

It follows that our approach to interpersonal skills is a developmental one. In the United Kingdom, the term competency has come to mean 'what people need to bring to the job in order to perform aspects of it to the required level'.[7] It may well be that our approach can be used in helping managers to bring their interpersonal skills up to the level deemed necessary in particular occupations or types of organisation. However, that is not our primary concern. We believe that everyone can improve his or her interpersonal skills and that such an improvement can have beneficial effects for both the individual and the organisation. Clearly, everyone cannot be equally good at everything and a high level of competence in one area may compensate for a lack of competence in another. For example, lack of interpersonal skills may be a small price to pay for the contribution made by an otherwise gifted organisational specialist in his or her own field. However, such people might still be able to perform their jobs *better* if they improved their skills, even though they might never reach normally expected levels. Similarly, managers whose interpersonal skills are already above the required level might also be able to enhance their job performance if they too improved their skills even further. Our aim, therefore, is to provide all managers with an opportunity to improve their interpersonal skills, whatever their current level, rather than to make judgements about what levels of skill are satisfactory or unacceptable.

Notes and references

1. For a general review, see B. M. Alban Metcalfe and P. L. Wright (1986), 'Social skills training for managers', in C. Hollin and P. Trower (eds), *Handbook of social skills training, vol 1: Applications across the lifespan*, Pergamon.
2. P. L. Wright (1986), 'A persuasive communication course for Water Authority Management Services Officers', *Interpersonal Skills Training Network Newsletter*, **1**, 16–23 (available from Human Resources Research Group, University of Bradford Management Centre).
3. D. S. Taylor and P. L. Wright (1988), *Developing interpersonal skills through tutored practice*, Prentice Hall; P. L. Wright and D. S. Taylor (1984), 'The development of tutoring skills for interpersonal skills trainers', *Journal of European Industrial Training*, **8**, (6), 27–32; P. L. Wright and D. S. Taylor (1984), 'Hiccups and nightmares: some problems in tutoring role play exercises', *Journal of European Industrial Training*, **8**,(7), 25–31.

4. A training programme designed to help managers to improve their skill in handling emotional interviewees has been developed by Dr Alistair Ostell of the University of Bradford Management Centre.
5. C. A. Callaghan and P. L. Wright (1992), 'Observing leaders at work: an alternative approach to the study of managerial leadership', paper presented at the British Academy of Management Conference, *Management into the 21st Century*, University of Bradford, September; P. L. Wright (1993), 'Interpersonal skills training: interactions between research and practice', paper presented at *6th European Congress on Work and Organizational Psychology*, Alicante, April.
6. See, for example: C. D. Tengler and F. M. Jablin (1983), 'Effects of question type, orientation and sequencing in the employment screening interview', *Communication Monographs*, **50**, 245–63; T. Johnston (1990), 'Leadership skills in work teams', unpublished PhD thesis, University of Bradford Management Centre; C. A. Callaghan (1991), 'Verbal leader behaviour in manager–subordinate interactions', unpublished PhD thesis, University of Bradford Management Centre; S. Baverstock (1993), 'Managing emotion at work: a study of manager–subordinate interactions', paper presented at the British Academy of Management Conference, *The Crafting of Management Research*, Milton Keynes, September; C. A. Callaghan and P. L. Wright (1994), 'Verbal leader behaviour in appraisal interviews: an observational study', paper presented at The British Psychological Society Occupational Psychology Conference, Birmingham, January.
7. P. R. Sparrow (1992), 'Building human resource strategies round competencies: a life cycle model', paper presented at the British Academy of Management Conference, *Management into the 21st Century*, University of Bradford, September.

Preface to the first edition

This book represents a new departure in the study of leadership. We believe that leadership is like most other human activities. The skilful person tends to perform better than an unskilful one. Yet the concept of skills is virtually unused in leadership theory. Early theorists took the view that it was the individual's personality which determined the degree of leadership success. When relatively little progress was made with this approach, theorists turned to the idea that it was what leaders did, their leadership style, rather than what they were, which determined their success. Thus we now have a vast and confusing vocabulary of terms describing the ways leaders behave, such as autocratic, democratic, authoritarian, employee-oriented, person-oriented, task-oriented, to mention only a few of the more common ones. However, the question of leadership skill is rarely, if ever, mentioned. Theorists are very concerned with *what* style or approach leaders should apply in different situations, but not with *how well* they apply them. This we believe is one of the major limitations of modern leadership theory. In this book, we have attempted to overcome this limitation by describing both a framework for the analysis of the interpersonal skills of leadership and methods for their training and development.

Our aim is to help managers to develop the interpersonal skills which they need to fulfil their leadership role effectively. We have no desire to develop a grand theory of leadership. To use an analogy, we would regard ourselves as tool developers rather than theory builders. We would rather supply managers with a set of behavioural tools from which they can select the one most appropriate to handle a particular leadership situation, than develop a grand theory which explains everything but has few real practical implications. Unfortunately, in our view, much of modern leadership theory falls into the latter category. We have taken a different approach to the study of leadership, at least in part, because our original interest was interpersonal skills training rather than leadership itself. Our interest in leadership grew out of what has come to be known as the 'Bradford Approach' to interviewing training. This was initially developed by Gerry Randell and his colleagues in the context of performance appraisal interviews.[1] However, it was later extended by ourselves and others into such areas as grievance, disciplinary and audit interviewing.[2]

The more we extended this work, the more it appeared to us that our basic approach – regarding the effective handling of relationships between people in terms of precisely defined interpersonal skills – was not limited to any one particular type of interaction. That is, although we were ostensibly training people to carry out a particular kind of interview, we were in fact training people in skills which had much wider managerial applications. In particular, it seemed we were training people in skills which would be useful in virtually any interaction between manager and subordinates. Rather to our surprise, therefore, we came to the conclusion that, implicitly, we were training people in leadership skills.

We were aware, of course, that interpersonal skills training had been successfully applied in such areas as counselling, encounter groups and mental health,[3] and developments in such areas had been a major source of influence in our approach to managerial problems. Indeed, we have occasionally received informal feedback from our course members that the training had also had beneficial effects on their personal and social lives. Nevertheless, there was, as far as we know, neither a fully developed practical nor theoretical framework for the application of an interpersonal skills approach to leadership theory and training. This book is our attempt to develop such a framework.

One other consequence of arriving at the study of leadership through interpersonal skills training is a belief in learning through practice with feedback and guidance. Simply reading a book may provide knowledge, but actual performance is unlikely to improve to any great extent until the reader has tried something out in practice, received feedback on what has been achieved and guidance on how to do better next time. In training in interpersonal skills, we have typically used interview role plays for this purpose. Obviously we cannot do this for individual readers. What we have done, however, is to include exercises which will enable readers to practice many of the skills we discuss and check their answers against the 'model' answers in the appendices. In the final section of the book, we also describe both a formal training course in interpersonal skills and a number of ways in which individual readers can practise their interpersonal skills and obtain feedback and guidance for themselves.

Notes and references

1. G. A. Randell, P. M. A. Packard, R. L. Shaw and A. J. Slater (1972), *Staff Appraisal*, London: Institute of Personnel Management.
2. R. W. T. Gill and D. S. Taylor (1976), 'Training managers to handle discipline and grievance interviews', *Journal of European Training*, **5**, 217–27; D. S. Taylor and P. L. Wright (1977), 'Training auditors in interviewing skills', *Journal of European Industrial Training*, **1**, 8–16.
3. See, for example, G. Egan (1975), *The Skilled Helper: A model for systematic helping and interpersonal relating*, Monterey, Calif.: Brooks/Cole; G. Egan (1976), *Interpersonal Living: A skills/contract approach to human relations training in groups*, Monterey, Calif.: Brooks/Cole; P. Trower, B. Bryant and M. Argyle (1978), *Social Skills and Mental Health*, London: Methuen.

CHAPTER 1

A skills approach to leadership

Introduction

The practice of leadership is concerned with influencing people's behaviour and feelings. Consider some examples:

An army sergeant yells what, to an outsider, would be an unintelligible command and a squad of thirty soldiers come simultaneously to attention, standing stiffly and impassively.

A sales director listens to one of her brand managers outline his plan for combating a competitor's newly introduced product. She merely nods and says 'uh huh' occasionally and, when he has finished, says, 'Yes, that seems like a good way of tackling the problem. Why don't you go ahead and implement it.' The brand manager leaves smiling and walks purposefully back to his own office.

A production foreman says to a sheet metal worker, 'For the last time, Joe, when you use that machine you must have the safety guard in place. If I see you using it without the guard again I'm going to institute formal disciplinary proceedings against you.' The worker looks resentful, but complies.

The departmental manager looks around his group and says, 'Now this is an important decision and, as you know, I don't believe in autocratic management, so I want the decision to arise out of a free and frank discussion among the group.' His subordinates look bored and resigned. 'Here we go,' one mutters, 'we will spend all afternoon being manipulated into accepting the solution he came in with in the first place. Why doesn't he simply tell us. At least an autocrat doesn't waste your time with tedious discussions.'

'You will do it my way, or else,' bellows the irate section leader. 'In that case, you can keep your job. I quit,' yells back the research chemist, throws her lab coat in the corner of the room and stalks out of the lab, slamming the door behind her.

1

In each of these examples, someone is trying to influence the behaviour of another individual or group of people in a particular direction. These attempts at influence also tend to have emotional consequences for the people concerned. They may feel enthusiastic about the task they are being influenced to do or resent it so much that they refuse to do it, or do it badly. They may regard the person attempting to influence them with admiration and respect, amusement and disdain, or fear and dislike. They may believe that their role within the leader's group is worthwhile and meaningful or feel so dissatisfied with it that they would leave at the first reasonable opportunity. Such beliefs and feelings are extremely important to the leader, whether he or she knows it or not. In varying degrees, they will determine not only the success of the leader's immediate attempt at influence, but also the probability of being able to influence the same individual successfully in future.

To summarise, we regard leadership as an activity, that of influencing the behaviour, beliefs and feelings of other group members in an intended direction. However, we shall not be concerned with all forms of influence or even all forms of leadership in this book. For example, influence may take place at a distance without any personal interaction between the people concerned. The marketing executive who plans an advertising campaign undoubtedly wishes to influence the attitudes and buying behaviour of potential customers. Similarly, the politician planning a political campaign undoubtedly wishes to influence the attitudes and voting behaviour of the electorate, most of whom he or she will not meet personally. On the other hand, each of these people is likely to have a group of subordinates or staff with whom he or she interacts on a more personal basis. It is with leadership in such situations, where influence takes place within a relatively small group allowing personal contact, that the present book is primarily concerned.

Furthermore, although much of what we say will have relevance to leadership in informal groups, our main emphasis will be on leadership in formal organisations. That is, we are primarily concerned with situations where people are appointed or elected to leadership positions and are expected by the organisation to be the major source of influence on the work behaviour of a particular group of organisation members. For the sake of convenience, we shall refer to the parties involved in such a situation as manager and subordinate or subordinates. In part, this is because the term 'leader' and 'follower' can sound rather stilted, but more important is the fact that we are mainly concerned with leadership in an organisational setting where the interaction would usually occur between manager and subordinate in any case.

Whilst our main concern is with hierarchical leadership, there are, of course, other relationships in which the ability to influence work behaviour is important. At times, managers may need to influence their fellow managers and even their own superiors in order to achieve their performance objectives. Many of the skills we discuss will also be relevant in such situations.

We realise that defining leadership solely in terms of influence can give rise to an apparent anomaly. If a successful leader is one who has considerable influence on the followers' behaviour, then a leader who makes the wrong decision and leads a group into disaster is a more successful leader than one who fails to influence the group and thereby avoids disaster.[1] However, we take the view that leadership is only one part of a manager's job.[2] To expand the concept of leadership to include decision-making skill, technical expertise, and all the other attributes necessary to succeed as a manager, would not be helpful. It would make the concept of leadership far too broad. Specifying what it is that enables a leader to influence follower behaviour is difficult enough, without having simultaneously to take into account other significant facets of managerial performance. Furthermore, expanding the concept of leadership in this way would render it synonymous with management, and make the term virtually redundant. We shall therefore be concentrating on one aspect of a manager's job, that of influencing subordinate behaviour and feelings, and this activity we shall call leadership.

The aim of this book is to help managers to be able to perform their leadership role more successfully by improving their ability to influence the work performance of their subordinates, and their feelings about their work. We would argue that one of the key factors in successful leadership, and certainly the one most readily improved, is the possession of certain specific interpersonal skills on the part of the manager. This emphasis on skills, rather than the leader's personality, attitude, style and so on, inevitably has implications for leadership training. We believe that successful leadership behaviour can be learned, and that the most effective way of learning it is by the acquisition of the relevant interpersonal skills through practice with feedback and guidance.

Current approaches to leadership theory

Most current theories of leadership are behavioural in the sense that they are concerned with the behaviours, rather than personality traits, which are presumed to be associated with effective leadership. Nevertheless, such behaviours tend to be described at a relatively high level of abstraction. This is particularly true of leadership style theories, where terms such as consideration, concern for production, employee-centred, participative, task-oriented, demo-cratic, and so on, abound. These concepts describe very broad classes of behaviour, but the behaviours themselves are rarely discussed in any detail. A few examples of the behaviours in question may be given, but it seems to be assumed that actual and potential leaders are fully aware of the complete range of behaviours which exist under any one heading and, what is more, can perform them perfectly if need be.

The inherent vagueness of the style approach was recognised by Vroom and Yetton in their normative model of leadership.[3] They advanced instead a number of different decision-making methods which the leader could employ, such as obtaining the necessary information from subordinates, sharing the problem with subordinates, delegating the problem to a subordinate, and so on. This undoubtedly comes closer to describing actual leader behaviour than the leadership styles approach, but Vroom and Yetton still do not tell leaders how they should go about obtaining information and sharing or delegating problems, let alone how to go about it skilfully. Again, it seems to be assumed that leaders will somehow know this intuitively and simply need to be guided to the right general approach to the problem.

In a more recent version of the theory, Vroom and Jago do acknowledge the importance of leadership skills.[4] They state: 'Ineffective decisions frequently result from using a decision process that is inappropriate to situational demands. However, the results encountered depend not only on one's method, but also on one's skill in using it. A surgeon may choose a correct operating procedure, but success also depends on the surgeon executing that procedure in an appropriate manner.' Nevertheless, the only skills which they describe at any length are those recommended some years earlier by Maier for effectively implementing consensual group decision making.[5] These apply to only one of Vroom and Jago's leadership styles and whilst some useful advice is given, it is also very general. For example, it is suggested that 'the leader should avoid dominating the discussion and instead encourage group members to do most of the talking', but no advice is given on exactly how the leader should go about encouraging the group members to talk. The skills required to carry out the other leadership styles effectively are not discussed, except to suggest that autocratic leaders must be intelligent enough to make high-quality decisions and that it is helpful if they are 'charismatic' or at least skilled in the art of persuasion.

Fiedler apparently avoids the question of leadership skills by arguing that leaders should not attempt to modify their behaviour, because this is too difficult, but should attempt to modify their situation instead. However, examining the methods that he suggests leaders should use to change their situation, one finds that they include such *behaviours* as 'organising some off-work group activities which include your subordinates (e.g. picnics, boating, softball teams, excursions, etc.)' or 'trying to be one of the gang by playing down any trappings of power or rank'.[6] As in other leadership style theories, such behaviours are merely given as a few examples of the *kind* of thing the leader might do. No attempt is made to provide a comprehensive account of the behaviours concerned nor is there any discussion of the skills required to perform them well. One doubts, for example, whether subordinates invited to play softball by a disliked, socially inept superior would necessarily find this a rewarding experience.

A recent development in leadership style theory has been a growth of interest in what has been variously called inspirational, visionary, charismatic or transformational leadership. Bryman refers to this approach to the study of leadership by the general term 'the New Leadership'.[7] Common themes in this approach to leadership identified by Bryman include having a vision or mission, communicating the vision, the empowerment of organisational members, creating an organisational culture which is consistent with the vision, changing organisational structures in line with the vision, and inspiring the trust of followers.

In many respects this is a confused and confusing area of leadership theory. Some writers take the view that charisma is a characteristic of certain outstanding individuals which allows them to inspire followers to greater things. According to House the term is commonly employed in the sociological and political science literature to describe leaders who, by force of their personal qualities, are capable of having profound and extraordinary effects on followers.[8] Others view charisma as something which is attributed to leaders by followers. Bennis and Nanus, for example, state that charisma is the result of effective leadership, not the other way round.[9] Bryman combines aspects of both these views, suggesting that charismatic leadership involves 'relationships between leaders and their followers in which, by virtue of both the extraordinary qualities that followers attribute to the leader and the latter's mission, the . . . leader is regarded by his or her followers with a mixture of reverence, unflinching dedication and awe'.[10]

The confusion concerning charisma is carried over into research into the effects of charisma on organisational performance. For example, research by Bass has shown that transformational leaders, who influence their followers through a combination of charisma, individualised consideration and intellectual stimulation, are more effective than transactional leaders who emphasise the giving of rewards if subordinates meet agreed performance standards.[11] If one examines the questionnaire which Bass uses to measure transactional leadership, however, one finds items such as 'the person I am rating has my trust in his or her ability to overcome any obstacle' and 'the person I am rating enables me to think about problems in a new way'. In other words, the rating of whether someone uses transactional leadership or not also contains an element of how effective he or she is, so it is hardly surprising that the two turn out to be related.

Indeed, most writers on the subject of the inspirational, visionary, charismatic or transformational leaders are only concerned with those who are successful. One rarely finds mention of someone who tried to be a charismatic leader and failed. Similarly, if someone who was once regarded as charismatic subsequently fails, there seems to be a tendency to question whether the person really was charismatic rather than question the effectiveness of their charismatic leadership. Bryman suggests, for example, that Lee Iacocca, once the epitome of the New Leadership, currently appears to be undergoing just such a process of 'decharismarization'.[12] Nevertheless, as Bryman points out, charismatic leadership is not always something which benefits an organisation. Charismatic leaders' arrogance about their own special abilities can lead to folly, their vision may become an unshakable obsession leading to catastrophe, or they may become autocratic, using their power over people as a means of getting their own way regardless of the views of others. Bryman goes on to suggest that more studies are needed which draw on failures of the kind of leadership that the New Leadership extols. It is hard to believe, he states, that they do not exist in greater profusion than is sometimes implied by many writers.

The approach taken by New Leadership theorists has two additional disadvantages from our point of view. First, it tends to be mainly concerned with top-level leaders. There are writers who say that the New Leadership should be disseminated throughout the organisation. Nevertheless, much of the writing about New Leadership has been concerned with leadership at the chief executive level. Furthermore it is difficult to see how lower-level charismatic leaders can operate successfully if their vision, regarded as one of the key aspects of the New Leadership, differs from that of their superiors. Secondly, like previous leadership style theorists, writers on the New Leadership tend to describe the behaviour of leaders only in very general terms. In the vast majority of cases, they do not say precisely what it is that such leaders do when interacting with their followers which produces the effects they claim. There is, however, one exception and, because of its rarity, it is worth describing in some detail.

Howell and Frost carried out a laboratory study of charismatic, structuring and considerate leadership, defining each in terms of the leader's verbal and nonverbal behaviour.[13] Those playing the leaders were trained to portray all three leadership styles used in the experiment.

When portraying the *charismatic* style, the leaders articulated an overarching goal, communicated high performance expectations, exhibited confidence in the subordinates' ability to meet these expectations, empathised with the subordinates' needs, projected a powerful, confident and dynamic presence, spoke in a captivating, engaging voice tone, alternated between pacing and sitting on the edge of their desk, leaned toward the participant, maintained direct eye contact, and had a relaxed posture and animated facial expressions.

Considerate leaders exhibited concern for the personal welfare of the participant, engaged in participative two-way conversations, emphasised the comfort, well-being and satisfaction of the participant, were friendly and approachable, spoke in a warm tone of voice, sat on the edge of their desk, leaned towards participants, maintained direct eye contact, and had a relaxed posture and friendly facial expressions (i.e. smiling, positive head nods).

When using a *structuring* style, leaders explained the nature of the task, decided in detail what should be done and how it should be done, emphasised the quantity of work to be accomplished within the specified time period and maintained definite standards of work performance. They acted in a neutral, businesslike manner towards the participants, being neither warm nor cold, and maintained a moderate level of speech intonation. They sat behind their desks, maintained intermittent eye contact and had neutral facial expressions (i.e. absence of smiling and positive head nods).

The task performed by the participants was an in-basket exercise. It was found that individuals working under a charismatic leader had higher task performance in terms of the number of courses of action suggested and higher quality of performance, higher task satisfaction and lower role conflict and ambiguity in comparison with individuals working under considerate leaders. In addition, individuals with a charismatic leader suggested more courses of action and reported greater task satisfaction and less role conflict than individuals with structuring leaders. The results further indicated that participants felt that they had a better quality of relationship with the charismatic leaders than with the structuring or considerate leaders, despite the latter's exclusive focus on establishing a strong emotional bond with subordinates by conveying warmth, acceptance, support and reassurance.

Inevitably, there are dangers in drawing far-reaching conclusions from a single research study. There seems no reason to assume that all structuring leaders behave in the neutral fashion portrayed in this study. For example, they could be equally expressive as charismatic leaders in the way they offer rewards and threaten punishments. The study did not address the question of individual differences amongst subordinates in responses to the different leadership styles. Finally, the findings are based on a 45-minute exercise. The participants did not formally join an organisation and knew that their participation would only last a short while. Thus the experiment did not take into account either the long-term effects of the leaders' styles or the real-life organisational leader's reward and punishment power over subordinates. Nevertheless the study suggests a number of intriguing possibilities and points the way for further research in this area.

In complete contrast to the New Leadership theorists are a group of leadership researchers who have based their approach on Skinner's operant conditioning model.[14] Their work is concerned with much more specific aspects of the leader's behaviour, such as rewarding good performance (e.g. giving recognition or recommending merit increases), punishing poor performance (e.g. giving reprimands or withholding pay increases), setting goals and providing feedback. In general, such studies show that setting goals, providing feedback and giving rewards based on performance have a marked beneficial effect on work performance, whilst punishment has little effect or even a detrimental one.[15]

Encouraging as this work is, it does not go far enough in our opinion. For one thing it considers only a narrow range of leadership behaviours. Leaders do much more than simply reward, punish, set goals and give feedback when interacting with their followers, important as these activities are. More importantly, it ignores the crucial issue of how skilfully the leader performs the behaviours in question. For example, praise done well can have beneficial effects, but done badly can equally give rise to adverse reactions, such as embarrassment, resentment and loss of respect. Similarly, punishment is something which can be done more well or less well. Often it seems to be done badly, perhaps because the behaviour usually represents an emotional response on the part of the punisher rather than a skilful attempt to influence subsequent behaviour. Some support for this view can be found in a study by Arvey, Davis and Nelson of the attitudes towards discipline of 526 hourly paid workers in a large chemical plant.[16] They found that the workers had a negative attitude towards supervisors who administered discipline in an inappropriate manner – in a childish or petty fashion, being typically angry, and so on – but a positive attitude towards supervisors who applied discipline in a consistent manner. Thus it may well be that studies which apparently show that punishment is an ineffective method of influencing behaviour may merely demonstrate that it is *unskilful* punitive behaviour which has negative effects. Furthermore there is a very fine line between negative feedback and punishment. Negative feedback may be necessary to help a subordinate to identify where an improvement in performance is desirable, but unless done skilfully, it is very likely that the subordinate will experience it as punishment.

Thus the practical implications of the leadership research based on operant conditioning are less apparent than they seem at first sight. An obvious conclusion would seem to be that managers should avoid punishing poor performance and concentrate upon rewarding good performance. However, it might be more advisable to learn how to perform such behaviours as giving praise, criticism and feedback skilfully, rather than to assume that one type of influence is necessarily more effective than another.

Finally, the research does not take into account the crucial question of individual differences between subordinates: some may resent criticism more than others, some may respond well to praise whilst others find it embarrassing, some might be highly motivated by the offer of a pay rise whilst others may prefer the opportunity to do more challenging work, and so on. Thus general solutions are likely to be less effective than those designed to suit the needs of specific subordinates. Recognising the individual needs of subordinates, and modifying the way they are treated accordingly, is also something which requires considerable skill on the part of the manager.

On the other hand, Honey argues that, when attempting to solve people problems, taking into account motives, attitudes and feelings unnecessarily complicates the issue.[17] People's behaviour can be much more effectively influenced, he claims, by manipulating the cues and pay-offs (consequences) which control it. He expresses doubts about the effectiveness of coaching, counselling and appraising as means of bringing about improvements in performance. Most managers do not have adequate skills to handle such face-to-face interactions well and the result is often embarrassing, even bruising, to both parties. He therefore advocates that instead managers should attempt to influence people's behaviour by applying the principles of behaviour modification, an approach which is also based on Skinner's work on operant conditioning.

Honey recognises the importance of taking into account individual differences when using operant conditioning principles as a means of influence. He says that managers should not assume that something is rewarding or punishing but should establish whether it is, by observing its effect on behaviour. However, as the effects on behaviour of selecting the wrong consequence as a reward or punishment could be adverse (e.g. resentment, poor performance, resigning, and so on), this could be an expensive form of trial and error learning. The manager observing the adverse consequences will know better next time, but by simply talking to the subordinate about his or her motives, attitudes or feelings beforehand, the manager might be able to avoid the error in the first place. Skinner did not have this option in his early work with rats and pigeons, and therefore had to rely on observation, but managers are not so restricted in their relations with subordinates.

Furthermore, whilst Honey's approach takes into account differences *between* people in what they regard as rewards and punishments, it does not take into account differences *within* the same person over time. Having established by observation what an individual finds rewarding or punishing, the manager may find that an influence attempt fails because the individual does not respond as expected. This may be due to a change in mood. A subordinate who has just suffered a bereavement or suddenly come into a large inheritance is likely to respond differently to the manager's attempts at influence from the way he or she did in the past. Similarly, people's motives change over time. A subordinate may become more concerned about monetary rewards due to increased family responsibilities or less concerned about promotion as he or she gets older. One cannot assume that just because someone found something rewarding or punishing in the past, he or she will necessarily respond in the same way now. It would be much more effective, therefore, to establish someone's probable reactions beforehand, by skilful questioning and observing nonverbal cues of acceptance or rejection, rather than passively waiting to see what happens before modifying one's approach. Thus, useful as operant conditioning is as a means of behavioural influence – a fact which has long been recognised by social skills trainers such as Egan[18] – it cannot replace the need for interpersonal skills in the management of people.

However, there are signs in recent leadership theory based on operant-conditioning principles that the importance of skills and individual differences is being recognised. Sims and Lorenzi, for example, give advice on how to deliver a constructive reprimand.[19] They also state that an effective manager must be concerned with individual perceptions concerning reward behaviour, because what the manager perceives as a reward may not be rewarding to the subordinate or may even be a disincentive. The manager therefore requires information concerning employee preferences for different rewards, information which can be obtained from the subordinate mainly on an informal basis through personal conversations. However, Sims and Lorenzi do not give advice on how to conduct such conversations skilfully.

One leadership theory which has taken into account interpersonal skills, and done so very effectively, is Graen's leader–member exchange (LMX) theory (also known as the 'vertical dyad linkage' model).[20] LMX theory differs from most other behavioural theories of leadership in that it is not based on the idea of leadership styles, but concentrates instead on the quality of the relationship between leaders and subordinates. It suggests that, on unstructured tasks, leaders may offer certain subordinates increased autonomy, influence in decision making, open communications, support for their actions, and confidence in and consideration for them. These subordinates may then reciprocate by expending more time and energy on their work, and assuming greater responsibility and commitment to the success of the entire unit or organisation. If this happens, such subordinates become members of an 'in-group' or 'cadre'. Over time, the in-group members become trusted assistants and the leader may become more dependent on them, not only to ensure adequate functioning of the group but also to deal with problems which may arise within the unit. Subordinates who are not offered such a relationship or respond inappropriately when an offer is made become members of an 'out-group'. As such, they have a more contractual relationship with the leader. In effect, they are 'hired hands', who agree to fulfil the requirements of the job and accept the legitimate authority of their specified superiors in exchange for wages, continued employment and other benefits.

Initially, the LMX model was simply a descriptive theory. It described different types of relationship between superiors and subordinates, but did not give any explicit advice concerning how such relationships could be changed. This question has been taken up in more recent research. In a field experiment carried out by Graen, Novak and Sommerkamp, managers of information-processing technicians in a large public service organisation were given training based on the LMX model designed to help them to develop higher-quality relationships with their subordinates.[21] In addition to learning about the LMX model and its uses, the managers were given training in how to conduct one-to-one conversations with their unit members. The training sessions, which included role-played practice, covered such things as the general structure of the conversations; the use of specific questions and techniques in order to stimulate discussion of subordinates' gripes, concerns and job expectations; active listening skills; and sharing the managers' own job expectations with subordinates.

Measures taken before and after the training showed significant improvements for the leadership-trained group as compared with the control group in a variety of areas, including productivity, leader–member relations, leader support, the motivating potential of the job, and member's loyalty and job satisfaction. The trained group and their subordinates improved their productivity (measured by number of completed cases per hour) by an average of over 16 per cent, with no significant effects on quality of output, resulting in projected system-wide annual cost savings of over $5 million.

An important additional finding was that the effect of the leadership training on productivity depended upon the strength of the subordinates' growth needs (defined as needs for personal challenge and accomplishment, for learning and for professional development). Subordinates with high growth needs showed a 52 per cent improvement in productivity, whilst those with medium and low growth needs showed no gains. Similar results were obtained in a field experiment on a comparable sample carried out by Graen, Scandura and Graen.[22] In this study, the high growth need subordinates showed an increase of 55 per cent in productivity (measured by weekly output records) over the control group, with a significant decrease in errors, whilst the medium and low growth need groups demonstrated no significant improvements.

Conversely, however, the LMX model says little about how to manage people who either work on structured tasks or have low growth need strength. In this case, the manager may have the more contractual relationship with the subordinate described earlier, but this is not explicitly stated, nor does the model say anything about how to manage such contractual relationships more effectively. Nevertheless, the leader–member exchange model makes a very useful contribution to bridging the gap between traditional leadership theory and interpersonal skills training.

Interpersonal skills training for managers

A wide variety of different methods of training managers in interpersonal skills have been developed. One approach, developed during the mid-1940s, which is widely quoted as being a method of interpersonal skills training, is what is variously known as sensitivity, laboratory or T-Group training. Procedures vary considerably, but T-Groups commonly consist of ten to fifteen people who meet without an agenda, pre-planned topics or activities, or designated roles such as chairperson. A trainer is usually present, but he or she refuses to accept a leadership role. The focus of the discussion is on the 'here and now' of what is happening within the group, such as people's behaviour, impressions formed, feelings elicited, reasons for these, and so on.[23] The ultimate objective of these discussions is to increase group members' ability to recognise clearly how others are reacting to them, to perceive accurately the state of relationships between others and to carry out skilfully the behaviour required by the situation.[24]

However, research into the effectiveness of T-Group training has produced mixed results. In some cases, there have been beneficial organisational effects, but in others the results have been insignificant or even negative. In a minority of cases, T-Group training has also been found to have damaging psychological effects on participants.[25]

One thing which is often unclear in descriptions of T-Group training is precisely what skills it is intended to develop and exactly how they are to be developed. This is more particularly true in the case of behavioural skills. Intuitively, one can see how receiving feedback from other group members about how their behaviour is perceived within the group could help participants to develop greater sensitivity to others. To what extent this actually happens, of course, will depend upon the *quality* of the feedback, and this in turn will depend upon the interpersonal sensitivity and verbal skills that the course members *already have* before joining the group. For this reason, Egan regards interpersonal skills training on an individual basis as a prerequisite for successful group training.[26]

When it comes to behavioural skills, however, it is difficult to see what mechanisms exist within T-Group training for the identification and acquisition of the specific behavioural skills that each participant most needs to develop in order to perform more effectively in the working environment. According to Smith, each member 'has the opportunity to test out and develop personal behavioural skills, where situations arise in the group requiring such skills'.[27] However, if the requirement to perform the behavioural skills which a participant most needs to develop does not arise in the course of the discussion, then the need to develop them may never be revealed. Moreover even if the requirement to perform the skills does arise, it is questionable whether untrained fellow T-Group members would necessarily have the ability either to identify precisely which skills were needed or to provide effective feedback and guidance on their development. Thus, T-Group training would appear to be somewhat of a hit-or-miss method of interpersonal skills training – if indeed it can be regarded as a method of interpersonal skills training at all.

Other approaches to interpersonal skills training have attempted to identify in much more precise terms the behaviours required to interact effectively with other people within organisations. Two examples are behaviour analysis and behaviour modelling. Behaviour analysis was developed by a group of trainers working with BOAC in the late 1960s.[28] In order to provide a list of behavioural categories which could be used to analyse the behaviour of people in groups, they carried out an analysis of video-taped recordings of working groups. A conscious decision was made at this stage to concentrate on verbal rather than nonverbal behaviour and on the *form* rather than the content of the verbal behaviour. The result was a dozen or so behavioural categories (e.g. supporting, disagreeing, building, summarising, and so on) which showed high reliability between different users. Since then a number of category sets have been developed, each of them designed for measuring a specific type of interaction (e.g. performance appraisal interviewing, selling and chairing group meetings).[29]

These behavioural categories provide the basis for giving feedback to participants on interactive skills courses. The extent to which each participant uses each behavioural category during training exercises is logged and fed back to the participant concerned. Thus, in later stages of the course, the participant can use this information to plan changes in the behavioural categories which they use and then receive further feedback on how successful they are in making these changes to their behaviour. Honey has also described how behaviour management can be used by individual managers to analyse their own communication behaviour and identify ways in which they can improve it.[30]

According to Morgan, behaviour analysis enables the trainer to give more helpful feedback concerning the trainee's manner of performance than any other form of feedback because it provides a complete objective, quantified record of what actually happened, rather than the trainer's interpretation of what he or she thinks happened or should have happened.[31] The greater objectivity of behaviour analysis is undoubtedly one of its important advantages as a training technique. However, it is questionable whether it provides a *complete* record of the participant's behaviour. The behavioural categories of behaviour analysis describe communication behaviour at what may be termed an intermediate level of analysis.[32] That is, they fall somewhere between the broad generalities of leadership style theory and the much more specific molecular[33] or microskills[34] level, which is of most use to interpersonal skills trainers. For participants to become skilful in the use of these behavioural categories, therefore, they still need to identify the specific behaviours required to use each category of behaviour and learn how to perform them well. For example, Morgan found that salesmen who were high on 'seeking information' made significantly more sales, but notes that this still left the problem of discovering the specific types of questions which the salesmen used in information seeking.[35] Similarly, Dyar and Giles comment that, when using their version of interaction analysis, they may supplement the analysis with direct observation of the questions used by an interviewer (e.g. whether they are open, closed or leading, whether they are flexible or follow a rigidly determined sequence, and so on).[36]

Behaviour modelling, on the other hand, provides training in much more specific behaviours. Course members are shown examples of the skilled behaviours portrayed by experts. Examples include starting a conversation, expressing a compliment, asking for help, responding to praise,[37] motivating the poor performer, discussing personal work habits with an employee, giving recognition to the average employee, and conducting a performance review.[38] Course members then perform the behaviours in question in role-played interactions and receive feedback on how closely they followed the steps demonstrated by the expert model, and social reinforcement (praise) according to the extent that they did so.

Behaviour modelling provides an effective way of developing some of the basic skills which are required in order to interact effectively within the working environment. It can be used to teach course members how to perform single behaviours, such as asking an open question or making a request, and ways of sequencing such behaviours which will typically be successful in relatively simple interactions. However, skilful behaviour involves more than simply following a set routine. Interacting effectively with other people inevitably involves reacting adaptively to the way they respond, and in longer and more complex interactions, this cannot be predicted in detail or with certainty. This element of reacting adaptively to the relatively unpredictable precludes the identification of a 'correct' or 'one best way' of conducting any particular type of interaction. The skilful leader not only knows how to ask an open question or make a request, but also when to use them and when a closed question or a direct order is more appropriate. Furthermore, as we have already noted, different people may well respond in different ways to the same behaviour on the part of the leader. Thus, the development of more advanced leadership skills involves not only learning how to perform particular skills, but also learning which skills are most appropriate for different purposes, how to adapt one's behaviour to the different ways in which people may react, and how to cope with the unexpected in interactions with other people.

In recent years, interest in the development of managerial skills or competencies has grown considerably.[39] Influential texts in this area include Whetten and Cameron's *Developing Managerial Skills*[40] and Quinn, Faerman, Thompson and McGrath's *Becoming a Master Manager*.[41] Such texts are typically concerned with a wide range of managerial skills, such as self-awareness, managing stress, motivating others, communication, delegation, managing conflict, creative thinking, and so on.

In dealing with such topics, however, they tend to emphasise conceptual learning at the expense of behavioural skills. For example, Whetten and Cameron base their advice on motivating employees on expectancy theories of motivation and operant conditioning. As McKnight points out, there is more to motivating people than understanding expectancy theory and operant conditioning.[42] They may help the manager to decide what motivation strategy to use, but motivating people in a face-to-face situation requires much more than the selection of the right strategy. The manager's behaviour, verbal and nonverbal, towards the people he or she is attempting to motivate is also vitally important. In McKnight's view, motivational skill is 'the ability to relate to employees in a way that inspires them to want to do their best' and in such interactions '*everything* is a stimulus – physical gestures, facial expressions, smiles, vocal inflections, and so forth'.

It is in this area that texts on managerial skills or competencies tend to be weakest. The crucial issue of what managers should say and do when interacting with others tends not to be covered in depth. In Quinn *et al.*, for example, questioning skills are described in the course of a one-page section on reflective listening and no other types of verbal or nonverbal behaviour are considered. Similarly, although Whetten and Cameron describe certain types of questions and statement in more detail, they restrict themselves to those required to establish supportive communication and ignore other forms of interaction which may need to be performed skilfully in order to manage people effectively.

In summary, the various approaches to interpersonal skills training we have discussed so far have all in different ways attempted to show how it is possible to develop the skills required to interact effectively with other people in the working environment. However, none of them has described in sufficient detail what leaders actually say and do when interacting with subordinates. One approach to interpersonal skills training which typically does involve the analysis of communication behaviour at this molecular or microskills level is interviewing skills training. For example, Maier described the skills which supervisors would need to carry out non-directive counselling with disturbed or frustrated subordinates, including listening, reflecting feelings and the use of questions.[43] Kahn and Cannel showed how techniques such as the use of open and closed questions, probing, summaries, the funnel sequence, reflecting feelings, and so on can be applied in a variety of information-gathering interviews, including the selection interview.[44] Maier described three different approaches to performance appraisal interviewing, identified the circumstances in which each should be used and outlined the skills required in each case.[45] Randell, Packard, Shaw and Slater described in more detail different questions and statements which could be used in appraisal interviewing and identified the different purposes for which it is most appropriate to use them.[46]

This approach tended to fragment interviewing skills training. Whilst the skills required in these different situations obviously overlap in varying degrees, they tended to be taught on different courses and described in separate books, or at best different chapters in the same book, each devoted to different types of interview. As Argyle put it, 'Management skills came to be seen primarily as a number of discrete set-piece performances, such as the various kinds of interview, each of which could be trained.'[47] What was lacking was a general model of the interpersonal skills required for the effective management of people at work in a wide variety of different situations. In the next section we will describe such a model.

A skills approach to leadership

We would suggest that the manager's behaviour in interactions with his or her subordinates can be examined in terms of three different levels of analysis, as follows:

1. *Primary components* Here we are concerned with what managers actually say and do – their verbal and nonverbal behaviour – in interactions with their subordinates. Verbal behaviour includes the manager's use of questions and statements to gather information from subordinates, provide information to subordinates, influence their work behaviour, handle grievances, and so on. Nonverbal behaviour consists of the tones of voice, gestures, body postures, facial expressions which accompany speech, often changing its meaning in significant ways, and sometimes even replacing it altogether.
2. *Structural factors* This refers to the way in which the primary components are sequenced, or in longer interactions to the way in which the interaction as a whole or topics covered within it are introduced, sequenced, resolved, linked together, and so on.
3. *The overall approach* The components used in an interaction and the way it is structured will depend at least in part upon the type of interaction the manager wishes to have with a subordinate. Two main factors are important

here. One is the extent to which the manager is prepared to allow the subordinate to influence the content of the interaction and the decisions which are reached. The other is the extent to which the manager wishes to conduct the interaction in a warm, friendly manner or one which is cold and businesslike, emphasising differences in status. It is at this level of analysis that our approach most resembles that of traditional leadership theorists. However, there are important differences, as we shall see later.

We would regard the interpersonally skilled leader as one who:

1. has a wide variety of verbal components (question and statement types) at his or her disposal and is able to select the one most appropriate for the situation and particular purpose at hand, and perform it well, with the appropriate nonverbal cues;
2. can structure interactions effectively by organising these questions and statements into purposeful sequences which steer the interaction towards its objective(s); and
3. can develop an approach to the interaction, which is appropriate to the objectives in question and the probable reactions of the subordinate.

Our analysis of the behavioural skills of leadership forms the central core of this book. Verbal and nonverbal components are discussed in Chapters 4 and 5 respectively, structural factors in Chapter 6 and approaches to manager–subordinate interactions in Chapter 7.

In addition to behavioural skills, however, two other types of skill are required for the successful management of people at work. First, there are the diagnostic skills which are required to identify what needs to be done to maintain high levels of work performance, and to improve it where necessary. To achieve this, the manager must have a good understanding of the range of factors which affect performance, such as motivation, abilities, feedback, and so on. Furthermore, the manager must know that actions can be taken to influence these various factors and, through them, performance itself. This question will be examined in Chapter 2. Secondly, the successful management of people requires accurate perception and evaluation of people and events. This is important in the analysis of work performance; for example, establishing what are the major factors influencing a subordinate's work performance and whether there are areas in which improvement is desirable. It is also important in interactions with subordinates where sensitivity to the other person's responses can enable the manager to pick up low-level cues concerning his or her beliefs, feelings and intentions which might otherwise have been missed. The perceptual skills of leadership are discussed in Chapter 3.

Finally, in Chapter 8 we examine ways in which the interpersonal skills of leadership can be acquired and developed, both in formal training courses and by the individual manager working on his or her own.

Ethical considerations

One subject which is rarely, if ever, discussed in books on leadership is the ethics of helping one person to exert greater influence over another. Early leadership style theorists neatly avoided the problem by claiming that showing consideration or concern for people was the most effective way of increasing subordinates' productivity. Thus there was no conflict for the manager being trained, who could be organisationally effective and a nice person at the same time. Even the later situational theorists avoided the problem to a large degree, by defining their leadership styles and the expected consequences of using them so vaguely, that one did not feel that real people were involved in the process. We, on the other hand, are concerned with much more specific leader behaviours aimed at producing specific subordinate responses. So the question inevitably arises: 'Who is to benefit from any increase in the manager's influence over his or her subordinates?' Are we, for example, preaching manipulation? As scientists we can, of course, avoid these problems by claiming that we are only concerned with what objectively does happen as a result of actions taken, not with what should happen. As trainers, however, we *are* concerned with the effects on other people, beneficial or otherwise, of the training we give. Thus the ethical implications of our work, we feel, are something which should not be avoided.

It seems to be a requirement of organisations that certain people are made responsible for the performance of others. How the role is distributed, whether it is unitary, shared or alternated, the way in which it is performed and so on, will depend upon the function, philosophy and culture of the organisation. Nevertheless where individuals are responsible for the performance of others, influence is inevitably involved. One cannot be held responsible for the performance of people over whom one has no influence.

However, this should not imply that the influence is necessarily authoritarian. It may be, but it need not be. Even the most democratic forms of management need someone to be responsible for sounding out members' opinions, organising, voting, ensuring that everyone has an opportunity to express their views, and so on. If, however, the democratic leader fails through a lack of skills to influence his or her followers to behave democratically, then the democratic process itself may fail.

Similarly, skilful influence does not necessarily imply manipulation. Again, it may do so. If the leader skilfully influences a follower to do something for the leader's benefit without the follower realising it, then manipulation is involved. On the other hand, if the leader influences a follower to do something for the follower's benefit, with the follower's knowledge and consent, then one would refer to the activity by a much kinder name, such as career development, job enrichment, and so on.

Much the same skills are involved in behaviour influence, whatever the motives of the manager concerned. Thus, providing leadership training does increase the danger that such skills may be used for selfish purposes. On the other hand, failure to provide such training may also prevent genuinely concerned managers from helping or developing their subordinates effectively, because they lack the necessary skills. Our response to this dilemma is to regard training in interpersonal skills as the lesser risk. Being managed by someone with an autocratic style but little real influence can be much worse than being managed by a skilful autocrat. Similarly, the skilful democrat may be a more pleasant boss to work for, but the chaos under an ineffective one can drive subordinates to despair. Whilst each subordinate may enjoy his or her own freedom of action caused by a boss with low influence, the unfortunate fact is that all the boss's other subordinates will have equal freedom of action. Thus, obtaining their co-operation when interests conflict can be a time-consuming and emotionally exhausting business. It is at times like these that one sometimes hears a heartfelt plea for a dictator to make a decision either way. Our view is that a more appropriate plea would be for a skilful manager with greater ability to influence subordinates. An authoritarian decision might be an appropriate way to solve the problem but, equally, a skilful democrat might influence the individuals concerned to solve the problems in a participative way to their mutual satisfaction.

Thus, in the final analysis, it comes down to a choice between being managed skilfully or unskilfully. Our own feeling, supported by research evidence, is that people prefer working for interpersonally skilled managers. It is the ineffective manager who is disliked most, irrespective of his or her managerial style or motives.[48]

Taking a skills approach to leadership also has implications with respect to racism, sexism and other forms of discrimination. We have defined leadership as the activity of influencing the behaviour, beliefs and feelings of other group members in an intended direction. If the other group members react differently to a leader who is a woman or a member of an ethnic minority, then the leader may find that ways of behaving towards followers which are effective in influencing followers for a male majority group member are less effective in his or her case. For example, Benazir Bhutto, the ex-President of Pakistan, has been quoted as saying: 'As a female politician I cannot embrace people or ruffle their hair like my father and brother used to do. Such actions often say more than words, but this camaraderie can only exist man to man.'[49]

Thus female and minority group leaders may find themselves in situations where they have to make a choice between behaving in the same way as male or majority group leaders and accepting that they will be able to exert less influence and may even alienate people, or behaving in ways which differ from those employed by male or majority group members. Such different ways of behaving may, for example, involve being less assertive, and employing persuasion because the other group members would not accept direct orders, or it may involve being more assertive than male or majority group members would have to be in order to obtain the same effect. In a survey of managers and management students, Rasmussen found that female respondents were more likely than male to regard active listening as representing a passive or nurturing stance.[50] Some female respondents stated that they had consciously distanced themselves from nurturing roles – or at least from entering additional situations in which they are expected to take a nurturing stance. One female manager said: 'I have a difficult enough time holding my own. If I don't go nose-to-nose with those guys [other managers in her organisation], they'll walk all over me.'

To make our own moral position clear, we regard it as regrettable that some group members may respond differently to particular leaders because they are women or minority group members, and would much prefer that this were not so. However, it does happen and such a choice of methods of influence may have to be made. It would be presumptuous of us to say *what* choice should be made, but we would hope that our description of the skills of influence would provide all leaders with a greater number of options from which to choose.

Similar considerations apply with respect to the way in which leaders behave towards female or minority group members. We would abhor the idea of them being treated worse than other group members simply because they were women or members of a particular ethnic group. This does not mean, though, that leaders should treat all their followers in exactly the same way. We have drawn attention to individual differences at several points during this chapter. People have different motives, attitudes, values, and so on, and thus treating people in the same way will have different effects on their feelings and behaviour.

This was powerfully illustrated in an interpersonal skills course run by the authors. In a role-played practice session, a manager in his late fifties interviewed a female 'subordinate'. He treated her in a somewhat avuncular fashion, showing a great deal of concern for her feelings and suggesting in a sympathetic manner ways of overcoming the performance problems she faced. After the interview, he received very positive feedback from the interviewee, who said that she felt that the interviewer had treated her very well. The interviewer was not surprised that the interview had been a success. He said that most of his staff were female and he knew how to manage them. In his second interview, by coincidence, the interviewee was also female. He used exactly the same technique and at the end of the interview, to his amazement, received vehemently negative feedback concerning his insultingly patronising manner.

To avoid problems such as those which arose in the second interview, it is necessary for the manager to avoid stereotyping, assuming that all members of a particular group have the same needs, feelings, attitudes, and so forth, simply because they are a member of that group. Problems of stereotyping are discussed in Chapter 3. In addition, the manager needs to gather information concerning the likely reactions of each of his or her subordinates. This could be done formally or could simply arise in the course of informal discussion. In either case, skilful use of question and statement types (Chapter 4) and the observation of nonverbal cues (Chapter 5) will be required.

All this takes time and effort, and the argument we sometimes hear on interpersonal skills courses when we raise the question of individual differences is that the manager should not have to worry about those differences and, in any case, there is not time to do so. In effect, some course members say: 'I can't afford to spend time worrying about whether the way I behave towards people upsets some of them; I've got a job to do.' If, however, the way a manager treats subordinates upsets some of them, then the price of not spending time understanding individual differences may be poor performance. Furthermore the effects may not be easily noticed. The degree of job satisfaction does not necessarily have a direct or observable effect on how job-holders fulfil the formal job requirements. However, dissatisfied workers are less likely to perform 'citizenship behaviours', such as helping a colleague who is having difficulties, and are more likely to indulge in non-compliant behaviours, such as criticising the organisation or the boss to outsiders, deliberately making mistakes, damaging or defacing equipment, and so on. The manager may not even notice the former, because the subordinate's output remains the same, and may not know about the latter because the subordinate makes sure that they are done in such a way that he or she cannot be found out.[51] Nevertheless both can have a marked effect on the quality of work for which the manager is responsible. Needless to say, the above comments apply to all subordinates, irrespective of gender or ethnic group membership.

Notes and references

1. D. Katz and R. L. Kahn (1978), *The Social Psychology of Organizations*, 2nd edn, Wiley.
2. H. Mintzberg (1975), 'The manager's job: folklore and fact', *Harvard Business Review*, **53**, July–August, 49–61.
3. V. H. Vroom and P. W. Yetton (1973), *Leadership and decision making*, University of Pittsburgh Press.
4. V. H. Vroom and A. G. Jago (1988), *The new leadership: managing participation in organizations*, Prentice Hall, 37–42.
5. N. R. F. Maier (1963), *Problem solving discussions and conferences*, McGraw-Hill; N. R. F. Maier (1970), *Problem solving and creativity in individuals and groups*, Brooks/Cole.
6. F. E. Fiedler, M. M. Chemers and L. Mahar (1976), *Improving leadership effectiveness: the leader match concept*, Wiley.
7. A. Bryman (1992), *Charisma and leadership in organizations*, Sage.
8. R. J. House (1977), 'A 1976 theory of charismatic leadership', in J. G. Hunt and L. L. Larson (eds), *Leadership: The cutting edge*, Southern Illinois University Press.

9. W. G. Bennis and B. Nanus (1985), *Leaders: The strategies for taking charge*, Harper & Row.
10. Bryman, *op. cit.*, 41.
11. B. M. Bass (1985), *Leadership and Performance Beyond Expectations*, Free Press.
12. Bryman, *op. cit.*
13. J. M. Howell and P. J. Frost (1989), 'A laboratory study of charismatic leadership', *Organizational performance and human decision processes*, **43**, 243–69.
14. B. F. Skinner (1953), *Science and Human Behavior*, Macmillan.
15. H. P. Sims (1977), 'The leader as manager of reinforcement contingencies: an empirical example and a model', in Hunt and Larson, *op. cit.*; A. D. Szilagyi (1980), 'Causal inferences between leader reward behaviour and subordinate performance, absenteeism and work satisfaction', *Journal of Occupational Psychology*, **53**, 195–204.
16. R. D. Arvey, G. A. Davis and S. M. Nelson (1984), 'Use of discipline in an organization: a field study', *Journal of Applied Psychology*, **69**, 448–60.
17. P. Honey (1980), *Solving People-Problems*, McGraw-Hill.
18. G. Egan (1975), *The Skilled Helper: A model for systematic helping and interpersonal relating*, Brooks/Cole.
19. H. P. Sims and P. Lorenzi (1992), *The New Leadership Paradigm: Social learning and cognition in organizations*, Sage.
20. G. B. Graen (1990), 'Designing productive leadership systems to improve both work motivation and organizational effectiveness', in U. Kleinbeck *et al.* (eds), *Work Motivation*, Erlbaum.
21. G. B. Graen, M. A. Novak and P. Sommerkamp (1982), 'The effects of leader–member exchange and job design on productivity and satisfaction: testing a dual attachment model', *Organizational Behavior and Human Performance*, **30**, 109–31.
22. G. B. Graen, T. A. Scandura and M. R. Graen (1986), 'A field experimental test of the effects of growth need strength on productivity', *Journal of Applied Psychology*, **71**, 384–91.
23. M. Dunnette and J. P. Campbell (1968), 'Laboratory training: impact on people and organizations', *Industrial Relations*, **8**, 1–27.
24. P. B. Smith (1981), 'The T-Group approach', in C. L. Cooper (ed.), *Improving Interpersonal Relations: Some approaches to interpersonal skills training*, Gower.
25. B. M. Alban Metcalfe and P. L. Wright (1986), 'Social skills training for managers', in C. R. Hollin and P. Trower (eds), *Handbook of Social Skills Training*, vol. 1, *Applications Across the Life Span*, Pergamon.
26. G. Egan (1976), *Interpersonal Living: A skills/contract approach to human relations training in groups*, Brooks/Cole.
27. Smith, *op. cit.*
28. N. Rackham, P. Honey and M. J. Colbert (eds) (1971), *Developing Interactive Skills*, Wellens.

29. R. G. T. Morgan (1980), 'Analysis of social skills: the behaviour analysis approach', in W. T. Singleton, P. Spurgeon and R. B. Stammers (eds), *The Analysis of Social Skills*, Plenum.
30. P. Honey (1988), *Face to Face Skills: A practical guide to interactive skills*, Gower.
31. Morgan, *op. cit.*
32. P. L. Wright (1993), 'Interpersonal skills training: interactions between research and practice', paper presented at the *6th European Congress on Work and Organizational Psychology*, Alicante, April.
33. R. M. McFall (1982), 'A review and reformulation of the concept of social skills', *Behavioral Assessment*, **4**, 1–33; J. P. Dillard and B. H. Spitzberg (1984), 'Global impressions of social skills: behavioral predictors', in R. N. Bostram and B. H. Westley (eds), *Communication Yearbook 8*, Sage.
34. A. E. Ivey and M. Galvin (1984), 'Microcounselling: a metamodel for counselling, therapy, business and medical interviews', in D. Larson (ed.), *Teaching Psychological Skills: Models for giving psychology away*, Wadsworth.
35. Morgan, *op. cit.*
36. D. A. Dyar and W. J. Giles (1981), 'Interaction analysis', in C. L. Cooper (ed.), *Improving Interpersonal Relations: Some approaches to interpersonal skills training*, Gower.
37. A. P. Goldstein (1981), *Psychological Skill Training: The structured learning technique*, Pergamon.
38. A. P. Goldstein and M. Sorcher (1974), *Changing Supervisor Behaviour*, Pergamon.
39. For a review of developments in this area see J. D. Bigelow (ed.) (1991), *Managerial Skills: Explorations in practical knowledge*, Sage.
40. D. A. Whetten and K. S. Cameron (1984), *Developing Managerial Skills*, Scott Foresman.
41. R. E. Quinn, S. R. Faerman, M. P. Thompson and M. R. McGrath (1990), *Becoming a Master Manager*, Wiley.
42. M. R. McKnight (1991), 'Management skill development: what it is; what it is not', in Bigelow, *op. cit.*, 209.
43. N. R. F. Maier (1952), *Principles of Human Relationships: Applications to management*, Wiley. N. R. F. Maier (1955), *Psychology in Industry*, 2nd edn, Harrap.
44. R. L. Kahn and C. F. Cannel (1957), *The Dynamics of Interviewing: Theory, technique and cases*, Wiley.
45. N. R. F. Maier (1958), 'Three types of appraisal interview', *Personnel*, **54**, 27–40.
46. G. A. Randell, P. M. A. Packard, R. L. Shaw and A. J. Slater (1972), *Staff Appraisal*, Institute of Personnel Management.
47. M. Argyle (ed.) (1981), *Social Skills and Work*, Methuen, p. xv.
48. P. J. Sadler (1970), 'Leadership style, confidence in management and job satisfaction', *Journal of Applied Behavioural Science*, **6**, 3–19.

49. *The Times*, 7 January 1987.
50. R. V. Rasmussen (1991), 'Insights into managerial skills', in Bigelow, *op. cit.*, 185.
51. P. L. Wright (1989), 'Motivation and job satisfaction', in C. Molander (ed.), *Human Resource Management*, Chartwell Bratt.

CHAPTER 2
The diagnostic skills of leadership

Geoff's performance

Geoff, a 20-year-old draughtsman, works in an architects' office. He has been with this firm of architects for three years during which time he has been accountable to four different architects, each of whom gave him drawings to do. The four architects have felt for some time that Geoff has been working at an unacceptable level. However, when any of the four have questioned him about his work, he has played one off against another. One architect recently left and a new one has just been appointed. It has been decided to channel all work for Geoff through the newly appointed architect, Clare, so that she can monitor the work.

From casual observation and interaction, Clare has noticed that Geoff spends a significant amount of time in personal activities, such as talking to the members of the typing pool, talking on the telephone to friends and relatives, and going for frequent drinks from the coffee/tea/soft-drinks machine.

His main work involves making drawings and plans for buildings from specifications and sketches produced by the four architects. Other tasks include filing these after photocopying, maintaining his own equipment, ordering supplies of paper, pencils, pens and ink, and other stationery items. Throughout Clare's period of observation and interaction there has been a backlog of work, causing frustration and anger to the architects. Further, some of the drawings have had to be returned by the architects because they have not been to specification, contain drawing errors and/or omissions.

One of the architects has no doubt about the cause of the problem or what should be done about it. 'He is bone idle and bloody-minded,' the architect said to Clare. 'He should be told that he either performs up to standard or he will be sacked.' However, Clare wonders whether there might be other explanations for Geoff's poor performance and other ways of dealing with it.

Before reading this chapter, list what reasons you think there might be for Geoff's below-standard performance and the steps which might be taken to improve it. Treat these as hypotheses to be checked out later. Do not worry if some of them are contradictory.

24

Introduction

All organisations face the problem of how to influence their members to work effectively towards the achievement of organisational objectives. The issue of managing employee performance is related to the notion of leadership. Management involves using resources to achieve goals, and probably the most important resources essential for the attainment of the required level of performance in high-achieving organisations are the 'people' resources. The need to motivate and inspire people in organisations signals the importance of the influence role of leadership. A distinction in leadership research has been made between supervisory and executive leadership.[1] Executive leadership is concerned primarily with the leader's ability to influence large numbers of followers, not simply immediate subordinates. The more micro-approach to leadership, which we are emphasising in this book, is concerned primarily with a manager's ability to influence employees on a one-to-one basis. (The employees are most likely to be subordinates but could also be peers or superiors.) Nevertheless, the micro-approach is also applicable to influencing the output of a group. With increasing complexity and interactions of technology and social systems, there has been an increase in interest in performance at the group level as opposed to the individual level. As a result, a manager's attempt to influence performance may, in some cases, be best applied to group perform-ance rather than to specific individual behaviours. Even so, a manager may still need to attempt to influence group behaviour by defining and assessing desirable and undesirable behaviour at the individual level. The diagnostic approach to analysing behaviour in this chapter can be successfully applied to the group as well as to the individual. The same questions can be asked of group behaviour as for individual behaviour. However, analysis at the group level may well require further analysis applied to individual members of the group.

Alternative approaches to the problem of influencing the effective work performance of organisational members are organisational development (OD) and organisational transformation (OT). These approaches typically view top management as the catalyst for changes in organisational culture and perform-ance. The changes are 'top-down' in that once introduced by top management the changes are expected to spread down throughout the whole organisation. Organisational development concentrates on work-setting and organisational systems changes as a result of some mismatch between the organisation's present capabilities and its current demands. Usually it also attempts to produce changes in individual employees' attitudes. Organisational transformation, in contrast, emphasises much more the cognitive changes – the creation of a new vision for the organisation – which will lead to radical changes in employees' behaviour. Both these are 'top-down' macro-approaches in contrast to the 'bottom-up' micro-approach taken in this book.

Organisational life would certainly be chaotic without systems. In contrast, the performance of a single individual may make little difference in organisational terms. Nevertheless, no matter how well designed the systems are, they cannot work on their own. They are managed by, and function through, individuals. How well they function depends on the summated performance of all the individuals involved. If, therefore, one can improve the performance of each individual by even a moderate amount, the difference it would make in organisational terms could be substantial! When an organisation develops the capability for continuous individual self-diagnosis and change it becomes a learning organisation that is constantly adapting to present requirements and anticipating future needs. Handling an employee well to maintain existing high levels of performance or to improve performance, besides being an important part of a manager's leadership role, should assist the development of individuals in terms of improved skills and abilities. In addition, the climate generated by the concerned manager's active leadership role can lead to individual self-diagnosis and self-development, typical of successful and adaptable organisational employees.

Improving the performance of all the members of an organisation can seem like a daunting task! Redesigning or tightening up controlling systems seems much easier. The latter can also be seen to be done and thus receive credit, whereas handling a subordinate well is much less visible and therefore more likely to be overlooked. To encourage managers to exercise their leadership role requires that such a role is better recognised and rewarded (through praise, promotion and financial rewards). Only when such managerial behaviours are recognised will managers exercise effective managerial responsibility. Whether an intervention focuses at the macro (OD/OT) level or at the micro (individual) level may matter less than how effective it is at producing change. In some cases, where systems have been outmoded or outgrown, OD or OT will be essential, but even in such cases the individual employee has to be successfully managed during the implementation of the change. Consequently, there will always be a great deal which an individual manager needs to do to influence the performance of each subordinate for which he or she is responsible.

Supposing, then, that a manager feels an employee's performance is below standard in some area, or even if adequate could be improved further, what should the manager do? Sooner or later, it will be necessary to talk to the individual or individuals concerned. It may be to tell him or her what to do differently, ask what is going wrong, or influence the individual's behaviour in more subtle and indirect ways. The more skilfully these interactions are handled, the more likely it is that the manager will achieve the desired performance improvement. These interactive skills will be discussed in later chapters. However, before the interaction occurs, three steps are necessary. The manager concerned must define precisely what aspects of performance it would be beneficial to improve, discover the reasons why performance is not satisfactory or not as good as it could be, and identify actions which can be taken to achieve the desired improvement in performance. If any of these steps are omitted, then performance improvement is unlikely to be successful. If the performance problem is incorrectly defined in the first place, time and effort will be wasted in attempting to solve the wrong problem. If the real reason for the problem is not understood, then an inappropriate solution is likely to be chosen, such as trying to motivate an individual who lacks the ability to do the task well in the first place. If effective actions to solve the problem are not identified, then the result may be increased understanding, but we cannot be sure that the outcome will be beneficial in organisational terms. The individual may know *why* his or her performance was unsatisfactory but not have a clear idea of *what* to do to improve it. We will now examine these three steps in more detail.

Identifying performance problems

Before a manager can identify the reasons for a performance problem and the steps which can be taken to solve it, he or she must be able to pinpoint precisely what the performance problem is. In dealing with the complexities of human behaviour, 'the successful manager must be a good diagnostician and value a spirit of enquiry.'[2] Where performance is obviously unsatisfactory, it will be relatively easy to identify that a problem exists. Quantity or quality of output may be below stated minimum standards. In interdependent situations, complaints from other members of the work group, or from other members of the organisation may have occurred. For finished products or services, complaints from outside the organisation – customers, clients, government inspectors and so on – may be the stimulus. On the other hand, when performance is acceptable or good, potential areas for improvement are less easy to identify. Unless there are some obvious minor or recurrent errors or failures, an in-depth review of the employee's performance may be necessary. Such a review could occur within the appraisal process where an assessment of an employee's areas of eminence (strengths) and areas requiring development (weaknesses – although we would not recommend the use of the term in the interview itself!) may reveal potential areas for improvement. In yet other cases, an area for improvement may not even relate to the individual's present job but may be seen as part of succession planning or to cope with new developments such as changing markets, changing production techniques or services. These approaches to performance improvement highlight the integrative areas of appraisal, training and development within the identification of performance problems and their solution. Organisation analysis, task analysis and person analysis all focus on identifying which groups and/or individuals require training and development.[3]

In addition, a personal analysis done separately or within the appraisal system can be used to assess whether employees have the prerequisite attitudes, knowledge and motivation to benefit from training. Individuals who lack basic skills or motivation prior to training and development are less likely to learn and may require remedial preparation prior to the learning experience. Relating to this, self-efficacy (the belief in one's ability to perform a specific task) has received increased attention in the training/development literature. Individuals with high self-efficacy tend to outperform individuals with low self-efficacy.[4] That is, individuals who participate in training believing they are capable of mastering the content are likely to learn more during the training. Similarly, individuals who after training believe they can successfully perform the task learned in training should be more resilient when meeting with obstacles to applying their learning[5] and more willing to try new things.[6] Self-efficacy then appears to be an important element in training and development as a predictor of learning success, as a process variable during learning and as a desirable outcome of learning.

This lays emphasis on the approach used to identify performance problems for individuals. Such an approach should be one which is supportive to the individual and maintains his or her self-esteem throughout the whole process of performance improvement. Making narrow and stereotyped assumptions about the nature of performance problems, whether it is that poor performers are 'bone idle and bloody minded', or that they merely need the right opportunity to release 'their natural energy and creativity' will not assist this approach. Further, because of the complexity of human beings and their work roles, such assumptions may only be right some of the time, and even where they are right, they give little assistance in determining how to go about rectifying the poor performance.

Thus, identifying that there may be a need for performance improvement is not the same as identifying what it is. For example, a complaint from a customer about the arrogant manners of a sales representative may signal that there is a performance problem, but it does not tell us *exactly* what the sales representative did to give this impression. It could be any one of several things such as the use of particular words or phrases, accent or tone, manner of presentation, and so on. Telling the sales representative to be 'less arrogant' will have little effect if he or she is unaware of the source of the problem. Thus it will be necessary to identify precisely what the person was doing or not doing before trying to solve the problem of 'behaving in an arrogant manner'. Furthermore, even if we did know, this does not tell us whether it is worth spending time and effort trying to solve it. Both these points will be taken up subsequently.

Causes of unsatisfactory performance

To improve diagnostic skills, we would suggest that the first requirement is the knowledge of the *range* of factors which can influence job performance. It is worth considering at this point the number of reasons you listed for Geoff's poor performance – the exercise at the beginning of the chapter. It is likely that the number of reasons you gave will be strongly influenced by your knowledge of this range of factors. Two key factors which all managers are aware of are motivation and ability. These are undoubtedly important. An individual will not perform well at a task unless he or she wants to perform well and has the necessary ability to do so. Early writers on work performance recognised this, and produced the much quoted formula:[7]

Performance = Ability × Motivation

The formula not only draws attention to two important performance variables, but also says something of the relationship between them. It indicates that this relationship is multiplicative, which suggests that there is little point in attempting to increase a person's ability if their motivation to do a task is zero, or vice versa, attempting to motivate a person who lacks the ability to do the task. For example, 'We've got a training problem because our workers aren't maintenance conscious.' Workers usually *know* they are required to follow certain maintenance procedures. Providing further instruction is unlikely to get the results you want.

Important as ability and motivation are, however, they are not the only factors which influence levels of work performance. The obvious omission is resources. How would you like to be operated on by a highly motivated, skilful dentist whose toolkit consisted of a hand-drill, a rusty penknife and a pair of pliers? An early modification to the formula therefore produced:

Performance = *F* (Ability × Motivation × Resources)

In an attempt to provide a more complex picture of the factors influencing work performance, more complex formulae began to occur. One example suggested that:[8]

Performance = *F* (aptitude level × skill level × understanding of the task × choice to expend effort × choice of degree of effort to expend × choice to persist × facilitating and inhibiting conditions not under the control of the individual)

Perhaps it would be worth using the formula itself to assess its influence on your performance in applying it. Do you have the aptitude or skill level, understanding of the task, and so on, for you to use it effectively? The likely answer is no! It probably fails on the two factors, ability and motivation, of the earlier formula! Its apparent complexity would probably put you off and you would probably have little motivation to use it, resulting in zero performance. Furthermore, if it were possible to use it to identify reasons for poor performance, it fails to indicate what actions might be taken to solve the performance problems. Finally, the pseudo-mathematical nature of the formula is open to criticism. The variables listed may influence performance but they would be extremely difficult to measure. In reality, therefore, such formulae represent no more than a convenient way of listing a number of relevant variables which can cause unsatisfactory work performance.

This alternative approach of simply listing factors has been attempted. Miner and Brewer (see Table 2.1) and Steinmetz (see Table 2.2) have produced such lists.[9] They avoid some of the problems of the formulae described earlier, but they are not without limitations. For example, both lists are long. Steinmetz's list includes factors that managers can do little about, such as sex and senility, and it omits others which managers can do something about, such as lack of feedback. Miner's list also omits lack of feedback along with target setting and, whilst both authors discuss methods of improving work performance, they do not link specific remedial actions to each of the suggested causes of poor performance. Their lists, therefore, may help managers have a better under-standing of the causes of poor performance, but they do not provide specific guidance on how to solve a performance problem once it has been identified.

An allied area, in which emphasis is placed on analysing tasks for performance development, relates to the analysis of tasks for training. Within the training literature there are numerous approaches to, and techniques for, systematic analysis of jobs and tasks for the development of training programmes.[10] However, such approaches are both difficult to apply and time-consuming. Evidence indicates that, because of this, analyses for training are infrequently applied in the development of training programmes. For example, a survey of employers of computer personnel in the United Kingdom indicated that fewer than one in five had carried out any formal analysis of the jobs of programmer, systems analyst and analyst programmer before developing training provision.[11] The content of training analysis does overlap to some extent with performance evaluation aimed at improving work performance. However, training is usually concerned with people who lack knowledge and/or skills for executing tasks,

Table 2.1 *Factors leading to ineffective performance in business organisation*

Intelligence and job knowledge
    Insufficient verbal ability
    Insufficient special ability other than verbal
    Insufficient job knowledge
    Defect of judgement or memory

Emotions and emotional illness
    Continuing disruptive emotion (anxiety, depression, anger, excitement, shame, guilt, jealousy)
    Psychosis (with anxiety, depression, anger, etc., predominating)
    Neurosis (with anxiety, depression, anger, etc., predominating)
    Alcoholism and drug problems

Table 2.1 (*continued*)

Individual motivation to work
    Strong motives frustrated at work
    Unintegrated means to satisfy motives
    Excessively low personal work standards
    Generalised low work motivation

Physical characteristics and disorders
    Physical illness or handicap, including brain damage
    Physical disorders of emotional origin
    Inappropriate physical characteristics
    Insufficient muscular or sensory ability

Family ties
    Family crisis
    Separation from an emotionally significant family
    Social isolation
    Predominance of family considerations over work demands

The groups at work
    Negative consequences associated with group cohesion
    Ineffective management
    Inappropriate managerial standards or criteria

The company
    Insufficient organisational action
    Placement error
    Organisational over-permissiveness
    Excessive span of control
    Inappropriate organisational standards or criteria

Society and its values
    Application of legal sanctions
    Enforcement of cultural values by means not connected with the
        administration of the law
    Conflict between job demands and cultural values as individually held (equity,
        freedom, morality, etc.)

Situational forces
    Negative consequences of economic forces
    Negative consequences of geographic location
    Detrimental conditions of work
    Excessive danger
    Problems in the work itself

Source: J. B. Miner and J. F. Brewer (1976) 'The management of ineffective performance',
in M. D. Dunnette, *Handbook of Industrial and Organizational Psychology*, Rand McNally.

Table 2.2 *Possible causes of poor performance*

Managerial and organisational shortcomings
  Lack of proper motivational environment
  Personality problems
  Inappropriate job assignment
  Improper supervision
  Lack of training
  Failure to establish duties

Individual, personal shortcomings of the employee
  Lack of motivation
  Laziness
  Dissatisfaction with job assignment
  Failure to understand one's duties
  Chronic absenteeism
  Alcoholism
  Mental illness
  Chronic illness
  Senility
  Sex

Outside influences
  Family problems
  Social mores
  Conditions of the labour market
  Governmental actions
  Union policies
  Climate

Source: L. M. Steinmetz (1969), *Managing the Marginal and Unsatisfactory Performer*, Addison-Wesley.

whereas performance evaluation is largely concerned with the further development of knowledge and/or skills: that is, with assessing people who are already in the job, against some criterion. Consequently, data from training analysis is usually more detailed than that required for performance evaluation. On the other hand, information from performance evaluation can be useful for providing objectives for training programmes. Consequently, utilising the training literature and approaches to task analysis, though helpful, was felt inappropriate to what we thought would be acceptable to managers in assisting the process of analysing performance problems.

An approach which appeared much more promising was that of Mager and Pipe, who used a flow diagram.[12] The first step in their flow chart is to describe the 'performance discrepancy': that is, the difference between someone's *actual* performance and his or her *desired* performance. However, according to them, merely identifying a difference between what one is doing and what you would like them to do is *not* enough reason to take action. For example, if you have done a task in a particular way and subsequently someone else takes over that task and does it differently, that in itself may not be reason enough to take action. Aside from your possible displeasure, what would be the consequences of ignoring it? If there are no serious consequences, it is not worth the effort of attempting to change the way the new incumbent performs the task. They note that it would be unrealistic 'to expect to be able to remould the world into an image of our own desires. We must be selective about which discrepancies to attack' (p.12): that is, we must be selective in choosing target behaviours. As managers, our goal is to increase or maintain the frequency of desired target behaviours and to decrease or eliminate the frequency of undesirable target behaviours. Not all behaviours fall into either of these categories from a managerial point of view. Many behaviours are neutral, neither contributing to nor detracting from organisational goals. Further, although a behaviour may fall into these categories, it may not become a target behaviour because it has only a relatively unimportant effect on overall employee performance. Target behaviours should be limited only to those behaviours having a major impact on overall performance.

This procedure for identifying target behaviours has been called *pinpointing*.[13] It is not always an easy task because some managers frequently confuse attitudes, feelings and personality attributes with behaviours. For example, an employee may be described as 'unco-operative, aggressive and disruptive'. These are personal attributes rather than behaviours. They are difficult to measure meaningfully and having such a description does not tell us precisely what effect they have on their own or someone else's work performance. However, the individual must have done something which results in this description, such as threatening another employee, extending breaks, failing to apply safety regulations, refusing to do tasks, and so on. These are behaviours which can be observed and, if found to be affecting the performance of self or others, can be tackled.

There are two good reasons for defining performance problems in terms of behaviour rather than personality. First, although personality influences people's behaviour, it is by no means the only determinant. The environment (including other people) also has a substantial impact. Thus people with quite different personalities may behave in quite similar ways when in certain environments, such as at a funeral service. Conversely, even though personality is relatively unchanging, a person can behave quite differently in different situations; for example, at a board meeting compared to an office party. In forming impressions of people and attributing a causal role to their influence on events, we frequently overestimate the influence of their personality and underestimate the role of the environment (including other people), as we shall see in the next chapter.

The second reason relates to an earlier point on pinpointing. As adults, our personalities are relatively stable. Thus bringing about a change in personality is difficult and is not something which managers have the expertise to do effectively, nor perhaps would it be ethical for them to attempt to do. Deciding that a problem has arisen due to someone's laziness, lack of confidence, lack of foresight or aggressiveness, renders the problem unsolvable. We do not observe such attributes directly, we infer them from observations of behaviour. The individual has done, or failed to do, something to give us this impression; for example, he or she has sat around doing nothing when there was work to be done, failed to speak up in a departmental meeting, or failed to order essential supplies on time. These more precise behavioural descriptions are much less complex to tackle and are aspects of behaviour which a manager can probably get an employee to change, if the right approach is used.

Having described the performance discrepancy and examined the consequences, whether important or not, Mager and Pipe then ask whether the cause of the problem is a skill deficiency. If it is, various questions are asked to establish its nature and the remedial actions which can be taken. If the cause is not one relating to skill deficiency, it is then assumed to be one relating to motivation or some obstacle preventing satisfactory performance. Again, various questions are needed to establish the specific cause of the problem and the remedial actions required.

Identifying solutions to performance problems

The main limitation of most of the approaches to improving work performance which we have described is that they do not specify what steps managers should take to solve a performance problem once they have identified its causes. The one exception is Mager and Pipe's flow diagram. It specifies a variety of remedial actions which can be taken, such as arranging formal training, arranging positive consequences, changing the job, and so on. Nevertheless, whilst their step-by-step approach makes it easier to identify specific solutions to certain types of performance problems, it provides a relatively limited account of the factors influencing performance, confined in the main to those factors relating to skills and motivation. Both the research literature and our experience in analysing real-life performance problems indicated that there were other important influences on work performance.

In an attempt to overcome this problem, we produced an expanded version of Mager and Pipe's flow chart, incorporating additional influences on performance. The result was a complex diagram spreading over several pages, which was reluctantly rejected as being too cumbersome to use as a managerial 'tool'. What was needed, we felt, was an approach which fulfilled two important criteria – ease of use and practical 'real-life' applicability. We therefore decided to develop a one-page checklist, on the grounds that this would be easier to follow and thus easier to use in practical situations. The resulting checklist is shown in Figure 2.1.

1. What is the problem in behavioural terms? What precisely is the individual doing or not doing which is adversely influencing his or her performance?
2. Is the problem *really* serious enough to spend time and effort on?
3. What reasons might there be for the performance problem (see column 1)?
4. What actions might be taken to improve the situation (see column 2)?

Possible reasons for performance problem	*Possible solutions*
Goal Clarity Is the person fully aware of the job requirements?	Give guidance concerning expected goals and standards. Set targets. MBO.
Ability Does the person have the capacity to do the job well?	Provide formal training, on the job coaching, practice, secondment, etc.
Task Difficulty Does the person find the task too demanding?	Simplify task, reduce work load, reduce time pressures, etc.
Intrinsic Motivation Does the person find the task rewarding in itself?	Redesign job to match job-holder's needs.
Extrinsic Motivation Is good performance rewarded by others?	Arrange positive consequences for good performance and zero or negative consequences for poor performance.
Feedback Does the person receive adequate feedback about his or her performance?	Provide or arrange feedback.
Resources Does the person have adequate resources for satisfactory task performance?	Provide staff, equipment, raw materials as appropriate.
Working Conditions Do working conditions, physical or social, interfere with performance?	Improve light, noise, heat, layout, remove distractions, etc, as appropriate.
Personal Problems For example, stress, substance abuse, family problems, etc.	Provide counselling if sufficiently skilled. Call in specialist helper.

5. Do you have sufficient information to select the most appropriate solution(s)? If not, collect the information required, e.g. consult records, observe work behaviour, talk to person concerned.
6. Select most appropriate solution(s).
7. Is the solution worthwhile in cost benefit terms?
    (a) If so, implement it.
    (b) If not, work through the checklist again, *or* relocate the individual, *or* reorganise the department/organisation, *or* live with the problem.
8. Could you have handled the problem better? If so, review own performance. If not, and the problem is solved, reward yourself and tackle next problem.

Figure 2.1 *Checklist for improving work performance*

A performance improvement checklist

The first step in the checklist is to define the problem in behavioural terms. What is the employee doing or not doing which is adversely affecting his or her work performance? This is the pinpointing of target behaviour previously mentioned. Again it is worth emphasising that the problem should not be expressed in vague terms of personality attributes because we are unlikely to be successful in changing personality, but we may be able to change behaviour if an appropriate approach is used. This also avoids an ethical problem. Asking employees to change their personalities could be regarded as an unacceptable invasion of personal privacy, whereas asking employees to change their behaviour is a legitimate part of a manager's role. Influencing work behaviour is largely what managers are paid for.

The second step, as in the Mager and Pipe approach, is to check whether the problem is really serious enough to spend time and effort on. If the behaviour in question has little effect on the individual's work performance or that of others, then spending time and effort in attempting to bring about change would not seem to be an effective use of the organisation's resources, as noted earlier. However, there may be times when we feel obliged to do so for reasons of expediency. The organisation may require compliance with apparently trivial rules, or our own superior may insist on his or her own foibles being imposed on our subordinates. By the same token, it may also be useful to examine our own reasons for believing that a performance problem exists. It is all too easy for us at times to say something is bad for morale, bad for the company image, will upset people, or will give a bad impression. But will it? In some cases, such beliefs may be justified but, on the other hand, they may be merely rationalisations providing justification for our own idiosyncratic assumptions about acceptable behaviour.

Assuming the problem is seen as a significant one, the next step is to review the possible causes and potential solutions. It is better to work through all the possible causes first, before thinking about solutions, because premature evaluation of causes for their solution can result in premature closure of the review procedure. As a result, the quality of the chosen solution may be substantially reduced.

Evidence indicates that problem solving is enhanced by the following measures:

1. Defining the problem so that it does not block possible channels of thought (for example, not defining the performance problem in terms of personality attributes but in terms of actual behaviour).
2. Providing conditions that allow the production of ideas to range as freely as possible (for example, using *aides-mémoire* to increase the number of factors considered, such as a checklist).

3. Postponing the evaluation (or judgement) of ideas for as long as possible (that is, until all possible factors have been considered.[14]

For ease of presentation, however, we will consider them together here.

Goal clarity

The employee may not know or may misunderstand the requirements of the job. For instance, the individual may not realise that a certain task is included as part of the job, may be unaware of what standard of performance is expected, or may not be clear of the priorities of the various tasks within the total job (for example, stressing quantity of output rather than quality, or vice versa; choosing to carry out one task at the expense of another because the former may be easier/more rewarding, such as spending more time on sales contract renewals rather than attempting to secure new sales contracts).

Where performance indicates lack of conformity to required expectation, some guidance or reminder will be necessary about the total tasks expected to be fulfilled, the standards to be achieved and the priority of tasks within the total job. According to the situation, this might be achieved from a quiet word pointing out the importance of certain aspects of performance, or a more rigorous goal-setting session with the individual, say, in a performance appraisal interview. In the latter case, where a problem relates to performance standards, goal-setting has been demonstrated as an extremely successful performance enhancer.[15] Research has shown:

1. Specific goals are more effective than ambiguous goals such as 'do your best', or no goals at all.
2. Difficult but attainable goals lead to higher performance than easy goals, with moderate goals in between.
3. Goal commitment is necessary for goal setting to affect performance, and is affected by expectations of goal success and the value of success. It is not necessarily affected by participation in goal setting, although some recent evidence indicates a positive role for employee participation in setting goals.[16] Further, self-set goals are an important element of self-management.
4. Feedback on performance, together with support for employee efforts (time, tools, information and other resources needed to do the job) must be provided by the manager and the organisation.

Goal setting is a simple, straightforward and highly effective technique for motivating employee performance. However, it is no panacea. It will not compensate for underpayment of employees or for poor management. Furthermore performance goals are less easy to set for some employees than others. In supervisory jobs, for example, what is achieved is often influenced by factors outside the supervisor's control and the supervisor's own contribution is often difficult to observe or measure. In setting measurable production goals, managers may also overlook employee development goals. Consequently, as with other techniques aimed at influencing employee work behaviour, goal setting should be tempered by good managerial judgement.

As a technique, goal setting is applied at the individual level. If the problem relating to performance standards is widespread, however, then a more formal system such as 'management by objectives' (MBO) may be more appropriately applied to a whole unit. MBO incorporates many of the attributes of goal setting, but in a top-down approach. It can be applied across the organisation or within a particular sub–unit of the organisation. From the organisation's overall objectives (derived, say, from a strategic plan) sub-units agree their own objectives. These are then used to derive and agree group and individual objectives so that a coherent plan involving all employees is derived. Early applications of MBO failed to achieve consistent success largely because of poor communication between superiors and subordinates and lack of accurate measurement of results against plans (feedback). More recent applications emphasise that all phases of MBO should be objectives oriented, have a problem-solving focus and be supported with effective communication and feedback.[17] The role of communication between the manager and individuals or groups, whose perceptions of performance requirements may differ, is critical.

Ability

The individual may lack the skills or knowledge necessary for satisfactory work performance. Ensuring that employees can perform organisational tasks effectively can be viewed from two aspects – selection and training. Within the United Kingdom, emphasis tends to be placed on selection rather than training to achieve employee effectiveness. The selection approach seeks to identify people with good potential for effective job performance, which can create a climate that discourages formal training activities. It can also encourage a problem mentioned earlier, that of defining an employee's performance problem in terms of a personality defect, such as laziness, lack of foresight, lack of confidence and so on. Because we have selected people on the basis of good potential for the job, if they fail, we are therefore led to believe that their lack of success is at least partly due to personality factors, such as poor motivation or bloody-mindedness, rather than ability. As a result, our first thought on how to overcome the problem created by poor performance is often one of transferring the individual to some other unit or terminating employment! In the case of emphasising a training approach, less stress is placed on identification of potential and more stress is placed on identifying and overcoming existing performance deficiencies in employees in their present job. It is highly likely that the latter will become the more dominant philosophy in the future as equal opportunities legislation begins to bite. This shift in emphasis has already occurred in North America due to legislation encouraging the recruitment and training of a culturally diverse workforce.[18] As a result, both valid selection techniques and effective training programmes will lead to more effective use of human resources and a more appropriate analysis of employee performance deficiencies in terms of behavioural rather than personality terms.

A second factor which can affect whether good work performance occurs relates to environmental constraints. These include poor communication of job-related information (goal clarity, for example), inadequate feedback, and lack of tools and equipment, materials and supplies (resources) including required services, and help from others, as well as supervisory practices. In addition, pay and promotional opportunities may affect motivation. The reason for dwelling on these points is, that what may often be seen as a problem of ability can be one where the organisation is exercising constraints which are preventing employees from demonstrating good work performance. Therefore, before one can diagnose a performance problem as being caused by lack of ability, managers must ensure that the environment of the apparent poor performer is not subject to situational constraints directly affecting their performance, or to organisational policies (particularly reward structures) which fail to motivate good performance.

If the individual's performance is diagnosed as a lack of some necessary skill or knowledge, and not one related to other constraining factors, then some kind of 'learning experience' will need to be provided. This might be a formal training course which often, understandably, seems to be the practising manager's favourite solution. Such training may be 'on-the-job' training in the actual work situation, either under the supervision of a presently experienced employee who guides and gives feedback to the learner, or provided by a training specialist. Alternatively, it may be 'off-the-job', either on some externally run training course or through secondment or transfer to another department where the ability can be acquired. Similarly, 'off-the-job' training can occur within the workplace using simulation techniques. These may take the form of supervised simulated projects, such as sales forecasting, budgetary planning or in-basket exercises emphasising particular workplace problems. In these cases, realistic information (such as historical data, for example) is provided for the projects/ exercises and, where necessary, assistance from qualified personnel is used for guidance and feedback. Simulation techniques can also be used in off-the-job training situations for the development of personal and interpersonal skills through role-play exercises. Again, guidance and feedback would be provided by qualified personnel or trainers. Most organisations do not use developmental assignments and other forms of simulated on-the-job training for management development in a systematic way. On-the-job development can also be achieved through coaching by the job holder's own boss. It requires a large investment of time by the job holder's superior and because of this is probably the least-used technique. At higher levels of management, such an approach may be replaced by 'mentoring'. There is, however, little empirical data available on the ways in which mentors facilitate managerial development. People with assigned mentors have reported receiving psychosocial benefits (encouragement, coaching, coun-selling), but only limited career benefits.[19]

One major influence on the success or failure of training and development is the importance of designing programmes which facilitate the development of self-efficacy.[20,21] Trainees whose self-efficacy is developed through training are more likely to transfer and demonstrate the learned behaviour on the job. A second major influence is related to managerial/supervisory practices in assisting the learner to apply the newly learned behaviour on the job. The manager must ensure that there are no situational constraints preventing the newly learned behaviour from being implemented, and must support and motivate employee performance by providing feedback, maintaining high self-efficacy and, where appropriate, setting goals for achievement on the task.

Task difficulty

In some circumstances, it may be more expedient to regard the job as being too difficult for an employee rather than attributing poor performance to the individual's lack of ability. For example, a job may be more complex, involve more different aspects, or entail shorter deadlines than a job holder can cope with. Coping can be viewed from at least two aspects.

First, it can be considered from the point of whether the work can be done effectively at all. For example, the job may contain too many tasks which prohibit completion in the time available, or the job may demand goals which are set at too high a level. Alternatively, the goals may conflict, such as setting high goals for both quality and quantity of output, either of which can be achieved, but only at the expense of the other. Thus, whatever the individual does in any of these cases, performance will be below standard. Under such circumstances, reducing the demands by reducing the number of tasks, setting lower or different performance goals, may be appropriate solutions.

Secondly, task difficulty can be viewed from the effect of the job on the job holder's well–being. It may be possible to do some jobs well in the short term, but in the longer term job stress may develop in the incumbent, which affects the efficiency and effectiveness with which the job is done. Convincing evidence exists for the relationship between certain job design features and increased stress. These include workload, number of hours worked, number of people worked for, job autonomy, increased cost responsibility and ability to exercise control over the working conditions.[22] In some cases, training in stress management may assist adjustment to job stress,[23] although there has been some doubt expressed about its validity.[24] In others, where it would be difficult for most people to adjust to the stressful conditions, even though they may have been trained to reduce the effects of stress, some form of job redesign may be necessary to reduce the effects. This may include simplifying the job or, alternatively, job rotation or additional time off may also be successful approaches.

In all cases where it is decided that task difficulty rather than lack of ability is the source of the problem, then simplifying the task by reducing workload, number of people worked for, hours worked, or setting lower performance goals, may be necessary. Alternatively, where ability to exercise control is a problem, it may be necessary to *increase* the incumbent's control over the work so that he or she can restructure the work to reduce stress and control their own performance more effectively. However, some consideration of the implications is necessary because, on the one hand, taking work off one person and giving it to another may just shift the problem from one to the other. On the other hand, even were this avoided, simplifying a job too much, although it may solve an overload problem, may create an even worse motivational problem.

Intrinsic motivation

An employee may not be motivated to do a task, or do it well, because he or she does not find it rewarding in itself. That is, it does not provide the interest, challenge, opportunities for feelings of achievement or pride which the job holder would like to experience. How the person perceives a task or job is an interaction between what the job has to offer – the content and context of the job – and what the individual would like from a job in terms of the particular needs which are most important to that individual at the time. If the two are congruent, then it is likely that both motivation and job satisfaction will be high. However, if a performance problem has arisen, and there is some indication that a possible reason might be motivational, it will be worth exploring with the employee his or her feelings about the job. Some indicators of a problem relating to intrinsic motivation might be spending an increasing amount of time in non-work activities (taking additional drink breaks, extended social interactions with other personnel, arriving late, leaving early, poor attendance record, and so on) or, when on the job, poor concentration leading to high error rates or low productivity.

People have such a wide variety of needs that one cannot hope to satisfy all of them. In addition, there are many needs which cannot easily be satisfied within the organisational context or which it may not be practical to solve within that context for one reason or another. Therefore, what a manager needs to discover is the need which the individual would most like to be fulfilled *next* that is within the manager's or the organisation's power to fulfil.

If the needs which are most important to the individual are intrinsic to the job, then some form of job redesign may be appropriate. A manager cannot simply give a subordinate such 'intrinsic rewards' as a sense of achievement, increased self-esteem or an interest in the job. All that can be done is to provide employees with the opportunity of experiencing such things by changing the content of the job. The most well-known and widely discussed theory of job redesign is the 'job characteristics model' of Hackman and Oldham.[25] The model specifies five dimensions of job content – skill variety, task identity, task

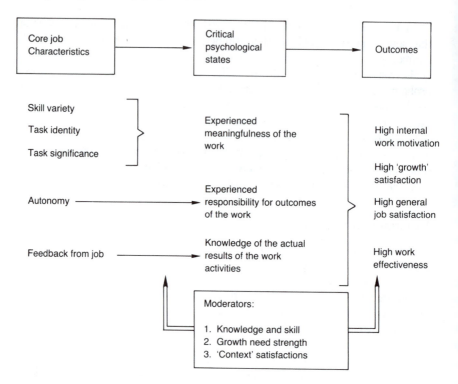

(Source: J. R. Hackman and G. R. Oldham (1980), *Work Design*, Addison-Wesley)

Figure 2.2 *The job characteristics model*

significance, autonomy, and feedback – that affect work outcomes via their influence over three critical psychological states: experienced meaningfulness of the work, experienced responsibility for outcomes of the work, and knowledge of the actual results of the work activities. These psychological states in turn lead to beneficial work and personal outcomes. They also suggest, however, that the strength of relationship will be moderated by the 'growth need strength' (GNS) of the employees concerned (see Figure 2.2). Employees with high GNS (those who value the fulfilment of higher-order needs such as needs for achievement, recognition and fulfilment of potential) are more likely to react favourably to enriched jobs than those with low GNS. The outcomes for employees who perceive their jobs as enriched on the five dimensions are predicted to be higher levels of intrinsic motivation, job satisfaction and work performance.

Empirical evidence largely supports the job redesign/job satisfaction link, particularly amongst those employees with high GNS,[26] but links between perceived job content, intrinsic motivation and job performance sustained only limited support, except where job redesign was associated with pay rises (extrinsic reward).[27] It may be that job redesign affects *quality* of performance rather than *quantity*. However, the literature on field and laboratory studies have used quantity rather than quality measures. A limitation of the model exists in that it tells us how to enrich jobs to suit high GNS employees, but not how to design jobs which would be satisfying to those with low GNS. Hackman and Oldham only state that low GNS employees will not respond as strongly as high GNS employees.

Another factor for consideration emerges from studies of the 'job characteristics model', that of pay. Although pay is an extrinsic reward (given by others) there is some indication that, in work situations, it can interact with other intrinsic rewards and affect performance. This seems self-evident when one considers the consequences of enriching jobs through job redesign. Most, if not all, enriched jobs require incumbents to demonstrate a wider range of skills and take more responsibility for the work they do. Under such circumstances there is likely to be an expectation for increased pay on a straightforward equity principle. Although there is some, largely laboratory, evidence that adding external rewards (e.g. monetary payments) to intrinsically interesting tasks may decrease task interest,[28] other evidence indicates that adding monetary incentives increases task performance without diminishing intrinsic interest.[29] Research, because of the necessity to single out variables for study, often simplifies reality. In consequence, the results when interpreted for application in the more complex organisational environment can appear questionable. It is important to bear in mind the complexity of why individuals engage in a task and what factors influence how well or badly they perform in the task. Present evidence tends to indicate that people probably expect both extrinsic and intrinsic rewards from work activities. For many people, intrinsically interesting jobs are unavailable and such people are likely to be strongly influenced by extrinsic rewards (monetary payments). However, for the fortunate people with intrinsically interesting jobs, extrinsic rewards will nevertheless be of great importance for reasons of pay equity, to fulfil expectations relating to their standard of living and for status reasons.

Another variable which can affect how job holders react to job enrichment through job redesign relates to social interaction. Job enrichment often provides a more interesting job at the expense of reduced opportunities for social interaction. Some evidence indicates that employees with high social needs may find this 'trade-off' unacceptable.[30]

Finally, as noted above, the aim of many job redesign programmes is to increase employee responsibility for work done, which is no doubt something that many people value. Others, however, may take the view that unless the increased responsibility is matched by a commensurate increase in pay, management is simply trying to trick them into doing a more difficult job for the same money.

We began this section on intrinsic motivation by stating that people have such a wide variety of needs that one cannot hope to satisfy all of them. Therefore, what a manager needs to discover is the need which the individual would most like to be fulfilled next that is within the manager's or organisation's power to fulfil. The complexity of this process may have been indicated by the content of this section and the importance for the manager of treating employees as individuals to achieve high levels of work performance. There is much that the individual manager can do to allocate responsibilities between subordinates in such a way that they more closely match the subordinate's own particular needs. Evidence shows that it is an effective motivational strategy.[31] Further, using such an approach is likely to lead to greater intrinsic satisfaction for the manager!

Extrinsic motivation

Extrinsic rewards are rewards which are provided by someone else. Whether an individual receives them is under the control of an external agent. In contrast, intrinsic rewards are those which the individual awards him- or herself. They come directly as a result of doing something and are basically related to feelings. The distinction is not entirely clear-cut and the two often occur together – for instance, doing a task well may trigger feelings of success (intrinsic reward) *and* be accompanied by praise from others, a bonus, a promotion and so on, which are extrinsic rewards. As noted in the previous section, in a work context our expectations are probably based on receiving both intrinsic *and* extrinsic rewards from organisational activities. Extrinsic rewards, then, include pay (wages, salaries, commissions, bonuses, etc.), fringe benefits (meal subsidies, vacations, discounts on company products, etc.), promotion, new title, increased office size, car parking space, praise, recognition, preferred task assignments, flexitime, time off, and so on. (Employees can also receive disincentives – for example, dismissal, pay reduction, and so on – the opposite of rewards.)

Where extrinsic rewards are considered important by the individual, then low motivation could be symptomatic of the fact that the employee does not perceive the rewards received as commensurate with the effort required to achieve them. The problem may be the size of the rewards or lack of recognition that particular required behaviours are rewarded at all (goal clarity) because there appears to be no apparent relationship between received pay and the required behaviour. For example, machine maintenance or an administrative task may not be perceived as important because doing or not doing it has no effect on pay.[32] In other words, pay is not contingent on performance. Further, employees may not be motivated to perform a task, not only because they believe it will not be rewarded but also because they believe they may actually be punished for doing it. For example: conscientious employees may be given disliked and tedious tasks because they are the only ones who can be relied upon to do them well;

	Good performance	Poor performance
Rewards	1	2
Negative or zero outcomes	3	4

Figure 2.3 *Extrinsic rewards and work performance*

poor performance on a disliked task is 'rewarded' by being taken off it, good performance is 'punished' by being given more of the same; people who continually cause conflict are treated with deference and rarely asked to do additional 'emergency' tasks and may even be given 'perks' to placate them; employees who get on with their work without any fuss are often ignored, whereas others who are less productive but spend unproductive time 'networking', receive merit awards or promotion as a result of their high profile. If the nature of the reward system is such that it does not pay to be a good performer, it is only to be expected that extrinsic motivation will be low.

We would suggest, therefore, that if managers feel that their staff lack extrinsic motivation, they should examine all the rewards at their disposal – verbal recognition, interesting work assignments, not being given last-minute or onerous tasks, time off, visits to conferences, salary and promotion recommendations, and so on – and ask themselves whether these go to the truly good performers. To help in this analysis we recommend that managers use the simple diagram (Figure 2.3) to assist their examination of reward application. In the four quadrants, simply list as follows:

1. The rewards which are likely to result from good performance.
2. The rewards which are likely to result from poor performance.
3. Negative or zero outcomes likely to result from good performance.
4. The negative or zero outcomes likely to result from poor performance.

If most items are in quadrants 2 and 3, then there is something wrong and changes should be made to give rewards for good performance and negative, or at least zero, outcomes for poor performance.

Another problem may arise as a result of additional or 'merit' awards being made contingent on good performance. These have been implemented widely and enthusiastically, not only in industry but also in educational establishments such as schools and universities. There is a popular belief in the power of merit pay for influencing performance which is not sustained by actual practice. Pay can be a powerful incentive for good performance but unless it can be directly linked to performance its influence will be severely restricted.

Real organisations are messy, often unpredictable places in which work is frequently interdependent and complex and requires as much co-operative as individual effort for successful organisational performance. Merit pay is usually based on *individual* performance on the assumption that overall organisational performance is the simple additive combination of individual employees' separate contributions.[33] Where this is not the case and where co-operation amongst employees is important, individual performance-based pay can provide disincentives for performing co-operative tasks essential for organisational effectiveness. And even where individual performance can be assessed, problems can arise due to the amount of merit awards given both absolutely and relatively. In absolute terms, a £300 merit award for someone earning £6,000 per annum may be viewed as reasonable for an 'outstanding' performance, but to someone earning £20,000 it will probably be viewed as derisory and act as a disincentive for future performance. In relative terms, if an outstanding employee is given a 5 per cent merit increase and an above-average employee a 4 per cent merit increase, the difference will probably not be sufficient to provide an incentive for above-average employees to strive for the outstanding category. Another similar situation occurs when a percentage of an organisation's wage bill is set aside for merit awards and in the first year the outstanding performers benefit. If, in the second year, rather than giving the same people a further award, the available money is shared amongst the next category, and so on, until most employees have had a share, again the process will lose its incentive value. Managing a pay reward system is one of the most complex tasks facing an organisation but, if properly designed, can be a key contributor to organisational effectiveness.[34]

As noted at the beginning of this section, the distinction between intrinsic and extrinsic motivation is not clear-cut. We have dealt with them separately for reasons of convenience, but people will have important needs in both areas. However, we have also noted that real organisations are messy, volatile and therefore often unpredictable places with not only complex work patterns but complex human beings working to fulfil organisational objectives. Consequently, rather than looking exclusively at either intrinsic or extrinsic rewards separately, it will be more appropriate for managers to seek ways of achieving an acceptable balance between the two. Approaches to applying rewards should therefore reflect the organisation's need to influence people to behave appropriately within organisational realities based around its own business strategy, the ways in which work is organised and showing congruence with its own managerial philosophy and leadership style.

Feedback

Poor performance may occur because the individual does not receive adequate feedback concerning his or her standard of performance and therefore does not realise the need for improvement. Alternatively, individuals may be aware that they are not performing as successfully as they might do, or are required to, but are uncertain about which specific aspects of their performance should be modified in order to improve their overall performance.

In the first case, the provision of some form of feedback is necessary. However, this assumes that the individual is aware of the expected standards of performance. It is worth checking before supplying the feedback that performance expectations or goals (see above under 'Goal clarity') have been set and that they are observable and assessable goals. Also, the performance must be assessable by both the manager and the job holder so that agreement can be reached about the partial or complete achievement of the set goals. Where employees can monitor their own performance, need for close supervision becomes unnecessary and can itself lead to improved performance. An example of performance self-monitoring is one implemented at Emery Air Freight. Employees believed that, nine times out of ten, they were responding to customer enquiries within ninety minutes. The company instituted a simple feedback system whereby the employees monitored and logged their own performance. It was found that the ninety minutes' response time was only actually being achieved three times out of ten. The self-monitored records were periodically inspected by supervisors who gave praise for performance improvement but simply ignored the results if no improvement occurred. A similar approach was used for container utilisation and delivery driving. The improved performance achieved by this combination of feedback and praise was estimated to have saved Emery Air Freight $2 million over a three-year period.[35]

The provision of feedback for multidimensional tasks, such as selling, patient care, interviewing, training, and so on, can create problems of providing precise quantitative information. Overall, performance may be reduced to a single measure (number of sales, patient recovery rate, performance improvement), but this will be of little use if, where performance is unacceptable, it does not enable the performer to identify specific aspects of his or her performance which need to be improved. For example, a golfer normally receives 'response-produced' feedback for each swing of the golf club. This relates information from the muscles (kinaesthetic) and joints (proprioceptive) with visual observation of the movement of the ball. The golfer will have a score for each hole plus eventually an aggregated score for the full round of golf. This response-produced feedback is all intrinsic to the task – information relating to performance available in the normal task situation. However, assuming the golfer is dissatisfied with his or her aggregated score and, on further analysis of the score for each hole, believes poor performance occurred on ten of the eighteen holes, what does he or she do then? Only if additional information is provided by a coach (or perhaps a video) concerning tactics, selection of clubs, the swing of the club and so on, will the individual have relevant information to relate to specific aspects of performance.

A similar situation arises in interviewing – the interviewer will have a context, a problem of some sort, a 'tool kit' of statement and question types and an objective to achieve (to persuade the interviewee, say, to do something different). The interviewer will tackle the problem using his or her 'tool kit' (questions and statements). Response-produced feedback will be available relating to the use of the questions and statements and their responses from the interviewee. However, assuming the interviewer is dissatisfied with the outcome, what can he or she do then? Again, only through the provision of additional feedback from a coach, mentor or trainer will the person have a situation which will enhance performance. This indicates the necessity, in some situations, to provide augmented feedback. This is feedback which is extrinsic to the performance of the task and not normally available to the person performing it, but which can be supplied from an external source. The external source in many cases will be the individual's manager. Augmented feedback can be provided on any required temporal basis – daily, weekly, monthly – or as part of an appraisal system. When supplied by a manager, it can be seen and included as an important aspect of his or her leadership role in influencing subordinate performance.

A final important consideration relates to group or team feedback. There has been little empirical study of feedback at the group or team level. Nevertheless, there are important differences between individual and group feedback. Whereas individual feedback relates to individual performance (whether performing an individual task or as a member of a group), group feedback relates to team performance and will usually require group debriefing/group problem-solving sessions. Despite its importance for both military and sporting activities, as well as occupational, there is little guiding information available from research. Sport psychology and physical education specialists emphasise the importance of team building. They emphasise aspects such as task, maintenance and process.[36] The latter two are factors relevant to team activities compared to individual activity, and may require separate attention for feedback to that relating to task outcomes. However, task outcomes themselves may need very different approaches since, although group outcomes depend upon the group as a unit, individuals and individual interactions are usually important variables influencing group performance.

Resources

If the individual is unable to perform to an acceptable level because of inadequate resources, then the manager will need either to provide the necessary resources or, in fairness, accept a lower standard of performance than otherwise might be expected. The allocation of resources can be one of the many sources of conflict which can affect individuals or groups. Resources are usually finite, particularly in relation to how personnel, finance, space or equipment are shared out. Thus, in the allocation procedure at the group or departmental level, one group's gain is likely to be another group's loss and, within the group or department itself, one individual's gain is likely to lead to another individual's loss. Resource allocation tends to take on a win/lose perspective.

A second related factor is that resource allocation can be linked to control. The way the resources are allocated initially by the organisation to groups/departments, and then by group heads/departmental managers to smaller groups or individuals, determines the expansion, maintenance or contraction of group or individual activity. Such allocations may be linked to the strategic plans of the organisation, in which case departments, groups or individuals may understand the need for such allocations, even though they may not like the result of the allocations in terms of winners and losers. On the other hand, resource allocation can be based on patronage, in which case feelings of discontent, or even anger, may arise. Employees may show little overt resistance to, or challenge, resource allocation based on patronage, nevertheless their behaviour and attitudes may be significantly affected.

A relatively recent area of research relates to the notion of organisational citizenship behaviour (OCB).[37] OCBs are actions that are not defined within the employee's formal job description but which can influence organisational effectiveness. A 'good citizen' attends work punctually, helps others, makes suggestions and volunteers for non-required activities. Dissatisfied employees are less likely to behave in such ways and more likely to complain, resist authority, avoid work and behave aggressively.

Occasionally complaints relating to resources may result from employees' general feelings of discontent or dissatisfaction. A lack of 'up to the minute' computer software by a secretary, or 'state of the art' laboratory equipment for a bench scientist, may produce valid complaints but have little effect on their organisational performance. Other individuals in the same departments may find not having these facilities of no consequence. In other words, there may be other sources of discontent behind the complaints, dissatisfaction or frustrations which are more difficult to crystallise or express, and resources become the scapegoat. Improving the resources could then have the opposite effect to that intended because if, after the novelty wears off, the frustration or dissatisfaction remains, morale is likely to drop even further until or unless another scapegoat is substituted. This does not mean, however, that nothing should be done about complaints concerning inadequate resources. These should be attended to and discussed. It may also be worth exploring, however, whether inadequate resources are the *only* source of the dissatisfaction.

Working conditions

As with resources, complaints about working conditions may simply represent something to gripe about or may be the symptom of some deeper source of dissatisfaction which is too complex to define. Again, therefore, it is a good idea to check whether working conditions are the real or the only source of the problem. Nevertheless, poor working conditions can adversely affect physical and psychological health and work performance.

There are many regulations concerning minimum acceptable standards with respect to certain aspects of working conditions, such as noise, illumination and temperature. Many of these are included in the Health and Safety at Work legislation. Minimum acceptable standards, however, rarely facilitate optimum work performance. Working conditions may not only be important in themselves but can also be indicative of a company's concern towards its employees, thus affecting the employee's perception of, and perhaps commitment to, the company.

More recently, a broader approach to work and well–being has developed within the context of work and stress. Factors relating to the physical environment and working conditions are viewed as potential 'stressors'. This broad set of potential stressors includes *task–induced* factors – speed or load demands of the task or job itself that impinge on the limits of an employee's ability to perform. *Situational and psychological* factors – heat, noise, lighting, hazardous conditions, long or unusual working hours, job insecurity, and so on. Finally, *personal factors* can increase or reduce the severity of task–induced and situational factors as a result of the physiological state of the body. Loss of sleep, illness, alcohol, drugs and other personal factors will all have an effect on the individual's adaptation to stressful working conditions.[38] This leads into the final checklist factor.

Personal problems

At the individual level, work performance can be affected by such problems as loss of sleep, illness, and drugs, as noted above. Other personal factors could include family problems, lack of social acceptance (for whatever reasons), lack of interest in the work, and so on. In such circumstances, unlike the factors discussed above, the solutions to the problems do not lie fully within the organisation's purview. Easing the person's work load may be appropriate as a temporary expedient, but it is unlikely to be a viable long-term solution. Furthermore telling an employee how to solve his or her personal problem is unlikely to be effective. A solution appropriate for the person giving the advice may be totally inappropriate or even unacceptable for the person with the problem. If the manager has the necessary skills, he or she can carry out a counselling interview, allowing the employee to talk through the problem and reaching their own solution *without giving advice*. Where the manager lacks these skills, then it would be more appropriate to refer the individual for professional help either from within or outside the organisation (e.g. specialist counsellors, Alcoholics Anonymous). Given that occupational stress is a quite prevalent problem, it may be worthwhile providing training in stress management for employees likely to be exposed to work stressors,[39] although, as noted previously, there has been some doubt expressed about its validity.[40]

Before leaving the factors influencing work performance, one further point is worth noting. For ease of presentation, it has been assumed that performance problems tend to arise because people lack something (e.g. ability, motivation, resources) and that the solution to the problem consists of finding some way of increasing such variables. This may not always be the case, however. Sometimes, too much of one of these variables may adversely affect performance. If the individual's abilities are too high for the task then he or she may become bored and careless. If motivation is too high it may cause anxiety, which will prevent an employee from making the best use of his or her abilities. If resources are too plentiful, a manager may spend valuable time managing resources rather than working towards the achievement of the unit's objectives, and so on.

In some cases, such problems will be picked up under other heads in the checklist. For example, 'too much ability' would reveal itself as 'lack of intrinsic motivation', and 'too many resources' as 'task too difficult'. Nevertheless, when using the checklist, it is worth remembering that a performance problem may occasionally arise because there is too much of one of these performance variables rather than too little. Therefore, rather than trying to maximise each variable, one should try to achieve an optimum level. Furthermore this optimum level will vary from job to job and person to person. Higher levels of anxiety, for instance, are less likely to have adverse effects on performance in simple rather than complex tasks. Similarly one individual may be able to work well under pressure whilst another may not; or one individual may like tightly defined objectives whilst another feels that this constrains his or her area of discretion. Thus, when attempting to solve performance problems, it should be remembered that we are never dealing with either the characteristics of the job or the characteristics of the job holder alone, but with the relationship between them.

Identifying specific causes and the solution

So far, then, the manager has generated a list of hypotheses regarding *possible* reasons for and solutions to a performance problem. The next stage is to narrow these possible solutions down to an action plan – those relatively few steps that are actually going to be taken to solve the problem. It may be that the manager already has sufficient information at his or her fingertips to select an appropriate solution. If so, this can be done immediately. Unless the problem is very straightforward, however, the manager is likely to require further information, either to check the validity of his or her hypotheses or to check whether there might not be other, as yet unconsidered but nevertheless plausible, hypotheses. This information might be obtained by, for example, consulting records, observing the individual's work behaviour or, probably most useful of all, talking to the person concerned. In addition, the manager may wish to talk to any other people involved to check out their feelings about the validity, feasibility or acceptability of the solution. In addition to diagnostic skills, these information-gathering processes will require observational and interpersonal skills, which we will discuss later.

What is the best solution?

Having collected any additional information required, the checklist next suggests that the manager should select the most appropriate solution or solutions and, if it is worthwhile in cost–benefit terms, then arrange for its/their implementation. It is worth re-examining the value of the solutions achieved at this stage because there is a danger that the manager may have become so deeply involved in the problem that he or she is determined to implement the 'perfect solution', even though it may cost more than the problem deserves and perhaps cause problems elsewhere in the system.

If the solution is not worthwhile in cost–benefit terms, then there are a number of options open. One could work through the checklist again looking for a better solution, relocate the individual, reorganise the whole department or organisation, or learn to live with the problem. We would argue, of course, that drastic steps like relocating the individual or reorganising the unit should not be taken until all possible measures which could be tried to improve the individual's performance have been exhausted. Also, the knowledge that all possible measures have been tried may help one to live with the problem if there is no other alternative.

Do I deserve a pat on the back?

Finally, we suggest that the manager should review his or her own performance in attempting to solve the problem, and ask whether he or she could have tackled it better. If so, then this is also a performance problem which might benefit from being analysed in terms of the checklist. Was it unclear objectives, lack of ability or motivation which resulted in an unacceptable level of performance and, if so, what should be done about it? On the other hand, if the manager performed up to standard and the problem is solved, then he or she may or may not be rewarded for it by the organisation, but there is no reason why he or she should not award him- or herself a feeling of achievement or a quiet glow of satisfaction before going on to the next problem.

The checklist in practice

It must be stressed that the aim of the checklist is *not* to enable managers to come to any final conclusions regarding the solution to a performance problem. We have already pointed out that further information will often be required which will involve other skills in addition to diagnostic ones. Rather the aim is to provide a means of thinking a problem over before collecting any further information, in order to clarify one's thoughts, decide precisely what information is required, and perhaps also to provide guidelines for a discussion with the person concerned. In place of single solutions which can be implemented without further consideration, the objective is to help managers to generate a *wider* range of hypotheses, concerning the possible reasons for and solutions to performance problems, than they otherwise would. Unless a wide variety of possible causes and solutions are considered, there is always a danger that a key factor in the situation may be overlooked and, as a result, the manager will too quickly accept an 'obvious' but invalid explanation and impose an inadequate or less appropriate solution.

The checklist does appear to fulfil this function. We have used it with managers and management students who have analysed either vignettes developed by the authors[41] or 'real life' problems from their own experience. What typically happens is that, starting from a small number of symptoms, participants generate a wider variety of possible reasons and an even wider variety of possible solutions. This was confirmed in a study which we carried out with forty-two business studies students. The control group was simply given a vignette of the type presented at the beginning of this chapter and asked to list possible reasons for and possible solutions to the performance problem. The experimental group were first given the checklist and a short talk explaining its rationale before analysing the problem. In both groups, subjects analysed the problem individually and were given forty minutes to produce their answers. The experimental group produced significantly more possible reasons and solutions than the control group.[42]

Conclusions

At the beginning of this chapter, we asked you to suggest possible reasons for Geoff's inadequate performance, together with actions that could be taken to improve the situation. In Figure 2.4, we show some of the reasons and solutions which might be generated using the checklist. Of course, these are not the only possible answers, nor are they necessarily 'better' than any other list which might be developed. However, the figure does show the wide variety of ideas which can be generated starting from a very small number of symptoms.

To managers who pride themselves upon being hard-headed realists, distrustful of the 'humanitarian' approaches of behavioural scientists, this may seem a great deal of trouble to take over a 20-year-old draughtsman. Would it not be much simpler and less time-consuming merely to call him in, tell him he has to mend his ways and sack him if his performance does not improve? In the end it may, in effect, come to this, but then Geoff will have to be replaced, the post advertised, applicants interviewed, the new draughtsman selected and put through the induction process. Going through the checklist concerning Geoff's

What is the problem in behavioural terms?

1. From Clare's casual observation, Geoff spends a significant amount of time in non-work activity (talking to members of the typing pool, social use of telephone, frequent visits to the drinks machine).
2. During the period of Clare's observation, many or all of Geoff's drawings/plans have been completed after the architect's expected deadlines.
3. Some of the drawings when completed have contained errors and/or omissions – i.e. they were not to the required specification.
4. Geoff responds evasively when questioned by the architects about his work.

Is the problem worth spending time and effort on?

Yes.

1. The problem is upsetting the architects for whom he produces work, causing frustration and anger. This may be affecting their work activities causing them to spend additional time on projects.
2. There is no direct evidence that customers have been affected, but his errors and late drawings make such a situation more probable. This could lead to a loss of business.
3. Geoff's interactions with members of the typing pool may be reducing their efficiency.
4. His behaviour may engender feelings of resentment in more assiduous employees or influence others to behave in similar ways.

Possible reasons for performance problem	*Possible solutions*
Goal clarity Geoff does not realise how important it is that drawings are completed on time.	Let Geoff know that completing drawings on time is essential. Set targets (e.g. not less than 9 out of 10 drawings shall be completed within the specified time).
Ability Geoff lacks the drawing skills to produce adequate plans both quickly and accurately.	Give him advice on drawing techniques (e.g. short-cuts which will enable him to work more quickly). Find out whether there is a suitable training course.
Task difficulty The architects are not giving Geoff long enough deadlines. All four of them give their own work top priority. Geoff has	Get the architects to schedule their work better so that Geoff is either given longer deadlines or work which is more evenly spread.

Figure 2.4 *Geoff's performance: model answer*

Figure 2.4 (*continued*)

Possible reasons for performance problem	*Possible solutions*
given up trying to achieve these deadlines because he knows they are impossible.	
Intrinsic motivation Geoff finds simply producing fair copies of other peoples' rough sketches boring. He does not even know what the plans are *for* in most cases.	Enrich Geoff's job in some way, (e.g. allow him to attend meetings or discussions at an earlier stage in the planning and design process so that he feels more involved in the work).
Extrinsic motivation Geoff never receives any recognition when his drawings *are* on time. When they are late people grumble, but nothing else seems to happen.	Train the architects to praise Geoff when drawings are on time. If there are any specific positive or negative outcomes, which can result from good or bad performance, point these out to Geoff. Then make sure they occur or lose credibility.
Feedback Geoff knows he is late occasionally but does not realise how often or appreciate the disruptive effect this has.	Institute a feedback system showing how many plans are on time and how many are late and by how much.
Resources Geoff's equipment is old fashioned and cumbersome, unsuitable for fast, accurate work.	Provide better equipment.
Working conditions Geoff's working environment is both hot and noisy, the main noise coming from the typing pool next door, which he finds very distracting. He is also the only person in his badly ventilated room and feels very isolated.	Improve ventilation and sound proofing. Involve him more in the work of the architects.
Personal problems Geoff is having to cope with some family problems, relationship problems or substance abuse, which is affecting his work performance through stress, loss of sleep or loss of concentration.	Carry out a counselling interview to determine the source of the problem. On the basis of this assess whether that is sufficient, whether a temporary solution is appropriate, or whether specialist help is required.

performance and interviewing him about it is likely to take little more time than preparing for and carrying out a *single* selection interview. At least, this will be true if the selection interviews are carried out thoroughly, and there is little point in sacking Geoff unless one makes a better job of selection next time. Thus sacking Geoff and replacing him could be much more time-consuming than improving his performance, with no guarantee that it will solve the problem.

Likewise it could be argued that the performance of a 20-year-old draughts-man is a rather trivial problem, hardly worth dignifying with such a grand-sounding term as leadership. It certainly does not evoke an image of some great man or woman inspiring an intrepid group of followers to victory, or at least glorious defeat against impossible odds. Yet marginally substandard performers like Geoff are very common in organisations, *at all levels,* and certainly much more common than opportunities for inspirational leadership. Dealing with their problems and improving their performance may seem too trivial to call leadership, but it *is* efficient and economic management of people, and that is what leadership is really about.

In this chapter, we have discussed the development of hypotheses concerned with improving performance at work. In the following chapters we shall look at techniques for narrowing these hypotheses down to an action plan.

Exercise 2.1
Critical incidents

'This is another fine mess you have got yourself into, Victor,' thought Bill Bean. Bill is administration manager at Solent Oil and Cake's head office in Southampton. He has four subordinates who share an open-plan office on the floor above his. They are the office manager (Victor Ridsdale) and the heads of the Order, Invoice, and Wages sections. Victor's main responsibilities are supervising the sixteen clerical staff in the general office, which is situated next door to his, and running the management information system (MIS) which supplies up-to-date financial, marketing, production and other information to all departments at the Southampton site and the SOC plants at Widnes and Ipswich.

Victor is in his mid-thirties. Until recently, Bill was very pleased with his performance. He is popular with his staff, who work for him willingly and efficiently. He has also put forward two schemes which have produced significant savings in administrative costs. Over the past year, however, a number of incidents have occurred which have caused Bill some concern.

When Bill returned from holiday last summer, the Personnel manager complained to him that Victor had been interfering in matters which were none of his concern. He had stopped a special bonus payment for six process workers and a strike had only narrowly been avoided. When Bill tackled him about it, Victor's excuse was that he had noticed that the payment note was ambiguous. He had tried to contact the Personnel manager, but she was out. Feeling that it would be extremely difficult to reclaim the money if a mistake had been made, he therefore decided to delay the payment until Bill could return and clarify matters.

About three months ago, two managers complained to Bill that some of the information which they were used to receiving was not now being provided. When asked about this Victor said that, in the interests of efficiency, he had checked through the information supplied via the MIS and eliminated items which he felt were relatively unimportant or duplicated elsewhere. As no one had complained to him, Victor felt that this vindicated his action. Bill did not agree and insisted that he reinstate the missing items.

Most recently, Bill received a complaint from the Technical manager that Victor had leaked confidential information concerning the impending promotion of James Smart, one of his Technical officers. When told he was being offered the post of Production manager at Widnes, Smart had expressed disappointment, saying that he had understood that the job was at Southampton. Apparently, he had heard this from his wife, Angela, who worked for Victor in the general office. Victor admitted that he had discussed the promotion with Angela Smart. She had told him that she had been offered a better-paid, but less interesting job elsewhere and was seriously thinking of taking it because she and James needed the money. As Angela was one of his best workers, Victor decided to pass on a piece of news he had heard on the grapevine, in the hope that it would persuade her to stay. He felt that his action had been in the best interests both of Angela and the company.

In view of this latest incident, Bill has decided that he needs to have a serious discussion with Victor concerning his recent work performance. He has also decided to tackle the problem systematically, identifying precisely what Victor had been doing, or not doing, which had adversely affected his job performance and reviewing the possible reasons for and potential solutions to problems. What do you think these might be?

A model answer to this question is given in Appendix I.

Notes and references

1. E. P. Hollander and L. R. Offerman (1990), 'Power and leadership in organizations: relationships in transition', *American Psychologist*, **45**, 179–89.
2. E. H. Schein (1965), *Organizational Psychology*, Prentice Hall.
3. W. McGhee and P. W. Thayer (1961), *Training in Business and Industry*, Wiley.

4. T. Bouffard-Bouchard (1990), 'Influence of self-efficacy on performance in a cognitive task', *Journal of Social Psychology*, **130**, 353–63.
5. R. D. Marx (1982), 'Relapse prevention for managerial training: a model for maintenance of behaviour change', *Academy of Management Review*, **7**, 433–41.
6. T. Hill, N. D. Smith and M. F. Mann (1987), 'Role of efficacy expectations in predicting the decision to use advanced technologies: the case of computers'. *Journal of Applied Psychology*, **72**, 307–13.
7. N. R. F. Maier (1955), *Psychology in Industry*, Harrap.
8. J. P. Campbell and R. D. Pritchard (1976), 'Motivation theory in industrial and organizational psychology', in M. D. Dunnette, *Handbook of Industrial and Organizational Psychology*, Rand McNally.
9. J. B. Miner and J. F. Brewer (1976), 'The management of ineffective performance', in Dunnette, *op. cit.*; L. M. Steinmetz (1969), *Managing the Marginal and Unsatisfactory Performer*, Addison-Wesley.
10. J. Patrick (1992), *Training: Research and Practice*, Academic Press. J. Patrick (1991), 'Types of analysis for training', in J. E. Morrison (ed.), *Training for Performance: Principles of applied human learning*, Wiley.
11. P. Spurgeon, I. Michael and J. Patrick (1984), 'Training and selection of computer personnel', *Research and Development No. 18*, Sheffield: Manpower Services Commission.
12. R. F. Mager and P. Pipe (1970), *Analyzing Performance Problems*, Fearon.
13. H. P. Sims Jr and P. Lorenzi (1992), *The New Leadership Paradigm*, Sage.
14. D. M. Johnson (1972), *A Systematic Introduction to the Psychology of Thinking*, Harper & Row.
15. E. A. Locke and G. P. Latham (1984), *Goal Setting: A motivational technique that works*, Prentice Hall.
16. P. Lorenzi (1989), 'Using self-efficacy to explain the effects of participation in goal setting', *Proceedings of the Midwest Academy of Management*, 46–50.
17. J. W. Leonard (1986), 'Why MBO fails so often', *Training and Development Journal*, June, 38–9.
18. A. Howard and D. Bray (1988), *Managerial Lines in Transition*, Guildford Press.
19. K. E. Kram (1985), *Mentoring and Work: Development relationships in organizations*, Scott Foresman.
20. Hill *et al.*, *op. cit.*
21. C. A. Frayne and G. P. Latham (1987), 'Application of social learning theory to employee self-management and attendance', *Journal of Applied Psychology*, **72**, 387–92.
22. P. E. Spector, D. J. Dwyer and S. M. Jex (1988), 'Relation of job stressors to effective health and performance outcomes: a comparison of multiple data sources', *Journal of Applied Psychology*, **73**, 11–19; R. Martin and T. D. Wall (1989), 'Attentional demand and cost responsibility as stressors in shop floor jobs', *Academy of Management Journal*, **32**, 69–86; R. Karasek and T.

Theorell (1990), *Healthy Work: Stress, productivity and the reconstruction of working life*, Basic Books.

23. A. E. Ostell (1988), 'The development of a diagnostic framework of problem solving and stress', *Counselling Quarterly*, 1, 189–209.
24. J. M. Ivancevich, M. T. Matteson, S. M. Freedman and J. S. Phillips (1990), 'Work stress management and interventions', *American Psychologist*, 45, 252–61.
25. J. R. Hackman and G. R. Oldham (1976), 'Motivation through the design of work: test of a theory', *Organizational Behaviour and Human Performance*, 16, 250–79; J. R. Hackman and G. R. Oldham (1980), *Work Design*, Addison-Wesley.
26. Y. Fried and G. R. Ferris (1987), 'The validity of the job characteristics model: A review and meta-analysis', *Personnel Psychology*, 2, 287–322.
27. J. Kelly (1992), 'Does job re-design theory explain job re-design outcomes?', *Human Relations*, 45, 753–74.
28. E. L. Deci (1975), *Intrinsic Motivation*, Plenum.
29. W. E. Scott Jr, J. Farh and P. M. Podsakoff (1988), 'The effects of "intrinsic" and "extrinsic" reinforcement contingencies on task behaviour', *Organizational Behaviour and Human Decision Processes*, 41, 405–25; J. A. Wagner III, P. A. Rubin and T. J. Callahan (1988), 'Incentive payment and non-managerial productivity: an interrupted time series analysis of magnitude and trend', *Organizational Behaviour and Human Decision Processes*, 42, 47–74.
30. W. E. Reif and F. Luthans (1972), 'Does job enrichment really pay off?', *California Management Review*, 15, 30–7.
31. G. R. Oldham (1976), 'The motivational strategies used by supervisors: relationships to effectiveness indicators', *Organizational Behaviour and Human Performance*, 15, 66–86.
32. S. Kerr (1975), 'On the folly of rewarding A, while hoping for B', *Academy of Management Journal*, 18, 769–83.
33. J. L. Pearce (1987), 'Why merit pay doesn't work: implications from organizational theory', in D. B. Balkin and L. R. Gomez-Mejra (eds), *New Perspectives on Compensation*, Prentice Hall.
34. E. E. Lawler III (1987), 'The design of effective reward systems', in J. W. Lorsch (ed.), *Handbook of Organizational Behaviour*, Prentice Hall.
35. E. J. Feeney (1972), 'Performance audit, feedback and positive reinforcement', *Training and Development Journal*, 26, 8–13.
36. J. Syer (1991), 'Team building: the development of team spirit', in S. J. Bull (ed.), *Sports Psychology: A self-help guide*, Crowood Press.
37. C. A. Smith, D. W. Organ and J. P. Near (1983), 'Organizational citizenship behaviour: its nature and antecedents', *Journal of Applied Psychology*, 68, 655–63.
38. For a general discussion of working conditions and stress, see F. J. Landy (1989), *Psychology of Work Behaviour*, Brooks/Cole, ch. 14.

39. For a more detailed discussion of the nature of stress and its treatment within the organizational context, see A. Ostell (1986), 'Where stress screening falls short', *Personnel Management*, September, 34–7; A. Ostell (1988), 'The development of a diagnostic framework of problem solving and stress', *Counselling Psychology Quarterly*, **1**, 189–209; see also references in n. 22 above.
40. Ivancevich *et al.*, *op. cit.*
41. P. L. Wright and D. S. Taylor (1981), 'Vignette analysis as an aid to psychology teaching', *Bulletin of British Psychological Society*, **34**, 57–60.
42. D. S. Taylor and P. L. Wright (1982), 'Influencing work performance: the development of diagnostic skills', *Journal of Management Development*, **1**, 44–50.

CHAPTER 3

Perception and judgement

Chris Broadbent, the newly appointed Sales Manager for ADU Manufacturing PLC, has been *inspecting* the previous month's sales figures. She was pleased to *see* that overall sales had increased. On *checking* further, however, she *noticed* that the increase was made up entirely of new sales and that repeat orders had in fact declined slightly. She *decided* to *analyse* them in more detail and *discovered* that one member of the sales staff, Peter Burton, had brought in a great deal of new business, but had not maintained sales with existing customers. She *decided* to discuss it with him and arranged a meeting. During the meeting, she *observed* that Peter seemed ill at ease when discussing repeat sales and asked him whether there were any particular problems in this area. He replied that they are a lot less exciting than going out and getting new business and he had therefore not really given them as much attention as necessary. Chris and Peter discussed the situation and they then agreed sales objectives for the next period, for both new and repeat sales. Chris indicated that she would be *monitoring* performance during this period and would discuss the matter further with Peter as sales figures became available.

After Peter had left, Chris considered her first real interaction with Peter. 'Very much an extrovert,' she thought, 'seems to have the ability to impress people and likes the challenge of selling to new customers, but then loses interest in maintaining the contact – prefers pastures new. Lacks some capacity for follow-through. Somewhat self-centred and wants to be liked. I'm not sure he'll achieve the objectives for repeat orders in the longer term. Not really management material, but likeable and probably good at maintaining an enthusiastic team spirit. Quick-witted and may well be good at developing new ideas. Worth following that up.'

Peter, on leaving Chris, thought, 'Put up a good show there – I think she likes me – at least she smiled a lot. I'm not sure I convinced her, though, about repeat orders – I'm going to put more effort in there. She obviously pays attention to detail – nobody else has "got me" on this point. Anyway, she does seem concerned about the company's success and that can't be bad, but she's going to exercise more control over us to achieve her objectives. She did seem to recognise what I was good at – and not so good at – but did keep praising me on my ability to get new orders. Not all that fast on her feet though – a bit pedantic, but seems open to new ideas. I think she might be OK, but only time will tell.'

Introduction

The ability to make accurate inferences concerning the factors which determine people's behaviour and events is one of the key skills of management. In the previous chapter, we outlined some of the main factors which influence work performance. However, a mere knowledge of these factors is not sufficient in itself to identify the specific causes of someone's behaviour in a particular instance, or to decide what should be done to change his or her future behaviour in a desired direction. Accurate perception and judgement are also required. They play a vital role, not only in the initial analysis of a performance problem, but also at several other stages during an attempt to influence behaviour at work.

This is illustrated in the case at the beginning of this chapter. Chris Broadbent notices a discrepancy in the sales figures. From this she infers that there may be a performance problem. She gathers further information which pinpoints a possible source of the problem. She talks to the person concerned and gathers more information both from what he says and from his nonverbal behaviour. Steps are agreed which are intended to remedy the situation, and the manager resolves to observe the subordinate's performance more carefully in future. Various skills are required at different stages during this process, such as the ability to analyse performance problems and to gather information and arrive at decisions with subordinates. Throughout the event as a whole, however, the manager is using and relying on her ability to perceive and interpret situations accurately in order to provide the basis for a series of decisions.

In addition, other processes are occurring. Each of the participants, in their first real interaction following the manager's appointment, are forming impressions of each other. On the basis of this impression formation, they are then attempting to predict future behaviour and its implications for organisational and personal objectives, which will in turn serve as a basis for future decision making. Hence the importance of accuracy in perception and judgement. Poor decisions based on ignorance or misunderstanding can be costly to an organisation. In order to provide a foundation for looking at perception and judgement, Figure 3.1 gives some indication of the processes involved.

At any particular time, a wide variety of information is available to the manager within his or her working environment. Certain pieces of information may be noticed or sought out by the manager, often those which past experience indicates are important in his or her job. Simply perceiving what has happened does not, however, provide an adequate basis for action. The same events could have entirely different implications depending on the circumstances. Throwing water on someone who has been accidentally splashed with a

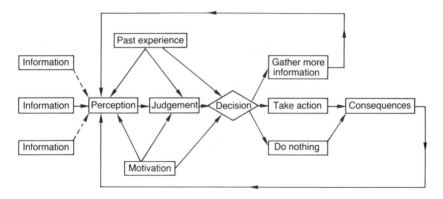

Figure 3.1 *Perception and judgement at work*

highly corrosive acid is entirely different from throwing water over someone for
a joke, although the actions involved might be very similar. Thus, once
perceived, the information must be evaluated, consciously or unconsciously, to
establish its meaning as clearly as the available data permits.[1] A decision is then
made, either deliberately or by default. This may be to clarify the situation by
gathering further information, to take action on the basis of existing data, or to
do nothing. Whether the manager takes action or does nothing, this will have
consequences which may also be perceived, interpreted and form the basis of
future decisions. Thus, we are concerned with a continual perception–
judgement–decision-making cycle.

Perception and judgement are pervasive and continuous activities. However,
the case at the beginning raises some interesting questions. How is it that both
Chris and Peter could develop such fairly strong impressions about each other
so quickly? On what basis can Chris decide that Peter is not really 'management
material'? How accurate are their perceptions of each other likely to be? These
are the types of question this chapter will attempt to answer.

Our viewpoint, and one reflected in this chapter, is that people are adequate
perceivers for dealing with a wide range of situations and problems in everyday
circumstances. We use the term 'adequate' rather than 'accurate' because
accuracy itself, in the context of social interaction, is relative. Accuracy is a
judged correspondence between some judgement and some standard, but in
most social interactions, the standard itself is based on someone's judgement,
either the perceiver's or an observer's. People are sufficiently accurate in their
own terms if they successfully achieve some intended goal. That is, it depends
on purpose. For everyday purposes, within their normal environment and with
their normal partners, friends or colleagues, the standards of accuracy often
need not be high. With the exception of racial and sexual stereotyping, in
interpersonal interactions of a sociable nature, either in social or work situations,
the consequences of inaccurate perceptions and judgements are rarely crucial.

They may cause inconvenience, but where necessary, and in the light of additional information or the use of acknowledgement of regret, they can be rectified with little long-term harm. In other words, people strike a workable balance between their goals and the effort required for accurate perception and judgement, which is sufficient to allow them to manage their social environment with some personally judged criterion of success.[2]

For some decisions in an organisational context, however, the consequences of inaccurate perceptions and judgements can be crucial. Selection decisions, promotion decisions, decisions about special posts of responsibility, appraisal, development, disciplinary decisions, and so on, can all have an important influence on both the short- and long-term success of an organisation, either directly or indirectly, through an accumulation of circumstances. Such decisions require the accurate judgement of people, their behaviour and abilities, in the decision-making process because, once made, the decisions may not be easy to rectify should they prove to be wrong. For example, selection and promotion decisions are usually contractual and, where inappropriate, may be costly to undo. Inappropriate appraisal decisions can result in disaffection and reduced commitment to an organisation. Bad disciplinary decisions can bring about fines from an industrial tribunal, and so on. Why might such organisational decisions sometimes go wrong with relatively costly consequences? It is our belief that organisational decisions are sometimes inappropriate because we tend to base our decision making on the same adequate rather than accurate processes of perception and judgement that we apply in our everyday social interactions – that is, the workable balance approach noted above.

Because we are, for most intents and purposes, apparently successful in our everyday social interactions with others in relation to our own standards, our perceptions, judgements, decisions and patterns of behaviour are, in principle, reinforced. These activities fulfil the workable balance between effort and intentions for successfully managing relationships. Our success breeds confidence and a belief that we can accurately judge other people's personalities and abilities, and thereby explain and predict their behaviour. However, what we are prone to forget is that the standards of accuracy which we apply to our everyday social interactions may be lower than those which we need to apply in an organisational context, where the consequences of imappropriate decisions can be much greater and the opportunities to rectify them are more problematic. The problem largely hinges on a transfer of learning context. Because we are generally successful in dealing with a wide range of situations and problems in our everyday interactions, which involves the use of certain processes, activities and standards, we utilise the same processes, activities and standards in other situations that for success may demand different ones. The standards of accuracy required may be higher and, as a result, require different approaches to processing information and different interaction patterns.

Organisations, when confronted with important decisions about people relating to selection, promotion and discipline, do tend to change their approach.

Decisions are shifted from individuals to groups, for example, in the belief that panel interviews will overcome individual biases. In many situations this does improve decision quality. However, although group consensus can improve accuracy of decision making, it is not a necessary or sufficient condition for it. Even group decisions are dependent upon the relevance of the criteria and standards, and the quality of information collected. As is often quoted regarding computer processing, 'garbage in, garbage out'! Along with changes in standards, therefore, what are also needed are more appropriate approaches to information gathering and processing, and the activities relating to them. It is a predominant theme of this book that sound decision making is 'information-based decision making' and, in order to achieve relevant information, information collection should be systematic. An important variable involved in the systematic collection of relevant information relates to the perception and judgement process.

In considering perception and judgement, first we shall look briefly at the process of perception and examine how the perceiver, the target or person being perceived, and the situation influence the process. Following this we will consider some of the variables which can have adverse effects on decision making.

Perception

Perception is the active process of obtaining and interpreting information from the environment to provide order and meaning. It is the process of making sense of the available data and, in order to do so, it usually involves going beyond the immediately given evidence of the senses. Perception also usually seems instantaneous and we are therefore not aware of this adding of information from memory to the available sensory data to provide interpretation and meaning. This additional stored information in memory which assists the process of interpreting can be a source of bias and distortion, as well as efficiency, and we shall return to it later.

Another important distinguishing feature of perception is its subjectivity. Each person's perceptions are private. Individuals relate to experiences in their own special way. Each individual's view of reality is unique in some way, based on their own individual experience. Perceptions are private, subjective and experienced from a first-person perspective. This presents difficulties both in describing and analysing a process which is the central core of our experienced existence. A characteristic error in considering perception is to ignore its essential subjectivity and to assume that people's views of their experience are objective. We cannot suppose that for a given input, as with a computer program, we can always achieve the same output, either for the same individual at different times or for several people experiencing the same event simultaneously. So, for example, in a panel interviewing situation, each member of the panel, though seeing the same target person and listening to the same words, may be experiencing different interpretations. However, we can attempt to increase correspondence and consensus of opinion by specifying criteria for judgement. In effect, what is happening by specifying criteria, as with the computer analogy, is that we are attempting to control the perception/judgement process for the observers by ensuring they attend to and process similar information within particular parameters. As a result, we hope to achieve improved accuracy, greater consensus and improved decision quality.

Finally, implicit in the above discussion is the notion that perception is the directive for action. The total environment in which perceiving takes place is not just a source of information, it is also an arena for action.[3] Perception is the source of information about the environment but this information is largely of value in assisting the adaptive functioning of people within their environment. The way we perceive is intimately related to our behavioural repertoire and our environmental opportunities. This intimate relationship between capabilities, opportunities and information selection can influence the judgemental process. For example, different people within an organisation will perceive and respond differently to the resignation of, say, a senior manager. Those people who may be eligible for promotion to the post will perhaps perceive the situation as competitive and respond in ways to enhance their chances of success in competing for the post. Other senior managers may see the situation as an opportunity to rectify discrepancies which arose as a result of the previous post-holder, each of them also perhaps having different views of what those discrepancies were. As a result, each will react differently. So although an agreed goal may be to replace the individual, the various people involved will view the situation differently and, as a result, their actions in relation to the situation will be different, based upon their interpretation of the new opportunity and the range of behaviours considered acceptable to take advantage of it.

In conclusion, then, perception is an active process which provides structure, stability and meaning to our interaction with the environment. This reduces uncertainty and assists prediction. Secondly, it is a subjective, private process and, as a result, can be subject to distortion and bias. Finally, as the directive for action, it is intimately and integrally related to our successful adaptation to the environment we live in.

For the remainder of the chapter we shall focus particularly on the perception of people, how we form impressions of them and interpret their actions – the study of social perception.

The components of social perception

Any social interaction has three predominant components: a perceiver, a target being perceived and a situational context in which the perceptual event is occurring. Each of these three components have characteristics which influence the perception and judgement of the target.

The perceiver

The important distinguishing feature of perception is its subjectivity, as we have already noted. Our past experiences, emotional state, motivational needs, gender, race, age and a number of other individual features influence our perceptions in idiosyncratic ways which can lead to misunderstanding and disagreement. These we shall explore more closely.

Past experience

Our previous experiences with others in social interactions is a major influence on our perceptions of people. From there, we develop expectations which affect current perceptions. In the introductory case to this chapter, past experience influenced Chris to believe that Peter would probably be a good team member but not a good manager. Peter believed that people who smile a lot indicate liking and he had formed an impression that Chris was pedantic but open to new ideas. Both of them had matched each other's actions to expectations about how certain types of people behave, developed either directly from past experience or indirectly from other people or through reading.

Our past experience also influences our special interests for both work and leisure. An interesting research exercise within an organisational context required executives in a development seminar to read and analyse a case study of a steel company and to specify the main problem affecting the company that a new president of the company should tackle.[4] The perceptions of the key problems differed amongst the executives, but in a consistent way. Sales executives saw marketing as the key, production executives cited production issues, and industrial and public relations specialists saw human relations as the most pressing problem. This is an example of 'perceptual set' where past experience influences people to attend to and perceive certain features in a situation or event, rather than others. It is as though to some extent we have 'tunnel vision' and such differences caused by this in our perception of people and events can lead to communication problems and conflict within organisations.

In general, we tend to perceive things which interest us and also things which we expect to see. The latter creates problems in proofreading. The illustration below is a good example.

Someone seeing this for the first time would very likely see 'Paris in the spring'. Did you? If so, check it again! Similar effects can occur when observing people's behaviour at work. Our previous experiences with others may often affect the way in which we view their current behaviour. When employees have consistently been given good performance ratings, and perhaps become known as 'high flyers', they may continue to be held in high esteem and perhaps promoted even though their performance has levelled of or perhaps even declined. The reverse situation may arise in the case of poor performers. In both cases, it is important that changes in performance should be recognised, the former for obvious reasons and the latter because if improved performance is not recognised, employees may quickly believe that whatever they do will make little difference and give up.

Emotional state

The particular emotions we are experiencing at any particular moment – happiness, depression, anger, hate, fear, and so on – can influence our perceptions and judgements. In anger, due to a machine breakdown or late report, we may abuse colleagues or subordinates assuming their personal responsibility for the situation, rather than gathering information to find perhaps more appropriate causes. An employee who has just been promoted may fail to notice the unhappiness of a colleague who was not promoted, and makes remarks seen as condescending or gloating by that colleague. It seems that, in general, emotional arousal reduces our capacity to use information and we tend to form simpler impressions and rely on stereotypes and prejudice, rather than treating people as individuals.[5] These capacity limitations which lead to the formation of simpler impressions can be created by anxiety, difficult social interactions, threats to self-esteem (for example, when being punished) and even by having to make decisions or act under time pressure. This is why emergency procedures, in the event of fire or other extreme situations, should be well practised and over-learned. When such procedures are over-learned, they can be automatically carried out in situations when our capacity to think and make decisions is limited by our emotional arousal. Experience then can help to compensate for the limitations imposed on perception, judgement and decision making by emotional arousal.

Motivational state

The third factor which may determine which stimuli are perceived or ignored is self-interest. Again, this is well known to advertisers who attempt to attract our attention by including in their adverts things which are likely to interest us, whether they are directly related to their product or not. There is also evidence from laboratory research that our needs can influence the stimuli which we perceive. In one study, for example, subjects who had been deprived of food for one, four and sixteen hours were asked to write down their impressions of very dim pictures projected on a screen. The projector operator went through the motions of inserting pictures into the machine, but did not actually project anything. Nevertheless the subjects did report that they saw meaningful perceptions and, the longer they were deprived of food, the more food related were the objects they reported seeing.[6]

Within the organisational context, too, our personal pattern of needs, interests, beliefs and attitudes will affect our selection and interpretation of information. An engineer and personnel manager being shown round a factory are likely to attend to, and seek out, information about different aspects of the operator-machine production system, relating to their interests and expertise. Furthermore, each one in his or her own area of expertise is likely to see more than the other. So, for example, the personnel manager may detect hostility between two operators by their body orientations and mannerisms, points which, even if brought to the attention of the engineer, may be difficult to perceive. Similarly, the engineer can point out machine operations to the non-engineer, which may be difficult to discriminate or understand. Thus people uneducated or without experience in areas of specialisation may be unable to perceive particular aspects of the situation even when their attention is drawn to them.

Our beliefs and attitudes will also influence what we pay attention to, and therefore 'register' and remember. Differences in beliefs and attitudes between union officers and management or subordinates and managers have implications for organisational behaviour. The manager probably ignores instances in which a subordinate is effectively working without supervision but quickly notices a subordinate 'hanging about' talking. His or her belief that workers are lazy and therefore need constant supervision causes the selection of those instances which reinforce his or her views and non-selection of disconfirming instances.

Individual features

Finally, relating to the perceiver, there are a whole host of idiosyncratic variables which can influence the subjectivity of the perceiver's interpretation of other people and events. Gender is an important variable. Attitudes formed from early cultural and social experiences relating to males and females form the basis of the perception and judgement of them. It was noted earlier that our perceptions seem instantaneous and we are unaware of how these are achieved. Much of the processing is automatic and unconscious and based on assumptions developed from our beliefs and attitudes. For example:

> Susan came across an old school friend she had not seen for ten years. Whilst chatting, a little boy walked up to them and took hold of her friend's hand. Susan said, 'I didn't know you had a son,' and turned to the little boy and asked, 'What's your name, then?', to which he replied, 'Same as my dad's.' 'Oh', said Susan, 'you must be called Peter.'

How did she know?[7]

Attitudes can be strong determinants of opinions, which influence our perceptions, judgements and decision making. In gender terms, society still purveys a view of the correct cultural roles of men and women, with males being expected to be self-contained, relatively unemotional and competent, and women as dependent and expressive. This has a significant influence on women's employment, particularly in certain sectors. For example, in a 1990 study, only 21 per cent of British managers were women, with only 2.5 per cent of women holding directorships.[8] Even in traditional women's employment, women fare badly. For example, although only 8.6 per cent of nurses are male, 50 per cent of the top nursing posts are held by men.[9]

Another variable which strongly influences perception and judgement is physical attractiveness. In general, both males and females rate physically attractive individuals of both sexes as:

- more sexually warm and responsive;
- more intelligent, poised, sociable and kind; and
- more likely to attain high occupational status,

than less attractive individuals.[10] Again, we are probably culturally influenced by 'fairy stories' (heroines and heroes are attractive – Cinderella, Sleeping Beauty, with handsome princes rescuing them; wicked people are ugly – Ugly Sisters, wicked witches, trolls, giants, whom the handsome princes quickly dispatch). The influence is maintained through Hollywood, TV and romantic novels. A longitudinal study started in 1955 with high-school students in America and followed up in 1970 and 1980 found, among other things, that men lower in physical attractiveness needed higher educational achievements to reach similar positions, high in job prestige, held by men of higher physical attractiveness.[11]

If we are perceived as attractive, then we are likely to be treated differently (usually more favourably) than if we are perceived as not very attractive. This will influence our opinions and attitudes of other people. The situation will be similar whether we are male or female. Other variables will also be pertinent, such as race or age or if we are a member of any minority group in particular situations. Also, whether we are fat or thin, tall or short, have a physical disability, and so on, all will have some influence on how we view and interpret the world and interact with others in the environment.

Finally, certain personality characteristics can affect how we view and interpret people and events. Whether we are self-confident or insecure, relaxed or anxious, has a bearing on how we handle information. In general, people who are insecure or anxious tend to form simpler impressions compared to non-anxious or self-confident individuals, as noted earlier under 'Emotional state'. Individual differences in the need for order and achievement tend also to affect information handling, with those high in this need showing more rigidity in their thinking and expectancy bias than those assessed low on these dimensions.[12] Perceivers, then, are complex information processors whose perceptions are influenced by their physical and mental abilities and personality characteristics. How they view the world – their opinions, beliefs and values that create expectations and standards by which they judge other people and events

– has developed as a result of their unique individual experiences, again emphasising the subjectivity of perception.

The target

Ambiguity

An individual's perceptions are affected by characteristics of the target, that is, the person or persons being observed. An important variable which relates to the target is its degree of ambiguity. Familiar people are less ambiguous in this sense. With familiar people, we will have formed some impression of them and developed habits of interaction with them that fulfil our need as adequate perceivers for successfully achieving some purpose. That does not mean that we are not occasionally surprised by their behaviour. Each of us who has developed strong relationships with other individuals will have developed expectations about them and made assumptions that have led us to make decisions on their behalf, usually in good faith, only to find it was a wrong one! Whilst working at a particular company, a colleague of the authors, browsing in the factory shop, saw some very expensive anti-wrinkle cream on sale, guaranteed to slow down or reduce facial wrinkles produced as a result of ageing. He thought his wife would be very pleased if he took her some back, so bought a couple of tubes of it. It was a pragmatic view of a current developing problem. His wife, however, did not perceive the situation in the same light. She saw it as a thoughtless act of her husband, drawing attention to changes resulting from the ageing process. For her it was not perceived as a pragmatic problem but rather as an emotional one and, instead of being pleased with her husband, she was very angry! It is similar in work situations in that we 'take for granted' that certain actions will be acceptable to work colleagues based on previous experiences with them. However, the context may shift slightly, which causes the action to be seen in a different light with often unexpected reactions.

For people with whom we are less familiar, the degree of ambiguity increases. This poses problems for us because we are less certain of them, their characteristics and their motives. In general, uncertainty creates anxiety, and in order to reduce the anxiety we need to resolve the ambiguity, so that we can interact with them with some measure of success according to need or purpose. As in the short case at the beginning of the chapter, both Chris and Peter were forming impressions of each other for their own purposes of interaction and influence. What factors might influence this process which relate to the target? The primary cues in initial meetings are likely to be those of physical appearance, including dress and verbal and nonverbal communication. These we use to ascribe characteristics and attributes to the target that provide meaning, which, in turn, helps reduce the ambiguity; for example, their likely occupation, status, interests and beliefs. The person's appearance, accent, verbal fluency, tone of voice and body language act as cues to trigger the process of categorising the target in some manner, based on learning from past experiences. As noted earlier, for familiar cues which trigger familiar categories (such as those based on gender, age or race), the process can occur automatically without awareness.[13] Only in uncertain or strange situations, or where events do not conform to expectations do we consciously search our memories to give direction to the imposition of meaning that will assist judgement and decision making.

Visual illusions, usually based on impression management, can occur in social perception. For example, the confidence trickster dresses soberly, usually in formal business attire, and communicates with an appropriate accent and vocabulary to create a belief in his or her bogus credentials. Similarly, in organisations, swiftly walking around the premises carrying material of some sort can give a correct impression, or illusion (if so intended) of being a very active, busy employee, and networking activity can given an impression or illusion of being an employee with influence. Only if the illusionist makes an error, such as dropping a folder which opens to reveal no contents, or a confidence trickster who inappropriately breaks into the vernacular, do we consciously seek for other cues which can defeat the illusion. In both these cases, some additional information about the target person has reduced ambiguity, particularly in relation to improving judgement and decision making.

However, gaining more information may not necessarily improve perceptual accuracy. This is because we are *selective* in what information we pay attention to and the selectivity is based on how we *categorise* target individuals. A research study looking at employment interviewing revealed that decisions were reached after less than five minutes in fifteen-minute interviews, with the rest of the time being spent selectively justifying the early decision.[14] Although a more recent study paints a somewhat better picture, there is still the problem that where several people interview the same individual separately, they tend to disagree in their ratings.[15] Thus, at least some of them must be wrong, and this emphasises the point that more information does not necessarily lead to better perceptions.[16] Rather, more and later information is frequently selectively gleaned and used to confirm our original early impressions.

In interpersonal interactions, particularly when meeting people for the first time, the reduction of ambiguity seems to be the predominant process preoccupying the perceiver. This process of resolving ambiguity has to be achieved from available cues. These include physical appearance and verbal and nonverbal communication, which may be the only cues available in some encounters, while in other instances we may have additional information that has been provided by other people in verbal or written form (e.g. references) or by the target person in the form of a written application or introductory letter. From all these cues we ascribe certain attributes to the individual which will then influence our perception of, and interaction with, them. Although our major concern in reducing ambiguity is to determine people's personal characteristics to assist the process of interaction, certain other attributes may also influence and modulate how we perceive those personal characteristics.

Ascribed attributes

Two factors which can influence ascribed attributes are the social status of individuals and their type of occupation. Taking the latter first, describing people as librarians, accountants, salespeople, engineers or research scientists can cue in stereotypes of these various people before any initial meeting. Such stereotypes can also be gender related, such as nursery teacher, nurse or secretary, which are generally linked with females, or surgeon, engineer or manager, which are generally male associated. In some situations – for example, in employment applications – people who deviate from expectations may never reach the first encounter stage (the interview) and even where they do, their lack of resemblance to those expectations may reduce their chances of being selected. A nursery teacher applying for a change of career to nursing may well stand a better chance of being interviewed than a bricklayer applying for a similar career change. Alternatively, a bricklayer applying for a job as a car mechanic may well stand a better chance of being interviewed than a secretary.

Status will also influence our perceptions of other people. Social status usually refers to the person's position in society and our assessment is generally determined by such data as income, occupational position, type of occupation and, when these cues are unavailable, where they live, how they dress and what model of car they drive. A person's status usually affects how he or she is evaluated by others. In general, even when they behave in similar ways, people with higher status are usually evaluated more positively than people with lower status.[17] They are also more influential than people with lower status.[18] For example, if a work colleague complained to you about your standard of work you would probably perceive that differently than if your manager complained.

Ascribed attributes can also be strongly influenced by the use of certain personal descriptors called central traits. A university lecturer at Massachusetts Institute of Technology told students that their regular teacher was absent and they would be having a substitute teacher instead. They were also told that they would be asked to assess the teacher at the end of the session. They were then given some biographical notes about the replacement teacher. All were given the same content in the notes, except that for one half, the description 'rather warm' was included, whereas for the other half 'rather cold' was used. Students who had the 'warm' notes rated the substitute teacher more favourably than those who read the 'cold' description, even though all experienced the same discussion. In addition, more of the 'warm' group (56 per cent) participated in the subsequent discussion, compared to the 'cold' group (32 per cent). This demonstrates an example of the 'halo effect'. Being told that a target person has a favourable characteristic seemed to have a major effect on the overall impression of the substitute teacher for the 'warm' group (a positive 'halo'). For the 'cold' group, being told that the teacher had an unfavourable characteristic created a negative halo – sometimes called the 'horns effect'. The halo/horns effect can influence many performance evaluation decisions. For example, a manager who places special emphasis on respect for superiors may rate an offhand employee low on quantity or quality of work even though that employee's work record is equivalent to others. It illustrates the principle of consistency. In information-processing and memory contexts, it is easier to regard a person as having all good or bad qualities than a mixture of both.

The situational context

Perception occurs in an environment which is not just a source of information but also an arena for action and, as stated earlier, perception is a basis for action. The total environment, other people and events, and the situational context in which it occurs, will influence perception and action. Situational contexts can to a large extent determine social roles – 'the slots or positions that we occupy in society'.[19] Most people have multiple roles – family roles (parent, spouse, son/daughter), occupational roles and social group membership roles – which influence how we behave at particular times. As a son/daughter we may behave differently than as a parent; in our occupational roles we will probably behave differently than in our social group membership roles, and so on. The context at any point in time will influence the modality of behaviour. At times, however, these multiple roles may conflict. For example, an organisation may require an employee to work on urgent business over a weekend whereas the employee's family is expecting a weekend vacation, an example of inter-role conflict. Intra-role conflicts can arise also, for example, where your boss requests that you carry out certain actions which you know breach company rules or ethical business standards. In such circumstances you may feel at a loss to know what you should do. Life, however, can produce added complications, and events may even require you to change roles from those normally exhibited in particular contexts. A subordinate's personal crisis, which is affecting his or her work, may cause you to shift from a managerial role to a parent role. A major emergency at work may require you to shift from your normal managerial role to that of deference to a subordinate, whose training makes him or her more skilled to deal with the emergency. Whilst visiting your parents at their home, which would normally trigger the obedient son/daughter role, a crisis due to illness may require you to exercise your organisational skills developed from, and normally exercised in, your managerial role. Any or all of these can occur, automatically triggered by the situation, which may, in some cases, cause role strain.

Despite there being expectations based on roles, individuals perform their roles in their own idiosyncratic ways, so reflecting something about the roles and also about the individual. At times, conflict may arise as a result of this, where people fulfilling their required roles do not do so in quite the way expected of them in the view of another. This can lead to what are often described as 'personality clashes'. In most cases they are not 'clashes of personality' but rather differences in expectations of the objectives to be achieved and of how the job should be approached within the scope of those objectives.

The importance and impact of the situational context on perceptions and behaviours are unlikely to surprise you even though our shift of roles, and the consequent changes in behaviour, generally occur automatically, particularly in familiar situations. Nevertheless, there are individual differences in sensitivity to situational cues which trigger these changes. Some of these can be accounted for through lack of experience, as in the case of a newly appointed manager failing to perceive a particular tone of voice of his or her superior used to indicate an expectation for a particular action rather than a choice of actions. On the other hand, people are either more or less sensitive to situational cues. Both circumstances – lack of experience to relevant situational cues, and variations in individual sensitivity to them – can cause conflict and communication problems due to the same situation being perceived differently by individuals. Such conflict and communication problems can only be reduced by being aware of the subjectivity of perception that stems from individual differences due both to differences in biological and physiological make-up and differences in life experiences. An awareness of this subjectivity can better prepare a manager in his or her systematic collection of relevant information. Being aware that people do things for all manner of reasons of which we, and even they, may be initially unaware, emphasises one of the important themes of this book – that of information-based decision making. Recognising that many inappropriate behaviours, as well as appropriate behaviours, may be triggered by situational cues can assist the process of exploring with colleagues and subordinates factors that influence both their successful and less successful work performances.

The perceptual process: a summary

Before we move on to see how the impressions we form of others, and how we interpret the reasons or causes for their behaviour, can be subject to bias and distortion, let us briefly recap on the process of perception.

Perception is a subjective process with each individual's view of reality being unique. It is also an active process of imposing meaning and stability through interpreting information from without, using stored information in memory from learning and past experience, to assist our ability to manage successfully our interactions with environmental events. Implicit in this is the notion that the process is the basis for, and provides continuity to, our behaviour and actions within the context of our capabilities and external opportunities/restraints.

That perception is an active process of imposing meaning indicates that in some situations, particularly where they are unfamiliar, we will actively seek out cues to extract information for reducing ambiguity. Because there may be literally thousands of sources of information to which we could attend at any particular point in time, and because we are limited in how much we can absorb, we are *selective* in what we do attend to. Selectivity is a subjective process influenced by perceiver characteristics (e.g. past experience, interests, needs) but cued by external sources of information, that is, things, people and events relating to what one is doing, needs or wants to do at any particular moment in time. Once information is selected, it needs to be assembled, related to both present circumstances and past experience, and processed as a basis for action. The processing will be influenced by the quantity, quality and relevance of past experiences, and by the emotional and motivational state and other idiosyncratic individual physical and mental features of the perceiver.

This apparently highly complex process seems to be experienced instantaneously in most situations and without awareness. In purpose, the process is successful for facilitating the need of individuals to manage their social environment with some personally judged level of competence.

Distortion and bias in person perception

In the introduction to this chapter, we stated our viewpoint that people are adequate perceivers for dealing with a wide range of situations and problems in everyday circumstances. We used the word 'adequate' rather than 'accurate' because in social perception, as in most other situations, accuracy is a relative term and has to be assessed against some standard. It was suggested that people are sufficiently accurate if, within their normal environment and with their normal partners, friends or colleagues, they successfully achieve some intended goal(s). For ordinary purposes this standard need not be very high and has led to the standard being qualitatively described as 'good enough perceptions'.[20] In other words, people strike a workable balance between their goals and the effort required for accurate perception and judgement which is sufficient to allow them to manage their social environment with some personally judged criterion of success.[21] Within an organisational context many employees' interpersonal interactions do not require goals of a higher standard than in normal everyday circumstances. That is, many of their interactions relate to those of a sociable nature or are not highly significant for work-related activities. Hence, the standard of perceptual accuracy to be achieved within the interactions to facilitate their social goals will fall within the 'good enough' area, so as to strike the workable balance between their goals and the effort required for accurate perception and judgement.

However, there are circumstances which, for successful achievement of behavioural and organisational goals, demand higher standards of accuracy because the consequences of failure to achieve those goals are much greater. These would include decisions relating to selection, promotion, appraisal, discipline and so on, all of which require a relatively high level of perceptual and judgemental activities if potentially costly errors are to be avoided. The remainder of this section will look at distortions and biases arising in perceptual and judgemental activities that may lead to lower probabilities of success in decision making where the decisions are more crucial but may not influence detrimentally our everyday social interactions.

Ambiguous events

As might be expected, events which are most likely to be misinterpreted are those which are ambiguous or cannot be clearly perceived because they are faint, distant, experienced in adverse conditions such as poor light or background noise, occur very briefly or unexpectedly, and so on. As we shall see, however, this does not prevent people from forming clear and unambiguous impressions of such events, sometimes leading to false conclusions or conflict with other people whose impressions are quite different but equally clear and unambiguous. Eyewitness testimony provides many examples of this process. For example, practically every car accident results in wide variations from one witness to another regarding how fast the cars were travelling and the sequence of events leading up to the accident.

There are also cases in which witnesses are willing to testify they saw something which has subsequently been shown to be impossible. In one case, a police officer testified that he saw a defendant shoot a victim as both stood in a doorway 120 feet away. Members of the jury, on going to the scene of the crime, found it impossible to identify the features of a person standing in the doorway from that distance and acquitted the defendant.[22]

Past experience

Knowledge from past experience is essential for perception to occur. It enables us to recognise and categorise information much more rapidly, and thus react much more quickly to what we perceive. Therein, however, also lies a danger. If the knowledge is incorrect or the past experience misleading, we may misinterpret the stimulus and react on the basis of incorrect information. Once such a premature categorisation has been made, it is often very resistant to change, just as any new information which could provide contradictory evidence is often distorted to fit existing beliefs.

A classic example is the case of eight researchers who voluntarily admitted themselves to American mental hospitals complaining of voices which said 'empty', 'hollow' and 'thud'. Immediately after admission to the psychiatric ward, these pseudo-patients ceased simulating any symptoms of abnormality. They behaved normally and when asked by staff how they were feeling, they replied that they were fine and no longer experienced any symptoms. Nevertheless, none of them was detected, and they were discharged from the hospitals with a diagnosis of schizophrenia 'in remission'; that is, in the hospital's view, the patient still had schizophrenia but was not showing signs of it at the moment. Oddly enough, the people who did notice the deception were other patients, who would say things like, 'You're not crazy. You're a journalist or a professor. You're checking up on the hospital.' At first, the researchers took notes secretly but they soon found this was unnecessary. Even their note taking was seen as pathological behaviour, such as compulsive writing. As far as the doctors were concerned, once a diagnosis of schizophrenia had been made, everything they subsequently learned about the patient, no matter how innocuous, was interpreted as supporting the original diagnosis.[23]

This case perhaps provides an extreme example, involving as it does formal categorising of people in terms of medical diagnosis. Nevertheless the more subtle informal and sometimes unconscious categorising of people which occurs in normal life can still have profound effects on the judgements we make about people. As has been pointed out, for example, some hunches we have about people may result from a chance resemblance to a former acquaintance.[24] If a previous employee who embezzled funds also happened to have widely spaced eyes, then a manager might experience vague feelings of distrust whenever encountering someone with widely spaced eyes without even realising the basis of these feelings. Some common sources of distortion in assessing people, directly influenced by categorisations developed from past experience, are as follows.

First impressions

We often form lasting impressions of people on the basis of limited information gained during a very brief period after we have first encountered them. Once formed, our first impressions are maintained by interpreting all subsequent information in terms of our initial conclusions. Thus we can never be wrong, at least in our own eyes. The rapid progress made by recruits identified as 'high flyers' is sometimes quoted as evidence for an organisation's ability to identify management potential at an early stage. Once someone has been identified as a high flyer, it is likely that their subsequent behaviour, unless grossly incompetent, will be interpreted as confirming this initial assessment. Evidence indicates that people who show successful performance before failure are judged as showing more ability than those who demonstrate failure before success.[25]

Sometimes, however, how we judge others is influenced by later rather than early information – a *recency* effect. This usually seems to apply for judgement of attributes that are likely to change over time – that is, those influenced by learning and experience – rather than stable traits such as intelligence, extroversion or emotional stability, and also where the observer's attention is drawn to later information.[26] Despite such examples of a recency effect, the primacy effect of first impressions seems to predominate in everyday experiences. Because each of us tends to vary in what we often consider as important characteristics in other people, it is probable that the impression different people form of a single individual will vary, depending both on what characteristics are considered important and on the circumstances of the first encounter.

In the short case at the beginning of the chapter, both Chris and Peter formed initial impressions of each other as a result of their meeting. These impressions would subsequently influence both their judgements about each other and the way in which they interact within the work environment.

The halo effect

Our impressions of other people may be strongly influenced not only by early information about them, but also by a single attribute which we regard as either very positive or very negative. For example, we may regard a person who is friendly as loyal, trustworthy and intelligent as well, even though evidence concerning these traits is lacking. This is an example of the halo effect, where information about one particular attribute of a person can colour our impressions of other attributes for which we have no evidence and which may be unrelated to those attributes. Regarding the latter, we may rate employees who have excellent attendance records higher on other aspects of job performance, such as quality or productivity, than those with poorer attendance records, even though attendance may not be related to actual level of performance.

The halo effect can also influence how employees view the organisation. A study of a company that was in receivership showed a generalised negative attitude to that company despite the company paying relatively high salaries, providing excellent working conditions and good supervision. The financial problem negatively influenced employees' ratings of individual features of the company in all areas, even those which could be viewed as positive features.[27]

This also serves as an example of the relative effect of negative information. In general, negative information more strongly influences impressions than positive information. It seems that negative information is automatically alerting and its overemphasis may be due to concern with avoidance of interpersonal threats and short- or longer-term problems of survival.[28]

Finally, we need to remember that characteristics which trigger a halo effect in one person may not have the same influence on other people. We all tend to have our own unique theory of personality – what people are like in general and which personality traits tend to co-occur in people. In addition, we each have our own opinions about which traits are more or less important in particular contexts. Consequently, we cannot assume that our own opinion about a particular individual will necessarily be shared by other people – a familiar point for those who have sat on selection panels of any type, from occupational ones through social committees to sports team selection!

The halo effect is probably the most pervasive source of error in performance evaluation. Furthermore, it is highly resistant to elimination. Even the knowledge of susceptibility to the bias is not sufficient to eliminate it completely. Evidence indicates that only the application of relatively sophisticated statistical control techniques is effective in reducing it.[29]

Stereotyping

Stereotyping is influenced by the same sort of inference process that underlies the halo effect. Given one piece of information about a person's character, we go beyond the information given to infer other traits for which we may have no evidence whatsoever. However, for the halo effect, the theories about behaviour and the influence of particular traits tend to be individually held, although there may be group influences on them, whereas for stereotypes the personality theories or beliefs are largely shared by larger groups of individuals or are part of a culture's beliefs. They can, of course, also be engineered by governments to engender 'group-think', particularly in times of danger as in situations of intercountry disagreements or wars.

Stereotypes are beliefs that all members of a particular group possess certain common characteristics or ways of behaving. They occur in what is probably their best-known and most pernicious form when they concern minority groups (e.g. gender, ethnic). Nevertheless, there are stereotypes for almost every class of people. There are stereotypes of engineers, librarians, nurses, managers, shop stewards, professors; people who wear glasses, pin-striped suits, or have beards; people who are thin or fat, old or young, male or female, and so on. Many of these stereotypes will influence how we see other people in organisations and, perhaps through this influence, how we interact with them. Therein lies the danger.

If we have no knowledge of a person who we are about to meet, information about who that person mixes with and the groups he or she belongs to may help to reduce uncertainty and increase our chances of successfully interacting with that person. However, the critical factor is the assumption that because that person belongs to a particular group he or she will behave according to our stereotype of that group. It could be that the stereotype is in general wrong, being based on false assumptions, or that the individual with whom we are concerned is atypical.

There are many examples of research which indicate that stereotypes affect the perceptual/judgemental process. For example, the more facial scars a person has, the more dishonest that person is judged to be. Physically attractive individuals of both sexes are rated as more warm, responsive, interesting, sociable, kind and poised than less attractive individuals and more likely to attain high occupational status.[30] Where males and females are candidates for jobs, even where both are equally qualified, males are given higher evaluations in general than are females.[31] This effect is greater when the interviewer is highly authoritarian.[32] Even where women were recommended for hiring as frequently as identically qualified men, they were offered significantly lower starting salaries and subsequent pay rises tended to increase the initial salary discrepancy.[33] Sex-role stereotyping seems to influence all facets of occupational life, usually to the disadvantage of women.

Stereotypes are learned from experience. We may encounter a few members of a group who possess some common characteristic and assume, perhaps mistakenly, that all other members of the group share the same characteristic. Alternatively, stereotypes may be acquired by accepting the views of other people without actually encountering any members of the group in question. The stereotype of the absent-minded professor, for example, probably exists amongst many people who have never even met a professor, let alone an absent-minded one.

Once formed, stereotypes can persist for a number of reasons. We may never come across a member of the group in question or, in some cases, may not realise that we have done so. Thus, we may never encounter any evidence to disconfirm our stereotype. Alternatively, we may give undue weight to cases which do appear to confirm the stereotype, ignoring contradictory evidence or regarding it as 'the exception which proves the rule'.

The dangers of stereotyping are all too evident. Individuals may be atypical of a particular group upon which the stereotype is based or the stereotype may, in general, be wrong. Whatever the case, we are not treating people as individuals and consequently our decisions about them may be biased or wrong. The results of this can include inefficient selection of personnel, poor development of personnel, inadequate problem solving and ineffective interpersonal interactions.

Interpreting people's behaviour

So far, we have largely been concerned with specific perceptual and cognitive factors which influence how we form impressions of other people. However, in observing people behaving within the context of their work performance, we are also concerned in determining the role they play in events that have a bearing on the achievement of work outcomes, whether successful or otherwise. The question of why people behave as they do influences how we interact with them on a daily basis, but it will also strongly influence our decisions of them at work in terms of selecting them, giving them special tasks to do, promoting them, and so on. The process of attempting to identify the causes of behaviour is called the attribution process. Such causal knowledge is assumed to provide a more stable, predictable and controllable environment, and thus a more apparently rational basis for making decisions for the dispensation of rewards and punishments and for selection and promotion decisions.

The behaviour of people at work can be influenced by 'internal' factors such as their personality, their beliefs or their motivational state. Thus an intelligent person is expected to behave in an intelligent way, a religious person dutifully, and a determined person decisively. On the other hand, behaviour is also influenced by the nature of the situation, including other people. Thus a less capable person may perform well at a task because the situation and supervision provide support to enhance performance, or a capable and determined individual may perform less well because the situation and supervision combine to create a frustrating and difficult climate. In these latter situations, factors 'external' to the individual influence behaviour in a predominant way. In general, however, behaviour is likely to be influenced by both internal and external causes. For selection and promotion decisions, for dispensing merit awards and so on, or in the event of accidents and where situations go amiss, we usually need to apportion individual influence in terms of capability or culpability. That is, to what extent were outcomes of events influenced by situational factors (external to an individual) or internal personality traits and dispositions?

In everyday life, including work situations, we often make such attributions to decide where responsibility lies for both successful and unsuccessful events. Under what circumstances we do so, how we decide whether causes are internal or external, and what errors or biases can influence the process, are three questions which are pertinent to the attributional process.

Conditions which cue the attributional process

We do not invoke attributional processing for all the actions people carry out. When people are performing in expected ways we accept the behaviour, usually without a thought. For example, if Maria is usually punctual for work we do not spend mental effort on considering whether this is because she enjoys the work or is afraid of arriving late (both internal), or whether it is a convenient time to arrive after taking her mother to work, or if she is avoiding traffic problems (both external), and so on. However, if Maria is normally punctual, but then over a period of several days turns up late, as her manager you will probably become concerned. Thus, when unexpected events or behaviours occur you are likely to ask the question, 'Why?' The cause of the unexpected behaviour, whether internal/dispositional or external/situational, will be important information which will then help you understand and consequently handle the problem. Is it a temporary situation caused by situational factors such as road works or illness in her family, or is it symptomatic of a personal problem within the work environment, which may have longer-term implications requiring a different solution?

A second obvious circumstance is when you are asked or required to make a judgement. Any evaluative or developmental situation is likely to invoke such a judgement. Appraising an employee, involvement in selection and promotion decisions, deciding on the provision of merit awards, or whether disciplinary action should be taken, are some examples. We may also make attributional judgements for interactive reasons. Is your co-worker pleasant and co-operative because the organisation requires it, or because he or she is friendly and helpful by nature? How you view your co-worker's motives will affect both your feelings towards and the nature of your interactions with him or her.

Two motivational factors which increase the likelihood of invoking the attributional process are *hedonic relevance* and *personalism*.[34] Hedonic relevance relates to a perceiver's emotional involvement in an event. For example, if you are responsible for the introduction of a newly designed production system and you are being obstructed by a particular individual, it is highly likely that you will attempt to discover why the person is being obstructive. Personalism refers to other people's actions which are seen as affecting you. You are more likely to make causal inferences if you overhear a co-worker making disparaging remarks about you than if the remarks are about someone else.

Finally, a third motivational factor, the *serious outcome effect*: the more serious an outcome of an event, the more likely we are to assess causal inferences.[35] A mistake by an employee which causes a minor production delay may be a source of irritation but be overlooked. The same mistake made by a different employee on another occasion, but which this time causes a major breakdown, will cue the attributional process, even though the two actions were similar.

Factors influencing attributional judgements

Our main concern in attributing responsibility for actions is whether the person or the situation is the cause. One approach to how we decide proposes that we act as naïve scientists. We interpret a given behaviour, such as poor performance, in the context of comparison of information in an experimentally based situation, using three principal variables, *consistency*, *consensus* and *distinctiveness* of poor performance.[36] That is, the manager should ask whether the employee has performed the task poorly in the past (consistency), whether other employees perform the task poorly (consensus) and whether the employee has performed poorly on other tasks (distinctiveness).

If other employees perform the task badly (that is, consensus is high) and the particular employee performs well on other tasks (high distinctiveness) but consistently badly on the task in question, then the more likely it is that the cause of poor performance is the situation – that is, the task is probably too difficult. If, on the other hand, there is high consistency (the employee always performs the task badly) and other employees perform well on the task (low consensus), the more likely it is that the causes of poor performance are internal to the individual.

However, such rules do not provide an explanation of the employee's poor performance and the reasons for the poor performance would need further exploration. It could be ability or motivation, for example. Alternatively, the assumption that all employees doing similar tasks are working under exactly the same conditions may not be the case. A manager, for instance, may treat one employee quite differently from another without necessarily being aware of it. Co-workers may also respond differently to each other, being supportive and co-operative to some individuals but not to others. Nevertheless the process described above will provide useful guidelines for analysing whether the causes of a performance problem are individually or situationally based, from which point discussion with the individual may draw out the reasons for the poor performance using both the diagnostic framework noted in the previous chapter and the techniques described in the next chapter.

Biases influencing attribution

The attribution process is an essential element of behaviour which assists the process of making sense of the world. Several conditions which cue the process have been noted earlier, as well as factors which can influence how we apportion responsibility. Yet there are natural tendencies and information-processing factors that can introduce bias into the attribution process, which has implications for managerial behaviour and decision making. Three factors were mentioned as conditions which cue the attribution process: hedonic relevance, personalism and the serious outcome effect. Evidence indicates that the relevance which an event or outcome has for us personally, and the more serious the event or outcome is, the more likely we are to credit causality to individuals rather than to external or situational factors. An unexpected machine failure in our own work group is more likely to be interpreted as individual negligence than one in another department. The more serious the effect of the breakdown the more blameworthy the individual will be rated.

Another bias with which we are all probably familiar is what has been called the *self-serving bias*. In any task-oriented situation, employees form causal attributions about their behaviour. Those attributions usually differ depending on task success or failure. Individuals are highly likely to take personal credit for success but blame failure on external factors. Three types of explanations have been suggested to account for this – motivational, impression management, and information processing:

1. Self-regard is the basis for a *motivational* explanation – the maintenance of self-esteem. It is interesting that evidence tends to indicate that, for individuals suffering from depression, this is not the case. When things go right for a depressive, success is attributed to luck, and when things go wrong they blame themselves.
2. *Impression management* relates to individual concern for gaining approval from, and avoiding disapproval of, significant others. Hence the need to seek public credit for success and deny personal responsibility for failure.
3. The *information-processing* explanation is linked to the viewpoint of events. When we are involved in tasks, our attention is largely drawn to factors in the situation which relate to the task. We view ourselves manipulating external situational elements. Consequently, where things go wrong, we tend to focus on changes in the situational elements which contribute to the failure and blame those. Where things go right, the focus for attention is likely to be individual skill in manipulating the situational elements successfully, based on past learning.

The information-processing explanation can also be applied to what has been termed *the fundamental attribution error*. This states that in judging the behaviour of others we tend to underestimate situational factors as significant influences on behaviour. Whereas with the self-serving bias the focus of our attention in viewing tasks done by ourselves is the situational task elements, when viewing other people performing, the primary focus of attention is the actual person carrying out the task. We see the person as influencing or manipulating the situation. As a result, we may frequently judge the person as being more influential or powerful than they actually are within the event. Such a focus of attention can hinder managerial learning as a result of faulty attributions. A good example of this occurs in interviewing skills training. Role-played interviews are usually the most appropriate way of developing interviewing skills. A role-played interview occurs after which interviewers are given feedback on their technique. A tutor who has observed the interview may have solicited from the interviewer that he or she had done most of the talking. On being asked to comment on this the interviewer is likely to say things like, the interviewee was very quiet, would not talk or, when they did, they were being uncooperative and therefore had to be told rather than asked, and so on. On the other hand, the tutor is likely to comment to the effect that the interviewer was failing to ask questions to gather information, making premature judgements on the basis of opinion rather than information and, as a result, failing to gain co-operation from the interviewee. For the interviewer, the focus of attention is the interviewee and the interviewee will therefore be seen as the major influence on the interview. The interviewer's explanation of the outcomes is likely to centre on the interviewee rather than the context of which the interviewer is a part.

This situation can interfere with the learning of the influence that interviewers have on the interview process. How can this problem be overcome? On the basis of the fundamental attribution process, getting interviewers to observe their interviewing performance should remedy the problem by shifting the focus of attention largely from the interviewee's performance to the interviewer's performance. This is what interpersonal skills trainers do. By recording the interview and having interviewers view their performance, they usually see themselves as being more influential on the course of events, in line with the tutor's views, than their own previous view.[37]

The fundamental attribution error is really a bias rather than an error, but it is a bias which pervades many managerial judgements, particularly in relation to appraisal situations. The self-serving bias and the fundamental attribution error can contribute towards managers and their subordinates seeing the same events quite differently, with managers often seeing performance problems caused by their employees, whereas the employees are much more likely to put forward situational causes for the problems. There do seem to be cultural differences in the generality of occurrence of the fundamental attribution error. Koreans, Japanese and Hindus are less likely to explain deviant behaviour in terms of personal dispositions than people in Western cultures. Eastern cultures tend to place greater emphasis on external situational factors.[38]

Two other attribution biases which have relevance to occupational situations are the illusory causation effect and egocentric attributions:

1. The salience of individuals in comparison to other people can lead to the *illusory causation effect*.[39] Individuals within groups who are more salient because they are more observable, more brightly dressed, better illuminated, louder, or possess any visual distinction that makes them stand out, are

judged as being more causally influential on events within the group than less salient individuals. This has obvious significance for rating people in the work environment. However, it has to be noted that such salient individuals may gain credit for successful events, but may also gain discredit for less successful or failed events.

2. When people are interacting with others as, for example, in group working activities, special projects, research collaborations and so on, they tend to recall more readily their own individual contributions than those of others in the group. As a result they see their own actions as more creditworthy (or blameworthy) for work outcomes than those of others. This is called the *egocentric bias*.[40] It can result in conflict in work situations where individuals believe that they are responsible for more of the work than others in the group, and that therefore the others are not doing their fair share of the work.

What, then, are the lessons to be learned from attributional biases? We should be aware that we often tend to underestimate the influence of situational variables on people's behaviour when making judgements about their responsibility for actions and events. Being aware, however, may not always have a practical influence on appraising and evaluating people and solving problems. In order to overcome naturally occurring biases, we usually need to develop systematic approaches which will reduce or eliminate their effect.

The previous chapter took a systematic approach to analysing work performance for improving problem solving and influencing more effective work behaviour. This chapter has indicated that making accurate inferences about the causes of people's behaviour is subject to many problems created by perceptual and judgemental distortions and biases which can detrimentally affect managerial decision making. How can we reconcile this with the viewpoint expressed at the beginning of this chapter that 'people are adequate perceivers for dealing with a wide range of situations and problems in everyday circumstances'?

Postscript

At the beginning of this chapter, the notion of a workable balance approach to perceptual and judgemental accuracy was proposed. The workable balance referred to a compromise between accuracy and effort for the achievement of some intended goal. For interpersonal interactions of a sociable nature, which tend to predominate in both social and work situations, the workable balance approach provides sufficient success. The biases and distortions which affect both the perceptual and judgemental processes, including the attribution of responsibility for actions, are rarely crucial in such social interactions. They tend to arise as a result of 'economy of effort', and where misunderstandings do occur which affect relations they can be rectified with little long-term harm.

Misunderstandings can be overcome through apologies from the guilty person or through rationalisations for the inappropriate behaviour by either or both the perpetrator and the victim.

For some organisational decisions, however, the criteria for perceptual accuracy need to be more stringent because the consequent judgements and decisions based on the data are more crucial, and more difficult to rectify once made. Therefore the standards against which we assess accuracy have to be much higher. The mistake we often make, because we are generally successful in our social interactions, is to fail to recognise that different approaches are needed to achieve this higher standard in order to overcome the inherent biases and distortions that are introduced by the economy of effort of the workable balance approach to everyday perceptual and judgemental activity. This chapter has discussed many of the common biases and distortions that can occur, and an awareness of them can help to sensitise us to them. However, a knowledge of and ability to handle situations in different ways, to eliminate or at least reduce their influence, is the better approach.

We have seen in this chapter that, in the absence of specific criteria to give meaning and stability to our experiences, we will generate our own, often inappropriate, criteria. For example, the pervasiveness of physical attractive-ness or gender as an influential bias triggers stereotyping which will affect judgement and decision making. Without setting goals, targets or standards against which we can assess the performance of employees, we are likely to evaluate or rate them on the basis of our opinions and beliefs developed from categorising them, often on the basis of relatively little and usually selective information. So, a crucial step required in reducing or eliminating subjective distortion and bias is to ensure that we have developed clear criteria that will clarify what is expected of employees in terms of targets or goals and standards of work performance.

The second crucial step is to ensure that decision making is information based. A major aspect of this is to be aware of the range of factors which influence work performance. The previous chapter explored this. Again, however, knowledge of this range of factors is insufficient in itself. The process of systematically exploring individual performance against each of these factors is essential to avoid jumping to premature judgements about those individuals on the basis of preconceptions, cued by our beliefs and opinions, that categorise or stereotype them. Again, clear expectations in terms of goals and standards, against which performance can be compared, are essential. It is also essential that employees themselves are aware of these expectations.

Finally, and underpinning the information-based decision-making approach, is the systematic collection of information relating expectations to the standards of work performance of individual employees in order to influence their perform-ance for the achievement of organisational goals and, within that context, their personal career goals. Again, this chapter will have highlighted some of the pitfalls which can influence detrimentally, through the introduction of bias, the process of gathering information. The opinions we hold about individuals, based on factors which trigger categorisations and stereotypes, will constrain or restrict exploration on the basis of our preconceptions relating cause and effect. The next chapter will explore what we consider to be one of the most important aspects relating to a manager's leadership role – the information-gathering and interpersonal skills component. Skilful application of this component, within the context of clear and publicised expectations of performance standards, based on relevant criteria, should lead to the reduction or elimination of bias and distortion in the evaluation of work performance.

Exercise 3.1
A perceptual analysis

Read through the case study and pick out any perceptual processes which you think illustrate those described in the chapter.

Bill Bean is administration manager at Solent Oil and Cake's (SOC) head office in Southampton. He arrived in his office in a pensive mood having received a complaint about Victor Ridsdale on the previous day. Victor is the office manager who reports directly to Bill. Bill was pensive because he held Victor in high regard, but over the last few months he had received several complaints about his performance.

The problem which caused Bill most concern was a near strike of six process workers which occurred whilst he was on holiday. The Personnel manager had formally complained to Bill, on his return, that Victor had interfered in matters beyond his remit by stopping a special bonus payment to these workers. Bill had been very angry because he had authorised the payment and left clear instructions to the Wages supervisor to pay it, although he had not informed, nor felt he needed to inform, Victor. He could not understand how Victor had become involved. Bill had called Victor in immediately he had received the complaint and told him in no uncertain terms that he should not have interfered and that he held Victor fully responsible for the near strike. He gave Victor no opportunity to defend himself and although Bill had given no indication that the interview had been a formal disciplinary one, Victor was left with the impression that it had been. Victor left Bill's office showing signs of suppressed anger – tight lipped, tensed jaw, slightly red in the face and walking stiffly.

Up to this point in time, Bill believed Victor had performed exceptionally well in his role as office manager. Bill had been the major force in Victor's appointment to this post. He remembered Victor's interview – the first time they had met. Victor's references had impressed him with glowing reports on his ability and intelligence reflected in rapid promotions from the shop floor as a plant operator, to despatch clerk, assistant statistics officer and then statistics officer, despite having no formal qualifications beyond GCE O-levels. Also impressive was his army record. Before joining SOC he had enlisted for three years. There, he had shown leadership ability having been selected for officer training and achieved the rank of lieutenant. Just the sort of background for an office manager, Bill had thought. He had a relatively wide knowledge of the company and its employees plus leadership ability. Victor's appearance and performance in the interview confirmed Bill's assessment and he insisted on Victor's appointment to the post, despite some opposition from other panel members based on Victor's responses to questions on managerial and administrative activities. Bill had felt that, although some of Victor's answers were not ideal, the stress of the interview situation could affect an interviewee's ability to think clearly. Nevertheless, Victor's work record spoke for itself and shows ability and accomplishment in the real world of work.

However, Bill was now having second thoughts. Over the past few months, he had heard occasional comments from other managers that they were not getting all the information they expected. On checking this out, Bill found that Victor had been cutting corners. Initially he had put this down to other managers overstating their need for information because, according to Victor, it was not vital information but more general or redundant information that had been omitted. Just last week, however, a further complaint had been received on lack of information which did appear more serious.

As Bill pondered on these incidents, other factors were recalled to which he had previously attached little significance. He remembered occasions when he had fleetingly thought that Victor allowed his staff to be too familiar with him and spent too much time in apparently idle gossip with them. A few particular occasions were recalled in which Victor and Angela Smart, an office secretary, seemed to be involved in long conversations, rather than getting on with their work. Nevertheless as far as Bill was aware, Victor's department was working efficiently and he had dismissed the occasions from mind.

Perhaps also, Bill thought, the credit he had given Victor for streamlining the paperwork system was overdone. On recall, Bill started to consider all the help he had given Victor in both the design and implementation of it. Victor's expenditure of effort, frequent discussions with him, early arrivals at work and late evening working had impressed Bill. He now felt less sure in retrospect. However, perhaps I'm being hard on Victor, thought Bill. When I look at his overall record he has performed well for the major part of his tenure, probably better than others in his position and he has also proved himself to be extremely competent in other positions he has held, otherwise he wouldn't have achieved such rapid promotions. Maybe what I need to do is to talk to Victor and find out the reasons for the recent problems.

Answers and guidance to this exercise are given in Appendix II.

Notes and references

1. It is worth noting that this process starts immediately something is perceived, otherwise all we would see or hear would be a meaningless jumble of senseless data. On the other hand, we may also consciously attempt to puzzle out the precise implications of some unclear information we perceived sometime previously. Thus although we are presenting perception and judgement as separate processes for the sake of convenience, and because judgement is sometimes divorced from the original events, the two processes are largely merged in practice.

2. L. Jussim (1991), 'Social perception and social reality: a reflection–construction model', *Psychological Review*, **98**, 54–73.

3. W. H. Ittelson (1973), 'Environment perception and contemporary perceptual theory', in W. H. Ittelson (ed.), *Environment and Cognition*, Seminar Press.

4. D. C. Dearborn and H. A. Simon (1958), 'Selective perception: a note on the departmental identification of executives', *Sociometry*, **21**, 140–4.

5. A. Tesser, C. J. Pilkington and W. D. McIntosh (1989), 'Self–evaluation maintenance and the mediational role of emotion: the perception of friends and strangers', *Journal of Personality and Social Psychology*, **57**, 442–56.

6. D. C. McClelland and J. W. Atkinson (1948), 'The projective impression of needs, I: the effect of different intensities of hunger drive on perception', *Journal of Psychology*, **25**, 205–22.

7. Susan's friend was a male friend! If you saw this possibility immediately – well done! If not, what assumptions were inhibiting the solution? Probably an assumption that, because she was Susan's school friend, she would be female. That the child took hold of her friend's hand may also help sustain this. We are also more likely to expect children to hold their mother's rather than their father's hand.

8. G. Nevill (1990), *Women in the Workforce*, The Industrial Society.

9. P. Darbyshire (1987), 'The implications of the rise in men in nursing', *The Occupational Psychologist*, December, 32–3.

10. K. K. Dion, E. Berscheid and E. Walster (1972), 'What is beautiful is good', *Journal of Personality and Social Psychology*, **24**, 285–90.

11. J. R. Udry and B. K. Eckland (1983), 'The benefits of being attractive: differential pay-offs for men and women', unpublished manuscript, University of North Carolina at Chapel Hill, quoted in G. L. Patzer (1985), *The Physical Attractiveness Phenomena*, Plenum Press, 118.

12. M. J. Harris (1989), 'Personality moderators of interpersonal expectancy effects: replication of Harris and Rosenthal (1986)', *Journal of Research in Personality*, **23**, 381–97.

13. J. M. Feldman (1981), 'Beyond attribution theory: cognitive processes in performance appraisal', *Journal of Applied Psychology*, **66**, 127–48.

14. B. M. Springbett (1958), 'Factors affecting the final decision in the employment interview', *Canadian Journal of Psychology*, **12**, 13–22.

15. J. M. Huegli and H. Tschirigi (1975), 'An investigation of the relationship of time to recruitment interview decision making', *Proceedings of Academy of Management*, 234–6.
16. For a review of the interview as part of the selection process, see R. D. Arvey and J. E. Campion (1984), 'Person perception in the employment interview', in M. Cook (ed.), *Issues in Person Perception*, Methuen.
17. G. N. Sande, J. W. Ellard and M. Ross (1986), 'Effect of arbitrarily assigned status labels on self-perceptions and social perceptions: the mere position effect', *Journal of Personality and Social Psychology*, **50**, 684–9.
18. J. Skvoretz (1988), 'Models of participation in status-differentiated groups', *Social Psychology Quarterly*, **51**, 43–57.
19. J. Gahagan (1975), *Interpersonal and Group Behaviour*, Methuen.
20. L. A. Zebrowitz (1990), *Social Perception*, Open University Press.
21. Jussim, *op. cit.*
22. R. Buckhout (1974), 'Eyewitness testimony', *Scientific American*, **231** (6), 23–31.
23. D. L. Rosenhan (1973), 'On being sane in insane places', *Science*, NY, **179**, 250–8.
24. A. Anastasi (1964), *Fields of Occupational Psychology*, McGraw-Hill.
25. E. E. Jones, L. Rock, K. G. Shaver, G. R. Goethals and L. M. Ward (1968), 'Pattern of performance and ability attribution: an unexpected primacy effect', *Journal of Personality and Social Psychology*, **10**, 317–40.
26. E. E. Jones and G. R. Goethals (1972), 'Order effects in impression formation: attribution context and the nature of the entity', in E. E. Jones, D. E. Kanouse, H. H. Kelley, R. E. Nisbett, S. Valins and B. Weiner (eds), *Attribution: Perceiving the causes of behaviour*, General Learning Press, 27–46.
27. B. A. Grove and W. A. Kerr (1951), 'Specific evidence on origin of halo effect in measurement of employee morale', *Journal of Social Psychology*, **34**, 165–70.
28. F. Pratto and O. P. John (1991), 'Automatic vigilance: the attention-grabbing power of negative social information', *Journal of Personality and Social Psychology*, **61**, 380–91; S. T. Fiske (1992), 'Thinking is for doing: portraits of social cognition from daguerreotype to laserphoto', *Journal of Personality and Social Psychology*, **63**, 877–89.
29. F. J. Landy, R. J. Vance, J. L. Barnes-Farrell and J. W. Steele (1980), 'Statistical control of halo error in performance ratings', *Journal of Applied Psychology*, **65**, 501–6.
30. K. K. Dion, E. Berscheid and E. Walster (1972), 'What is beautiful is good', *Journal of Personality and Social Psychology*, **24**, 285–90.
31. R. D. Arvey (1979), 'Unfair discrimination in the employment interview: legal and psychological aspects', *Psychological Bulletin*, **86**, 736–65.
32. K. Simas and M. McCarrey (1979), 'Impact of recruiter authoritarianism and applicant sex on evaluation and selection decisions in a recruitment interview analogue study', *Journal of Applied Psychology*, **64**, 483–91.

33. J. R. Terborg and D. R. Ilgen (1975), 'A theoretical approach to sex discrimination in traditionally masculine occupations', *Organizational Behaviour and Human Performance*, **13**, 352–76. Although this study is now nearly twenty years old, evidence still tends to show pay differentials for similar work, e.g. Equal Opportunities Commission (1991), *Women and Men in Britain*, London, HMSO.

34. E. E. Jones and K. E. Davis (1965), 'From acts to dispositions: the attribution process in person perception', *Advances in Experimental Social Psychology*, 2, Academic Press, 220–66.

35. E. Walster (1966), 'Assignment of responsibility for an accident', *Journal of Personality and Social Psychology*, **3**, 73–9.

36. H. H. Kelly (1967), 'Attribution theory in social psychology', in D. Levine (ed.), *Nebraska Symposium on Motivation*, XV, University of Nebraska Press, 192–238.

37. M. D. Storms (1973), 'Videotape and the attribution process: reversing actors' and observers' points of view', *Journal of Personality and Social Psychology*, **27**, 165–75.

38. J. G. Miller (1984), 'Culture and the development of everyday social explanation', *Journal of Personality and Social Psychology*, **46**, 961–78.

39. L. Z. McArthur (1980), 'Illusory causation and illusory correlation: two epistemological accounts', *Personality and Social Psychology Bulletin*, **6**, 507–19.

40. M. Ross and F. Sicoly (1979), 'Egocentric biases in availability and attribution', *Journal of Personality and Social Psychology*, **37**, 322–36.

CHAPTER 4

Verbal components of manager–subordinate interactions

Introduction

In this chapter, we come to what we consider to be the most important aspect of the interpersonal skills of leadership – what managers actually say and do when interacting with their subordinates. Undoubtedly, many other factors contribute to successful leadership. The manager may already have carried out a detailed analysis of the factors influencing the subordinate's performance, and also have cleared his or her mind of any preconceptions which could lead to distortions of perception or judgement. The manager may also have decided how to structure the interaction – which topics are to be dealt with and in what order – and decided on his or her general approach to the subordinate – friendly, considerate, stern, unyielding and so on. Nevertheless this still leaves the manager with the problem of what he or she is to say to the subordinate and how to say it. Throughout the interaction, the manager must decide what to say or do *next* in order to achieve his or her objectives. As we noted in Chapter 1, this is an aspect of leadership on which the practising manager will receive remarkably little help from leadership theories. Yet it is crucial. If it is mishandled – if the manager says the wrong thing, or perhaps even says it in the wrong way – then the interaction may fail, no matter how careful the manager's preparations or how good his or her intentions.

In our view, what is required as a first step towards helping managers to develop this aspect of leadership skills is an inventory of the various things which *could* be said and done in interactions with their subordinates, and guidelines which will help them to select those which would be most appropriate for a particular purpose. We would suggest that the manager's behaviour in interactions with his or her subordinates can usefully be regarded as being made up of a number of primary components. These are the basic building blocks out of which the manager's contribution to the interaction as a whole is constructed. Such components may be verbal or nonverbal. Verbal components include the various questions and statements employed by the manager during the interaction. These will be discussed in the present chapter. Nonverbal components, which we will examine in Chapter 5, consist of such things as tone of voice, gestures, body posture, facial expressions, and so on, which accompany speech and sometimes replace it. To rephrase the statement at the beginning of this paragraph, then, our aim in these two chapters is to provide an inventory of the various verbal and nonverbal components that are available to managers in interactions with their subordinates, and guidelines that will help them to select those components which are the most appropriate for the particular purpose at hand.

The objectives of manager–subordinate interaction

In our view, apart from idle conversation, there are four main objectives which a manager may wish to pursue in an interaction with a subordinate. These are: gathering information, giving information, influencing behaviour and handling emotion.

In some cases, the manager may be primarily concerned with achieving only one of these objectives. For example, in one interaction, the manager's main aim may be to discover the subordinate's opinion concerning a particular piece of equipment before deciding whether a repeat order should be placed. In another, the manager may provide information which the subordinate needs in order to make a more effective decision. In yet another, the manager's prime concern may be to let the subordinate know that an improvement in work performance is necessary in some particular area. Again, the manager may simply wish to listen sympathetically, thus allowing a subordinate to get a grievance or personal problem off his or her chest. Often, however, it will be necessary to fulfil all four objectives during the same interaction. If the manager does not simply wish to act as a 'sounding board', but actually wants to help the subordinate towards a solution to the problem, then further information will be required and perhaps also a change in the behaviour of the subordinate. Similarly, deciding precisely how someone should improve his or her performance may also require additional information and the attempt to get someone to change his or her work behaviour may lead to adverse emotional reactions. The interpersonally skilled manager must be able to perform each of these activities well. Let us examine each in turn.

Gathering information

The ability to obtain precise, valid and relevant information from people is an extremely useful aspect of a manager's repertoire of skills. It can be used in a wide variety of managerial situations, such as selection interviewing, identifying customer needs, pinning down suppliers on precise specifications or delivery dates, obtaining information from one's own boss or fellow managers, and so on. It is also an extremely important aspect of leadership skills. At one time, it was thought that each manager should be able to do their subordinates' job at least as well, if not better than they did. This, combined with relatively simple incentive systems, meant that managers could simply tell subordinates what to do. With the increasing complexity of modern organisations and of the work of their employees, managers are likely to find themselves managing a number of specialists, each of whom knows more about his or her job than the manager does. Furthermore, people's expectations of their employing organisation have also become more complex, and the potential adverse repercussions of leaving such expectations unfulfilled have become more serious. Thus, modern managers need much more information to manage people effectively than did their nineteenth- and early twentieth-century counterparts.

An important source of such information are the subordinates themselves. They may be able to provide information which will help the manager do his or her own job more efficiently. They will almost certainly be able to identify factors which influence their own performance, either beneficially or adversely. Furthermore, they may be able to suggest changes which can be made which would enable them to improve their work performance. This does not mean that such information will invariably be totally accurate. Like anyone else, subordinates may misunderstand the real factors influencing their performance, or may consciously or unconsciously distort the information in the direction of their own self-interest. However, this does not render the information valueless. Rather it means that more skilful questioning is required, despite the possibility of misunderstanding or distortion on the part of the subordinate.

The questions and statements used to gather information fall conveniently into three groups: eliciting information; managing the flow of information; and checking agreement concerning actions and events.

Eliciting information

First there are those which are specifically concerned with eliciting information. In different ways they all ask the subordinate to provide information on a particular topic, however broadly or narrowly defined. Included here are the following:

Open Questions
Open questions ask for general information concerning some topic area. For example:

What do you think of the new stamping machine?

Tell me what steps you have taken to deal with the absenteeism problem?

How do you see your career developing in the immediate future?

By asking the question in this form, the manager allows the subordinate to decide what information he or she thinks is relevant within some general area. They are also couched in such a way that simple 'yes' or 'no' answers are not appropriate. Thus, open questions are useful for encouraging a subordinate to talk about a particular topic area at some length, expressing his or her thoughts, feelings and opinions about it, when the manager does not have a clear idea of the specific information he or she requires. At the very least, therefore, open questions should provide useful background information concerning a particular topic. They may also elicit the more specific information the manager requires, either by chance or because the subordinate is perceptive and realises what the manager is looking for. If they do not, however, a different kind of question is needed.

Probes

Probing questions are useful for obtaining more detailed information, opinions, feelings, and so on. They often follow open questions, and are used to pin down more precisely something described in more general terms in response to the open question. For example:

> What particular complaints have the operators made about the new stamping machine?
>
> What is the most serious problem you have to deal with when absenteeism goes over 10 per cent?
>
> What is it that particularly attracts you to that kind of work?

The information gained from such questions is likely to be much more precise than that provided in response to open questions and, if used skilfully, should take the manager closer to the specific information he or she requires. However, if the manager has not collected more general information first – say, through the use of open questions – there is a danger that probing questions may be directed towards less relevant areas. Furthermore, when probing sensitive areas, care needs to be taken not to employ too threatening or demanding a manner as the interaction could take on the attributes of a 'third degree' and arouse resistance and resentment.

A type of probing question which is particularly useful when exploring the reasons for performance problems is the precise behavioural probe. This asks for precise information about what the subordinate actually said or did and the effects this had. In response to open questions concerning performance problems, subordinates often give general answers. This is not only because open questions encourage such responses, but also because the subordinate may not wish to describe in detail what he or she did if this led to adverse consequences. However, if such generalities are accepted, the manager may never discover exactly what happened, which in turn will make it more difficult to identify alternative courses of action which would have been more effective. The following is an example of how precise behavioural probes might be used to establish exactly what happened during an incident:

MANAGER: So, what did you say to her?

SUBORDINATE: Well, I let her know that I wasn't satisfied with her attendance record.

MANAGER: No, what exactly did you say to her?

SUBORDINATE: Well, I said that she had the worst attendance record of anyone in the department and I wasn't going to put up with it any longer.

MANAGER: And what did she say to that?

SUBORDINATE: She said that it wasn't her fault if her car wouldn't start.

MANAGER: And you replied?

SUBORDINATE: I told her that her excuse wasn't good enough.

MANAGER: And those were the exact words you used?

SUBORDINATE: Well, no, actually I told her that she should get a more reliable car or get another job.

MANAGER: And those were your exact words?

SUBORDINATE: Well, there were a few swear words in there. . .

Closed questions

These are useful for establishing specific points of fact; for example, simple 'yes' or 'no' answers, numbers, dates and so on. Examples include:

What is the delivery date for the replacement stamping machine?

How many days were lost last month due to absence?

Would you be interested in a secondment to Product Development for three months?

Obviously, if the manager wishes to obtain such specific pieces of information, and the subordinate is ready to supply them, there is little reason to talk round the subject by asking open questions. Conversely, however, they are much less useful for obtaining general background information, particularly with relatively taciturn subordinates who may simply give such answers as 'March 26th', '114' or 'Yes'. Thus, attempts to gather information employing a predominance of closed questions run the danger of being short and lacking in background information, additional details, comments about opinions, feelings, or reservations, which might completely change the complexion of the information given. This can, of course, be blamed on the taciturn nature of the subordinate, but equally the fault lies with the manager for not asking the right sort of questions.

Comparisons

Comparisons can be used to get the subordinate to explore facts in a new light or reveal his or her own needs, values and opinions. For example:

What do you think are the relative merits of the current stamping machine and the new machine which will become available later this year?

Are there any major differences in patterns of absenteeism between employees who live locally and those who have to travel further?

Would you prefer to develop your career on the technical side or in line management?

Obviously, the 'pairs' chosen must be relevant and realistic, so that it is within the capability of the subordinate to make a considered judgement. Also, it may be useful to set the scene by explaining why the question is being asked, otherwise the subordinate may suspect an ulterior motive and be reluctant to give his or her true opinions (see 'Trap setting' in Chapter 6).

Hypotheticals

Hypothetical questions represent another way of encouraging the subordinate to explore his or her ideas, feelings or opinions about a particular subject. For example:

If we were offered a replacement for the existing stamping machine, do you think we should take it?

Supposing absenteeism were to exceed your predictions for any reason, how would that affect your production forecasts?

How would you feel if you were offered a promotion which involved a move to a different part of the country?

It must be stressed that the main aim of hypothetical questions should be to get the subordinate to consider new ideas, or allow the manager to assess the subordinate's depth of knowledge in a particular area, or ability to come to reasoned conclusions about a particular problem. It should not be assumed that the answers necessarily represent what the subordinate would really do should the situation actually arise. After further thought outside the interview, perhaps triggered by the question itself, the subordinate might later change his or her mind. If the outcome is important to the manager, therefore, a further check at some later date may be useful. Furthermore, as with comparisons, the hypothetical situation which is posed should be selected carefully and, where necessary, background information given. Otherwise, there is a danger that the subordinate may lack the knowledge or experience to come to a meaningful conclusion. Alternatively, the question may raise unrealistic expectations which cannot be fulfilled at a later date, causing resentment, or the subordinate may suspect a trap and refuse to fall into it.

Hypotheticals often fail spectacularly if they are used in an attempt to make someone see another person's viewpoint or feel shame, perhaps because people have learned how to cope with them from early experience. For example:

MANAGER: How would you feel if I reprimanded you like that?

SUBORDINATE: I wouldn't make such a stupid mistake in the first place, so you wouldn't have to.

MANAGER: But supposing you did, how would you feel?

SUBORDINATE: I would think that I deserved to be reprimanded, and I would accept it.

MANAGER: But wouldn't you feel resentful if you were reprimanded like that?

SUBORDINATE: I might at first, but I would soon realise that it was entirely justified. Did you see what he did? He. . .

This is rapidly turning into a win–lose interaction (see Chapter 7 for more detailed discussion of this problem). Someone is going to have to back down, either the subordinate by showing compliance (e.g. 'OK, I take your point'), or the manager by changing the subject, with very little gained on either side. An alternative method of tackling such a problem ('causal analysis') is discussed in Chapter 6.

Multiple questions

These are the only type of question or statement amongst those we identify which we regard as serving no useful purpose whatsoever. They consist of a string of questions linked together without pauses for the other person to respond to. Sometimes they occur because the manager wishes to have answers to a number of related questions and cannot wait to ask them one at a time, and sometimes because the manager is not satisfied with the way he or she has expressed a particular question and therefore rephrases it in several different ways. The following is an example incorporating both aspects:

Have you done anything to reduce the high rates of absenteeism in your section? How many days did you lose last month? Did you notice any significant patterns in the absenteeism data? I mean, were there any particular jobs which had higher absenteeism rates or any particular people who were off more than others? Did you check out how your section compares with the others in the department?

It is very unlikely that the subordinate will be able to remember this string of questions and therefore answer all of them. Even if the subordinate could remember that, the answer might be, 'No, I've been too busy, 36, yes, no, yes, yes, and they are worse', which would be of little use to the manager. The most common response is to answer the last question asked, because it is freshest in the subordinate's mind. Alternatively, however, the subordinate may consciously or unconsciously select the question in the list which is easiest, or least incriminating, to answer and reply at length, hoping to lead the discussion on to less threatening topics. For example:

> Yes, there is one of the employees who has a particularly poor attendance record. That's Mrs Burns. Her daughter has been ill recently, and she says that there is no one else who can take her to hospital. I've talked to her several times about it but, from what I've heard, her daughter really is sick, so I don't feel I can lean on her too hard. What do you think I should do in a case like that?

What makes things worse is that often, buried amongst the string of questions which the manager asks, is a particularly good one which would have produced relevant and useful information, but which is never answered as the discussion changes direction. This raises some important general points about information gathering. First, simple questions are better than complicated ones. Secondly, having asked a question, listen to the answer. Do not be tempted to change it or ask a supplementary question before or during the interviewee's response. Despite having been asked a poorly phrased question, the interviewee may answer the question you meant to ask, rather than the one you actually asked. Even if the interviewee does not answer the question you meant to ask, it is still possible to listen to the answer and then pose a rephrased question to obtain the information you really wanted. Thirdly, silence is not merely golden, it is also powerful. Having asked a good question, wait for the answer. If the other person needs time to think, allow him or her to do so. Having been given time to think, the answer is likely to be all the more informative when it does come. Silence can also be used to elicit further information. If the answer to a particular question does not produce the information required, follow up probes can be used to elicit it, but sometimes simply saying nothing and merely waiting for the other person to continue can be a highly effective way of obtaining further information which may not otherwise have been forthcoming.

Managing the flow of information

The second major group of information gathering components are those concerned with managing the flow of information. Included here are what we refer to as 'lubricators', 'inhibitors' and 'bridges'.

Lubricators

Lubricators include such words, phrases and vocalisations as 'yes', 'go on', 'I see', 'mmm', 'Uh huh', and so on. If accompanied by the appropriate nonverbal cues of interest (see page 145), they encourage people to continue talking on a particular subject.

Inhibitors

Examples of inhibitors are, 'I see', 'Oh', 'Yes, but', and so on, which, if accompanied by nonverbal cues of disinterest (see page 145) or signs that the manager wishes to take over the speaking role (see page 160) indicate that the subordinate has said enough on a particular topic. Tone of voice is particularly important here. Thus a word or phrase (e.g. 'Yes') could act as a lubricator if said slowly and relatively softly, or act as an inhibitor if said shortly, sharply, repetitively and relatively loudly.

Both lubricators and inhibitors operate at a largely unconscious level. Unless the manager is very self-aware, he or she probably does not realise that a subordinate is being encouraged to continue to speak or to abandon some topic by means of lubricators, inhibitors and their associated nonverbal signals. Similarly, the subordinate is unlikely to realise quite how much he or she responds to such signals. Most people, in fact, seem to use such cues effectively most of the time, without thinking about it. However, there are occasions when problems can arise. Some people habitually do not display signs of interest or emotion very clearly, and are therefore very difficult to 'read'. Thus, lack of lubricators could be mistakenly interpreted as lack of interest. In other cases, the use of lubricators or inhibitors could be inconsistent with other aspects of the manager's behaviour, perhaps due to a conflict of motives. For example, a manager may use an open question because he or she thinks the subordinate should be encouraged to talk, and then follow this up with inhibitors or at least an absence of lubricators, because the manager is not really interested in what the subordinate has to say. The manager may then blame the subordinate's short and incomplete replies on the fact that the latter 'isn't very forthcoming', rather than his or her own questioning technique.

Bridges

In longer interactions, bridges provide a smooth transition between one topic and the next. For example:

> Well, I think that we have got as far as we can with the absenteeism problem for the time being. Let's turn to another topic which I think we need to discuss. I've been wondering whether we should replace the stamping machine. What do you think?

This is perhaps not the most important component in the manager's repertoire of interpersonal skills. Nevertheless, it does signal to subordinates that a new topic is being introduced and give them an opportunity to collect their thoughts on it, and it does add a certain amount of elegance to the discussion.

Checking agreement concerning actions and events

The final group of information gathering components are those involved in checking agreement concerning actions and events. Included here are restatements and summaries.

Restatements

Restatements involve restating or paraphrasing the subordinates' comments. Said in a slightly questioning, but nevertheless accepting, tone of voice their aim is to allow managers to check on the accuracy of their perception of what the subordinate has just said or to get the subordinate to crystallise ideas which have been clearly expressed. For example:

> What you seem to be telling me is that the machine is ideal for routine work, but cannot easily be reset for one-off jobs.

This not only ensures that the manager has not misunderstood the subordinate's comments, but also allows time to think about how to proceed with the issue in question. However, care must again be taken with accompanying nonverbal cues. Said in the 'wrong' tone of voice or with the 'wrong' facial expression, such restatements could indicate rejection, surprise, ridicule, disgust, and so on. Alternatively, if said with force and conviction, they could lead a compliant subordinate to agree, even though the restatement did not accurately reflect their views (see 'Leading questions' in the next section).

Summaries

Summaries draw together the main points of a discussion. They can be used at the end of an interaction to draw together all the major points discussed or, in the longer interactions, they may be used at the end of a particular section of the discussion before proceeding to the next. For example:

> What we have agreed so far, then, is that you will provide a breakdown of absenteeism figures by individual employees, type of work, day of the week, and so on, over the next month, and see whether any patterns emerge. We will then go through this data together at our next meeting and see what steps can be taken to solve the problem. In the meantime, I will talk to Personnel to see whether they have any useful suggestions, or at least will be willing to back us if we do try to do something, and you will have a word with some of the persistent offenders to see whether there are any particular problems we should know about. OK?

The advantage of an interim summary is that it ensures that there is agreement before going on to the next issue, thus reducing the likelihood that manager and subordinate will be at cross purposes during the subsequent discussion. It also makes it much easier to carry out a final summary, because the main conclusions have already been agreed at strategic points throughout the discussion.

Interim summaries can also be used in the middle of a discussion as a means of overtly identifying what issues require further discussion. Used in this way, these summaries in effect set up an agenda stipulating the items to be dealt with in the next stage of the interaction. The need to do this may arise for a number of reasons. The manager and subordinate may each contribute several ideas to the discussion as it progresses. The subordinate may not answer the question the manager asks, but provide different information which also happens to be important. Even more confusingly, the manager may ask a single question, but receive a multiple answer which provides several pieces of relevant information on the same issue. If the manager attempts to continue the interaction without overtly identifying the different issues or pieces of information which have emerged from the discussion, then it is very likely that one or more of them will be forgotten. On the other hand, overtly identifying such issues or pieces of information, perhaps writing them down, and agreeing an order in which they can be discussed can ensure that they are all dealt with. For example:

> Let's just hold for a moment. We started off talking about machine efficiency, then got on to the question of maintenance contracts and now you have just raised an interesting point about the difficulty of motivating part-time staff. I think these are all important issues, but let's deal with them one at a time or we'll both get confused. Let's finish off the question of machine efficiency first and come back to the others when we have wrapped that up. Now my original question was: "Have you noticed any difficulties in the efficiency of the new stamping machine as compared with the previous model?"

Final summaries serve several useful functions. They reduce the likelihood of subsequent differences of opinion between manager and subordinate concerning the main outcomes of the discussion. In longer discussions, they serve to remind participants of points made earlier which might otherwise have been forgotten. Given that there is a tendency for memory as well as perception to be selective, it is sometimes useful to ask the subordinate to do the summary. This will enable the manager to check on whether the subordinate has in fact remembered the main points of the discussion accurately, or at all. Finally, summarising and gaining agreement to do something can also help in gaining the subordinate's commitment to put into action any specific decisions or plans which emerged from the discussion.

The various types of question and statements described in this section are summarised in Table 4.1, together with an indication of the situations in which their use would be appropriate or inappropriate.

Before leaving the subject of gathering information, however, it is worth considering the nature of the response. No matter how appropriate the question

Table 4.1 *Components for gathering information*

(a) Components for eliciting information from the subordinate

Component	Appropriate use	Inappropriate use
Open questions e.g. 'Tell me about . . .' 'Could you describe what you think are . . .'	For introducing topics and encouraging subordinates to talk at length so avoiding simple 'yes' and 'no' answers.	For obtaining specific details.
Probes e.g. 'Could you tell me more about . . .?' 'What do you mean by . . .?'	Generally follow open questions to elicit more information about a particular topic or event.	Can miss point if more general information not collected first. Pointed and persistent probing on sensitive issues can be seen as intrusive.
Closed questions e.g. 'How long did it take?' 'Did you receive my draft report?'	Establishing precise information (dates, numbers, etc.) and receiving simple 'yes' and 'no' responses.	For gaining broad information, opinions, feelings, etc.
Comparisons e.g. 'What are the relative merits of . . .?'	Getting subordinates to explore and reveal their own needs, values and opinions.	Where the 'pairs' are unrealistic or irrelevant.
Hypotheticals e.g. 'What would you do (have done) about (if) . . .?'	Getting subordinates to think about a new topic or area.	When a subordinate lacks knowledge or experience of the situation described.
Multiples A stream of questions or statements strung together covering several points.	None. The respondent usually answers the last question or the one most convenient for him or her to answer.	Always inappropriate.

Table 4.1 (*continued*)

(b) Components for managing the flow of information

Component	Appropriate use	Inappropriate use
Lubricators e.g. 'Ye–es' 'Go on', 'mmm', 'Ah ha'	Indicating to subordinates that you are listening and want them to continue.	With over-talkative subordinates. Over-used they become intrusive and inhibiting.
Inhibitors e.g. 'Oh!', 'I see', 'Yes but . . .'	Signalling that enough has been said. Tone of voice may indicate surprise, indignation or non-acceptance of views expressed.	With reticent subordinates. For frank and open discussion. Where frustration or emotion is being expressed.
Bridges e.g. 'I think that's all we need to say on that topic, now let's turn to . . .'	Providing a smooth link between one topic and another and indicating clearly what the next one is.	When the previous topic has not been adequately dealt with from the subordinate's point of view.

(c) Checking agreement concerning actions and events

Component	Appropriate use	Inappropriate use
Restatements e.g. 'What you seem to be telling me is that . . .'	To confirm or crystallise ideas.	When used disparagingly or reproachfully, sarcastically or cynically.
Summaries e.g. 'What we seem to have discussed and decided so far is . . .'	Drawing together the main points of a discussion and avoiding discrepancies. It can also help in gaining commitment to action.	If used prematurely.

or how well expressed, it may not elicit the information which the questioner wants because the respondent either deliberately or inadvertently fails to supply it. Dillon lists a variety of ways in which a respondent may fail to give the information which the questioner wants, including silence, changing the topic, making excuses, evading the question, stonewalling, giving correct but misleading information, withholding or concealing information, distortion and lying.[1] In fact, according to Dillon, most responses are non-answers. This would not be a major problem if the questioner recognised the fact and re-posed the same question. In our interpersonal skills training sessions, however, it never ceases to amaze us how many times the respondent fails to supply the information requested by means of quite unambiguous questions, and the person who asked the question either does not notice or chooses to ignore the fact. What often happens is that the questioner responds to something the respondent said during his or her non-answer rather than to the fact that the question asked has not been answered. Sometimes the unrequested information may be useful, but often the information which is not obtained is equally, if not more, important and the fact that it is not obtained may prevent the manager from getting to the bottom of an issue. Thus, continually restating or refining a question may be necessary in order to ensure that it is answered. To do this, however, the manager needs to realise that the question has not been answered in the first place and this requires good listening skills. The question of listening skills will be discussed in more detail in Chapter 6.

Giving information

In this section, we are concerned with some of the types of statements which managers can use to give information to other people. Only a small number are identified because we often give information to other people in order to influence their behaviour or their feelings, and these uses are dealt with in more detail later. Nevertheless there are certain types of statement which can be used to give information in a more or less neutral form, in the sense that they allow the other person to decide how to make use of it, and these are discussed here.

Factual statements

These are intended to provide the other person with information which he or she can use to solve a problem or make a decision. For example:

> There is a detailed review of the main alternative types of stamping machine in the current edition of *Technology Today*.

> I understand that the Personnel Manager is setting up a working party to look at problems of absenteeism and time-keeping and will be asking for someone from our department to join it.

Self-Disclosure

Self-disclosure involves revealing our own 'weaknesses' or difficulties to another person who is concerned about his or her ability to cope with a particular problem or activity. For example:

> I think most people feel nervous before a major presentation. I always used to get butterflies in my stomach when I had to do one, and I still do to some extent.

> I can understand your feelings. When I first took over this job, I had serious doubts about whether I could handle it. In fact, I almost asked for a transfer at the end of the first week.

Used appropriately, self-disclosure can increase trust and respect between people because it shows a willingness to be open and honest about one's own problems, doubts, failures and so on. It can also help the other person to feel less insecure by realising that he or she is not unique in facing such problems. Unfortunately, it can also have the opposite effect if used inappropriately. Expressed in an offhand manner, it can indicate lack of concern, in effect saying 'We all have our problems, why are you so concerned about yours.' It can lead to premature advice about the way we handled such a problem ourselves before fully understanding what the other person's problem actually is, and it can be a seductive way of turning the topic of conversation to ourselves and our concerns rather than those of the other person. Finally, self-disclosure must be done in such a way that indicates a belief in our ability to cope successfully with the problem and that the other person, despite any doubts he or she may have, can be similarly successful. Done in an anxious, self-doubting way, self-disclosure will probably make the other person even more anxious and could lose their respect as well.

Evaluative statements

These statements tell other people our beliefs about what we regard as important or unimportant and whether our attitude towards particular people, actions, ideas and so on are favourable or unfavourable. For example:

> I wouldn't even consider buying one of their stamping machines. They have the worst after sales service of any company I have ever come across.

> The most important problem facing the department at the moment is the high rates of absenteeism among part-time staff.

In some circumstances, such evaluative statements can serve a useful function. They can provide important information concerning the criteria against which we are likely to judge other people's behaviour. It can be very useful, for example, for a manager to know that his or her superior believes that it is better to have a satisfied workforce than to attempt to achieve maximum productivity at all costs – or vice versa. From the subordinates' point of view, of course, it is important to assess when the manager is expressing sincerely held beliefs or merely paying lip service to socially acceptable views. With some managers, for example, it may be politic to agree that a satisfied workforce is important, because that is what the manager *says* that he or she believes in, but actually put more effort into obtaining high productivity, because that is what the manager really believes is important.

Where the values expressed are shared by the other person, this can also have a beneficial effect. Having shared values is one of the important factors which increases people's liking towards one another. Thus, expressing shared values, even over relatively trivial matters, can help to engender more friendly, co-operative and supportive relationships between a manager and subordinates. Inevitably, the reverse is also true. We may take our own beliefs and values so much for granted that we assume that other people will naturally hold similar views. This can lead to the expression of beliefs or values which other people find offensive. This may in turn result in an overt expression of anger or resentment on the part of the other person, which could be damaging to the relationship unless handled well. Alternatively, the other person may not respond overtly to the specific remarks causing offence, but may nevertheless become less friendly or co-operative, leaving the manager wondering what has gone wrong in the relationship. Even where the expression of values which differ from those of the other person does not cause offence, it may inhibit the expression of alternative views, particularly where the other person wishes to make a good impression. This can also be counterproductive, if the manager wishes to obtain honest, unbiased opinions from his or her subordinates.

When the evaluation is concerned with the other person, it shades into praise and criticism, which will be examined in more detail in the next section. It is also worth noting that any of the question-and-statement types we have discussed earlier can have an evaluative content. For example:

How on earth could you make such a stupid mistake?

Let me summarise some of your major failings over the past six months.

Why did you interfere when the decision was not your responsibility?

Responses to the implied criticism in such questions and statements are likely to be at best defensive and at worst a full-blown counterattack. Thus they are much less likely to elicit useful information about the issues concerned than the same question or statement expressed in a more neutral way. Even slight differences in expression can make a considerable difference. Substituting the word 'intervene' for 'interfere' in the third example asks the same question but without the implied criticism and is likely to produce an entirely different response from the subordinate.

Feedback

Feedback is intended to give people information about the effects of their actions. It is a crucial aspect of learning. Without feedback, we cannot know whether our performance has reached an acceptable standard, whether we need to do something to improve it, and, if so, what it is we need to improve. Often, of course, we obtain feedback in the course of performing the task itself. We ask someone to do something and he or she either agrees or refuses. Sometimes, however, the effects of our actions may not be immediately apparent to us, or we may not know why our actions did not produce the effect we had hoped for. In such cases, feedback from another person who is in a better position to observe the consequences of our actions can be very useful. For example:

Your report went down very well with the board. They were particularly impressed with your ideas on using non-monetary incentives as a means of encouraging regular attendance.

From what I hear, the reason your proposals concerning the new stamping machine weren't accepted is that most of the people at the meeting didn't understand the technical jargon you used.

The above examples illustrate two important points about feedback. First, it can be positive or negative. This is an obvious point, but one which is still worth making because it is easy to overlook the value of positive feedback. It can be very useful to know when we did something right, so that we realise that it would be worthwhile to do the same thing again in similar circumstances. In the absence of such positive feedback, we may wrongly assume that what we did was not important and neglect it in future.

Secondly, it will be apparent that positive and negative feedback can have considerable emotional impact. To the person receiving it, it may be indistinguishable from praise and criticism. This is less likely to be a problem in the case of positive feedback. If a subordinate responds too favourably to positive feedback, there is the possibility that he or she may become complacent, but for the most part positive feedback will have the beneficial effect of motivating the person to continue to perform well in the area in question. Negative feedback may also motivate the subordinate to do better in future, but if handled badly, it can also induce adverse emotional reactions that will make it difficult to conduct a constructive discussion of ways in which the problem could be avoided in future. For example, subordinates given insensitive negative feedback may become apathetic because they have been made to feel a failure or angry because they think that they are being blamed for something which is not their fault. To be effective as a motivational technique, therefore, negative feedback should be directed towards an area of performance which the subordinate can improve and it should describe the subordinate's actions and the effects they had without making negative evaluations of the subordinate as a person. In fact, positive evaluations of the subordinate may be helpful in some circumstances. For example:

> **Despite your best intentions, your intervention unfortunately prolonged the dispute.**

It must be admitted that giving negative feedback is no easy task and no matter how carefully done, adverse emotional reactions may still occur. Nevertheless non-evaluative feedback about the subordinate's behaviour may help to reduce them.

A summary of the components described in this section is given in Table 4.2.

Influencing behaviour

Although the primary purpose of the question-and-statement types we have just described is to gather or to give information, under certain circumstances it is also possible to use them as a means of influencing behaviour. With able and experienced subordinates, a combination of information gathering and giving techniques can be used to stimulate them to analyse their own performance problems or development needs and formulate their own solutions in personal development plans. This requires the skilful use of open questions, probes, hypotheticals, restatements, feedback and so on to guide the subordinate to restructure or reorganise problems so that new ways of tackling them can be explored. This approach is discussed in more detail in Chapter Six (see 'The double funnel' and Causal analysis').

There are several advantages to this approach. First, it is likely to develop high levels of commitment to the solutions reached because they are largely the subordinate's own solutions. Secondly, the subordinate may come up with a better solution than the manager would have. Thirdly, it is likely to improve the subordinate's problem-solving ability because the manager is, in effect, coaching the subordinate in methods of analysing and solving performance problems. Such a non-directive approach, though, is not always appropriate, for several reasons. It can be relatively time-consuming and, due to pressure of work or because rapid decisions have to be made, the manager may not be able to set aside sufficient time for a lengthy discussion. Also subordinates may lack the ability or experience to identify solutions to their own performance problems. Finally, the manager may have learned from past experience that the subordinate is likely to produce 'solutions' which are impractical or irrelevant and become frustrated or annoyed if they are not accepted. In some situations, therefore, more directive methods of influencing behaviour are called for, and it is necessary for the manager to spell out what behaviour is expected from the subordinate. It is these more directive methods of influencing behaviour which we will be examining in the remainder of this section.

Behavioural influence components do not fall neatly into distinct categories, as

Table 4.2 *Components for giving information*

Question/statement	Appropriate use	Inappropriate use
Factual statements e.g. 'I shall be in conference all morning.' 'The next train to London is at 4.30.'	When they help the subordinate to solve a problem, make a decision, etc.	When they are irrelevant to the problem or decision, often the result of an inaccurate evaluation of the subordinate's situation.
Self-disclosure 'I always feel anxious before giving a presentation.' 'I had a similar problem back in 1967 . . .'	Establishing increased rapport, decreasing subordinate's self-consciousness or feelings that he or she has a unique problem.	When disclosure deflects discussion away from subordinate's problem, particularly if leading to premature advice, or dumps additional problems on to subordinate.
Evaluative statements 'Accountants are typically narrow-minded; they don't see the broad picture.' 'It is better to be honest with a customer even at the risk of losing a sale.' (NB Shades into praise/criticism if about subordinate.)	Where it would be helpful for interviewee to know manager's feelings on a particular subject.	Can antagonise, alienate or lead to lip-service if subordinate has different values.
Feedback 'Your action nearly caused a strike.' 'Your manner is upsetting me.' (NB Shades into praise/criticism when evaluative.)	When it provides subordinate with important information which will allow him or her to respond to a situation more adaptively in future.	When punitive (seen as criticism), smug, or unnecessary (negative information already known).

do those for gathering information. Still, two main aspects can be identified, direction and inducement. Components which give direction tell the subordinate what the manager wants or expects him or her to do. Inducements, on the other hand, are components which are intended to persuade the subordinate to do it. Some components, as we shall see later, can fulfil both functions if used skilfully.

Direction

Components which provide direction include orders, requests, advice and suggestions. These vary in the extent to which the manager indicates that the subordinate is obliged to follow the manager's wishes.

Orders

Orders give the subordinate least room for manoeuvre. They indicate that the manager expects his or her wishes to be carried out without question. No participation in the decision is invited. Thus, subordinates cannot express their own opinions or preferences without running the risk of overt conflict. For example:

> In future, you will not order replacement parts for the stamping machine without first consulting me, and then only if I give you permission in writing.

Requests

Like orders, requests indicate the manager's wishes but, in theory at least, give the subordinate the right to refuse, express reservations, or express alternatives. For example:

> In future, I would appreciate it if you would consult me before ordering replacement parts for the stamping machine and preferably obtain my permission in writing.

Advice/suggestions

Advice and suggestions are similar to requests, but imply that the subordinate should comply because it would be in the subordinate's own interests or it would be organisationally more effective, rather than simply because the manager says so. Thus they stress the authority relationship between manager and subordinate much less than orders or requests. For example:

> In future, why don't you come and discuss the matter with me beforehand and get my signature on any requests for spare parts for the stamping machine? I think you would find that things would go a lot more smoothly if you did.

Which particular component is the most appropriate in any one situation will depend on a variety of factors. These include the organisational climate, the power of the manager, the preferences of the subordinate, and the severity of the consequences of non-compliance on the part of the subordinate. In some organisations, giving orders is an accepted way of influencing behaviour, whereas in others it would be regarded as inappropriate. Even within the same organisations, subordinates are likely to vary in their preferences with respect to the way in which their managers make their wishes known to them. Some may prefer clear-cut orders which leave the responsibility for the decision squarely in the manager's hands. Others may respond with enthusiasm to a mild suggestion, but would resent being ordered to do something and thus do it with much less commitment. The organisational power of the manager is important in that it determines the extent to which the manager can enforce compliance with his or her wishes should the subordinate refuse or fail to obey a direct order. If the subordinate is likely to refuse an order, and can do so with impunity, then more persuasive methods may be more appropriate.

Finally, much will depend upon how strongly the manager feels that non-compliance on the part of the subordinate would have serious organisational consequences. If the consequences are likely to be very serious (e.g. a strike, major loss of business, a serious accident), the manager may feel that he or she cannot risk non-compliance and issue a direct order. Similarly, if the subordinate has not responded to requests, advice or suggestions in the past, with adverse consequences, then the manager may decide that it is better to give an explicit order, rather than risk a further repetition. On the other hand, if the consequences of non-compliance are unlikely to be severe, the manager may well think it worthwhile to use a milder request or suggestion because this would increase the subordinate's self-esteem, positive feelings towards his or her boss, enthusiasm for the task, and so on.

Ultimately, then, the component selected should be the one which is most likely to ensure that the manager's wishes are carried out with commitment. All this assumes, of course, that the manager is in full possession of all the facts and is sure that his or her decision is the right one in the first place. If not, and time is available, then it may be that an information-gathering approach would be more appropriate.

Inducement

The components so far discussed simply let the subordinate know what the manager's wishes are. Inducements, on the other hand, give the subordinate reasons, either personal or organisational, for complying with such wishes. These include promises, threats and explanations.

Promises

Promises indicate that compliance with the manager's wishes will have beneficial outcomes for the subordinate. For example:

> And, on my part, I will put pressure on Purchasing Department to do all they can to speed up delivery on essential replacement orders.

> We will look at the situation again in six months' time and, if it isn't working as smoothly as we would like, we will then reconsider our current procedures.

One way in which promises can vary is in the extent to which their fulfilment is made contingent upon performance. If the promise is 'without strings' and requires no further action on the part of the subordinate, it may serve to increase his or her level of job satisfaction, reduce any feelings of resentment or frustration, and engender a more favourable attitude towards the boss. This in turn may result in the subordinate being in a more receptive frame of mind for the rest of the discussion. Where the promise concerns the removal of some factor which is impeding the subordinate's work performance, it may also increase or rekindle the subordinate's enthusiasm for the task. However, there is little evidence that improving job satisfaction will in itself lead to improved job performance.[2] If the manager wishes to use promises to motivate the subordinate to improve his or her job performance, therefore, fulfilment of such promises must be made contingent on the subordinate achieving the desired performance improvement. Thus they are useful in situation where subordinates cannot see a clear link between their performance and the extrinsic rewards they receive or where they do not regard existing rewards as being insufficient to merit the effort required to achieve them. Under such circumstances, promises can be used to spell out in more detail the existing relationships between performance and rewards and, where these are inadequate, identify additional rewards which can be linked to performance.

Used in this way, promises can provide a useful way of motivating subordinates to whom extrinsic rewards are important. They have the advantage over threats in that subordinates are more likely to work with greater enthusiasm and commitment towards the achievement of a desirable goal in order to avoid an unpleasant outcome. Also, if the rewards promised are both equitable and achievable, the subordinates are more likely to develop favourable attitudes towards their jobs, the manager and the organisation as a whole.

At the same time, promises can have disadvantages as means of influencing behaviour. They become 'addictive'. If the manager always promises something, and fulfils the promise whenever the subordinate shows reluctance to do something, the manager is, in effect, rewarding the subordinate for showing reluctance. This could lead to a situation where the subordinate shows reluctance with increasing regularity and the manager rapidly runs out of things to promise. Care should be taken therefore to ensure that what is promised is a legitimate and equitable reward for the performance in question, rather than simply a sop to appease an unreasonably disgruntled subordinate.

Threats/warnings
Threats and warnings indicate that failure to comply with the manager's wishes will have adverse consequences as far as the subordinate is concerned. For example:

> If there are any further incidents of this type, I shall have no alternative but to express strong reservations about your current performance and future career prospects in your annual report. Furthermore, I will instruct Purchasing Department not to accept any of your orders unless countersigned by me personally.

As we have already indicated, the use of threats clearly has disadvantages in that they may reduce the subordinate's enthusiasm for his or her job and cause resentment towards the manager or the organisation as a whole. Yet they still represent a useful and legitimate means of influencing behaviour under certain circumstances. If the subordinate's work performance is clearly inadequate in some respect, and other methods of behavioural influence have failed, then threats may represent the only alternative to doing nothing. The manager who simply ignored a subordinate's inadequate performance would also be failing in his or her own job. Furthermore, in many cases, it would not be fair to the subordinate either. Inadequate job performance often has its own adverse consequences, such as being overlooked for promotion, poor salary increases, lower bonuses, and even the ultimate sanction of dismissal. It is much better to let the subordinate know that such consequences may occur if performance is not improved, than to apply them later when it is too late for the subordinate to do anything to remedy the situation. Applied in this way, threats shade into warnings which can be very useful to the subordinate if they permit him or her to avoid adverse consequences.

In the case of both promises and threats, what is promised or threatened is extremely important. They must involve outcomes which matter to the subordinate and they must be pitched at the right level. With respect to promises, the manager must identify precisely what the subordinate would like to have *next* which would be sufficient to motivate the desired behaviour and which is within the manager's power to grant. This means that the manager must have a good understanding of what motivates the subordinate in question. To offer something which does not interest the subordinate will obviously not have the desired effect. Thus the promise of promotion could be a powerful inducement for some subordinates, but others may be so uninterested in promotion that they have to be offered other inducements to get them to accept it. Similarly, offering a subordinate less than he or she thinks is worthwhile in terms of the effort involved is likely to be ineffective, and the subordinate may resent the implication that he or she can be 'bought' so cheaply. Conversely, offering the subordinate significantly more than would be necessary to motivate the desired change in behaviour could represent a waste of organisational resources. The improvement in performance may be insufficient to justify what has been promised and, in any case, it will reduce the range of things which the manager can offer for an improvement in performance time.

Similar considerations apply with respect to threats. The outcome threatened must be something which the subordinate would prefer to avoid, and the consequences sufficiently severe to motivate the desired change in behaviour. Again, however, threatening a more severe outcome than would be necessary to produce the desired behaviour change would be counterproductive. Not only is this likely to cause unnecessary resentment, but it could actually have an adverse effect on performance rather than improve it. High levels of anxiety, particularly on complex tasks, may make the person too tense and nervous to be able to perform well. This effect will be increased if the subordinate cannot see any way of avoiding the threatened negative consequences. If used, therefore, threats should be accompanied by directive components describing specific, constructive and feasible actions that the subordinate can take in order to avoid the threat being fulfilled.

It is also important, when using promises or threats, that the manager is both willing and able to carry them out. There is little point in describing, however dramatically, the most attractive or adverse outcomes if the subordinate knows from past experience that neither are likely to be fulfilled. A primary source of credibility is the person's reputation for fulfilling past commitments. Research evidence shows that consistent enforcement of past threats increases compliance to current threats and consistent enforcement of past promises enhances the effectiveness of current promises.[3] Managers should only promise or threaten what they know is in their power to deliver.

Explanations

Used as an inducement, explanations tell the subordinate why he or she should, or should not, take certain actions in terms of their effect on organisational performance, other people within the organisation, or even the subordinate in question. In other words, they are concerned with the 'logic of the situation' rather than any subsequent actions the manager might take to reward or punish the subordinate. For example:

> We need to co-ordinate the ordering of replacement parts on a departmental basis. If everyone ordered parts independently, it could lead to unnecessary duplication, and the loss of any economies which could be made through bulk purchase. And, of course, it could lead to considerable resentment on the part of your colleagues if you were allowed to bypass the formal system and they were not. Not to mention the fact that I could look very stupid if my

boss asked me why we were making one-off replacement orders, and I didn't even know anything about it.

Explanations can provide an effective way of influencing behaviour. Many people respond much more willingly to an attempt to get them to do something, or change what they are doing, if it is explained why it is necessary for them to do so. It can add to intrinsic motivation by making the task more meaningful. It can also add to, or at least not detract from, their self-esteem, because they are being treated as thinking human beings with a need to understand what they are doing.

Nevertheless explanations may not always produce the desired motivation to change. The subordinate may disagree with the manager's assessment of the situation and the organisational consequences of his or her current way of doing things. Alternatively, the subordinate may be more concerned with the effect of any changes on his or her own self-interest than with their effect on the organisation, other people, and so on. Such self-interest may not, of course, emerge overtly in the discussion. It may instead, consciously or unconsciously, distort the subordinate's assessment of the situation and its organisational consequences. Equally, it is possible that the manager's initial assessment of the situation was distorted in much the same way. So there may ensue a long counterproductive difference of opinion, or perhaps even argument, in which the real issues are never discussed. Providing the manager is sure that his or her assessment of the situation is unbiased, therefore, other methods of influencing behaviour (e.g. promises, threats, a straightforward order without explanation) may be more appropriate.

Inducement and directive components are, of course, often used in conjunction with each other. It is possible to use a directive component, such as an order or request, without adding an explicit inducement, relying on the manager's implicit reward and punishment power or the subordinate's trust in the manager's judgement of fairness to ensure compliance. Similarly, it is possible to use inducement, such as threats or promises, to influence a subordinate's general emotional state by issuing them without conditions or any indication of how the threatened outcome can be avoided. On the other hand, if such inducements are used in an attempt to influence a specific aspect of performance, then it is necessary to spell out the behaviour required, which in turn requires the use of directive components. Thus, for example, an order, request, suggestion or advice not to wedge fire doors open whilst transferring files from one office to another might be combined with such inducements as:

... because a fire would spread more quickly if they are wedged open. (explanation)

... because I will institute formal disciplinary proceedings if you do. (threat)

... and I will look into alternative methods of transporting the files. (promise)

One of the ways in which both direction and inducement can vary is in their precision. 'Keep up the good work and I will see that you are all right', includes elements of both direction and inducement, but neither is very clearly spelled out. 'Keep up the good work and I will put you up for promotion in the next staff review', provides a very specific inducement combined with vague direction. Conversely, 'if you wedge those fire doors open again, I will not be responsible for the consequences', combines a very precise direction with a rather vague inducement.

One of the more subtle skills of leadership is achieving the appropriate degree of precision with which both aspects are spelled out. Going over the details of a task which the subordinate already understands, or giving someone precise orders to do something which he or she was going to do anyway, is likely to be at best irritating and at worst highly demotivating (see 'Hammering the point home', Chapter 6). On the other hand, if directions and inducements are not spelled out clearly enough, subordinates may not know what it is the manager wishes them to do or may not understand the consequences clearly enough to be motivated to do it. The situation is further complicated by the fact that subordinates will undoubtedly differ in the speed with which they grasp the implications of what the manager is saying. One may quickly understand the point being made, whilst another may need to have things spelled out in much more detail. Similarly, the same subordinate could grasp things very quickly on one occasion, but take much longer to understand an apparently simple point on another. This could be highly misleading if the manager has preconceived ideas about the subordinate's speed of comprehension, and fails to notice that the subordinate is not reacting as quickly – or as slowly – as the manager has grown to expect. Moreover a verbal agreement or acquiescence is not necessarily a sign of comprehension or commitment. The subordinate may not wish to appear stupid or may wish to avoid further criticism. One of the quickest ways to terminate the discussion is to agree. Thus, a comment such as, 'OK, I take your point, I'll make sure it doesn't happen again', may simply be a means of escaping from an unpleasant situation. It is all too easy to say, 'Good, I'm glad you got the message.' However, a follow-up probing question such as, 'What exactly would you do differently if the same situation arose again?' might reveal that the subordinate had not fully understood the problem.

Hard and fast rules cannot be given. It is a matter of spelling out directions and inducements in sufficient detail to ensure that the desired change in behaviour is forthcoming, but not going beyond this and labouring the point. Observational skills are, therefore, particularly important. The manager must actively listen and look for the various verbal and nonverbal signs of understanding or confusion, acceptance or rejection, interest or irritation, commitment or mere compliance, and be prepared to modify his or her approach accordingly.

The components we have described so far serve either to give direction or to provide an inducement and can only fulfil both functions if used in conjunction with each other. As we noted earlier, however, there are certain components which can fulfil both functions at the same time, if used skilfully. These are praise and criticism.

Praise

Praise tells the subordinate that his or her performance is appreciated and admired by the manager. If the subordinate values praise from his or her manager, this is likely to increase the subordinate's self-esteem, sense of achievement, and feelings of doing something worthwhile and meaningful, which many people find highly motivating. Furthermore if the praise is sufficiently detailed, it will let the subordinate know what types of behaviour the manager thinks are praiseworthy and are therefore likely to be appreciated in future. For example:

> I must congratulate you on the way you handled the fault on the stamping machine yesterday. If you hadn't been so alert and switched it off when you did, the whole machine might have seized up and we could have had a major repair job on our hands. As it was, we hardly lost any production at all. Well done!

However, using praise effectively requires much more skill than is generally recognised. Praise, it has been said, should be *personal, proximate* and *precise*. In other words, an individual is more likely to respond to praise if it is directed towards him or her personally, if it is close in time to the event being praised, and if it describes in detail what the person has done which is worthy of being praised. It is the latter which seems to cause most difficulty. We all seem to be able to describe precisely and at length what someone has done wrong, but find it much less easy to tell someone in precise detail what he or she did right. Simply saying, 'Well done, keep up the good work', may let someone know that he or she is appreciated, but it does not tell the individual precisely what is appreciated. Also, because general praise is so easy to give, there is a danger that it will be dismissed by the subordinate as 'mere flannel', whereas a manager would be unlikely to go to the trouble of praising in detail unless he or she actually meant it.

In the same way, praise which is done without conviction is also likely to have little effect. Comments such as, 'Overall, your performance has been quite good over the past year', said in an offhand manner as though the manager wishes to move quickly on to more important things, is unlikely to have much influence on subordinates' level of motivation or subsequent behaviour. They are much more likely to be waiting for the inevitable 'but', followed by the bad news. Simple rules such as, 'always precede blame with praise', are of little help if the subordinate knows that brief, weak and general praise is always followed by lengthy and detailed criticism (see Chapter 6). Again the answer seems to be precision. If the manager makes a point of never using praise without identifying precisely what the subordinate did to merit it, then the danger of weak general praise is considerably diminished.

Criticism

Criticism lets the subordinate know that the manager is dissatisfied with his or her performance. Used effectively, it should also let the subordinate know what he or she should have done differently in order to avoid the criticism. For example:

> You should have shut down the stamping machine as soon as you realised a fault had developed. I realise that there was a chance that it might have lasted out until the end of the shift and saved us interrupting production. As things turned out, however, the whole machine seized up and we now have a major repair job on our hands. In future, remember that it is much better to close the machine down for repairs rather than risk a major breakdown.

Like praise, criticism should be directed at a particular person as soon after the event as possible. Criticising a whole group of people is likely to be ineffective because at least some of them may feel, rightly or wrongly, that they were not at fault and are, therefore, being blamed unfairly. Similarly, criticising someone long after the event serves little useful function. Whether criticism should be precise or not is another matter. If the person is already aware of what he or she did wrong, and what he or she should do differently next time, then detailed criticism may simply cause resentment without adding further learning. This is not to say that the incident should be ignored. The subordinate may be waiting apprehensively for the manager's reaction, and feel very uneasy if nothing is said. However, a brief comment such as, 'I know you must feel as badly about that as I do, but at least we know how to avoid the problem in future', may be sufficient. On the other hand, if the person does not know precisely what he or she did which caused the problem or what to do differently to avoid it in future, then it may be necessary to provide more detailed feedback and guidance.

Like threats, criticism has the disadvantage of being likely to cause resentment and dissatisfaction. It can thus make the subordinate less co-operative in future, and less satisfied with and enthusiastic about the job generally. Therefore, if alternative methods of solving the performance problem can be found, these should be seriously considered. 'Causal analysis' is one possibility (see Chapter 6), as is non-evaluative feedback. However, such methods may not always be appropriate. The subordinate may either not be able to identify what went wrong or may not accept personal responsibility for the consequences of his or her actions, blaming instead other people, bad luck, and so on. In this case, it is better for the manager to let the subordinate know that he or she is dissatisfied with the subordinate's actions, rather than to ignore the problem and risk the same thing happening again.

Two points should, however, be made. First, the criticism should only be in sufficient detail to ensure that the subordinate understands precisely what he or she did wrong. Secondly, the main emphasis should be on what can be done to avoid the problem arising again in future and, where appropriate, what the manager can do to help the subordinate to achieve this improvement in performance. In other words, the criticism should be constructive.

Leading questions

The final technique for influencing behaviour superficially resembles an information-gathering component. It is a form of question which signals quite clearly the answer which the respondent is expected to give. For example:

> You do realise how important it is to follow agreed safety procedures, don't you?

> You do agree that absenteeism does give rise to serious problems in this department, don't you?

> You would like to go on an interpersonal skills training course, wouldn't you?

It would obviously be unwise to take affirmative answers to such questions at face value. They could represent the subordinate's genuine opinions, but there is always the danger that the manager is simply being given the answer that he or she apparently wishes to hear. Thus leading questions are inappropriate as means of gathering information. Nevertheless, they can be of limited use as a means of influencing behaviour. Agreement with a leading question cannot be taken to indicate the subordinate's wholehearted commitment to the idea being proposed by the manager, but they can be used simply as a means of obtaining explicit verbal agreement, either for the record or to provide the basis for a more detailed argument using other components such as requests, explanations and orders.

A summary of the various components described in this section is given in Table 4.3.

Handling emotion

Emotion is a significant influence on people's behaviour at work. Experiences both at work and outside the working environment produce feelings of pleasure, excitement, sadness, anxiety, anger and so on, and these in turn influence how people respond to their jobs, to other people and to the things which happen to them at work. Despite this, emotion is hardly ever mentioned in organisational behaviour texts,[4] perhaps reflecting a 'cultural, especially Western male, predilection to suppress, deny or minimise the role of emotions'.[5]

A number of reasons can be advanced for this tendency to ignore the role of

Table 4.3 *Components for influencing the behaviour of the subordinate*

Component	Appropriate use	Inappropriate use
Orders e.g. 'Do it now.' 'This is the way it will be done.'	With staff who need or prefer clear, precise instructions. Where compliance is vital due to special circumstances (e.g. time constraint, emergencies, etc.).	Where the benefits do not justify any resentment or stifling of ideas which may result.
Requests e.g. 'I have a problem . . .' 'Could you next time then, please . . .'	With subordinates who are more motivated by being asked or may contribute useful ideas to the problem.	With subordinates who need or prefer clear, precise instructions.
Advice/suggestions e.g. 'You could improve on that by . . .' 'The disadvantage of that is . . . but this way . . .'	With staff who prefer guidance and may be influenced in the desired direction by the 'logic of the situation' (e.g. those lacking experience).	Where compliance is essential and advice may be ignored.
Promises e.g. '. . . then I'll give you the opportunity to tackle bigger projects.'	Where the task may lack intrinsic reward and extrinsic reward must be introduced for motivational purposes.	Where the promises cannot be fulfilled. When the subordinate will perform the task effectively anyway.
Threats/warnings e.g. '. . . I will make you regret it.' '. . . and I shall begin formal disciplinary proceedings.'	Where compliance is essential and cannot otherwise be achieved (e.g. advice ignored, no available rewards, etc.). Where foreknowledge of potential adverse consequences would be useful to the subordinate.	When more positive methods are available. Where threats cannot be fulfilled. When the subordinate would perform adequately anyway.

Table 4.3 (*continued*)

Component	Appropriate use	Inappropriate use
Explanations e.g. '. . . because . . .' 'The reason is that . . .'	With those subordinates who are more motivated by understanding the reasons for doing something.	When the explanation will be rejected, leading to unproductive argument.
Praise e.g. 'I think that was well done because . . .'	To provide immediate feedback about the subordinate's standard of performance in a specific area and appreciation of it.	If too general, imprecise or late. When used in a patronising way without conviction.
Criticism e.g. 'Where you went wrong was . . . but this could be overcome by . . .'	To provide feedback on substandard performance in a particular area with emphasis on how to do it better next time.	When used negatively without emphasis on how to do it better. When it is likely to impair performance further due to resentment aroused.
Leading e.g. 'You must agree that . . .' 'Don't you think that . . .' 'You *do* see the point why . . .'	To gain compliance or acceptance by signalling the expected answer. Can be used to emphasise, or check on, a point made.	For encouraging a subordinate to express his or her views, feelings, etc. with reticent staff. For gaining commitment.

emotions in organisational life. One is a belief that emotions do not belong at work. Behaviour at work should be based on rational considerations and therefore emotions should be left at home. Another is failure to recognise emotions which are expressed at a relatively low level. In the next chapter, we will examine some of the nonverbal cues associated with different emotions. A third reason is fear. When managers on our training courses do not attempt to deal with emotional reactions on the part of 'subordinates' in practice interviews, the reason commonly advanced is that handling emotions is very difficult and rather than run the risk of exacerbating the problems, they thought it better to ignore them. Almost invariably the interaction is an unsuccessful one. Of course the manager may be right. Handling emotions badly could make matters worse. Equally, however, handling emotions well can lead to a highly successful interview.

Finally, managers may deliberately ignore emotional reactions because they believe that giving subordinates an opportunity to talk about their feelings would lead to a lengthy discussion and take up valuable time which could more profitably be spent on more important matters. Again, however, what often happens is that the subordinate's emotional reactions continually intrude on and disrupt the manager's attempts to achieve his or her primary objectives. Taking time to handle emotions may be time-consuming, but ignoring them can also result in an unsuccessful interaction or one which takes even longer to achieve its objectives. This is particularly true in the case of strong emotions. People experiencing strong emotions are unlikely to be either able or willing to take part in a logical analysis of a problem. It is only when strong emotional feelings begin to decrease that a rational discussion can take place.[6] Faced with someone experiencing strong emotions, therefore, it is almost invariably better to deal with the emotions first and attempt to reach a solution to the underlying problem only when the emotions have been dissipated.

In summary, ignoring emotions will not make their effects disappear, and dealing with emotional reactions in an effective manner when they arise can result in a more successful and less time-consuming interaction, and also enhance the long-term relationship between manager and subordinate. In this section, we will examine some of the ways in which emotional reactions can be handled more effectively.

Reducing negative emotions

One of the key skills in the effective handling of emotion is the ability to diminish or dispel adverse emotional reactions, such as anger, frustration, dissatisfaction, anxiety, despair and so on. This may be required because subordinates themselves raise issues with the manager which are causing them to feel aggrieved or distressed. For example, the manager may be faced with an angry or resentful subordinate who believes that he or she has been badly treated, either by the manager or by others within the organisation. Another subordinate may feel anxious or depressed about domestic problems or difficulties at work and come to the manager for guidance or reassurance.

Adverse emotional reactions may also be aroused or aggravated by the manager's behaviour during an interaction with a subordinate. We have already noted that remarks which are regarded as racist or sexist may give offence and ways of avoiding them have been discussed in earlier chapters. Negative emotions may also be aroused by the use of insensitive words or phrases in discussions of the subordinate's work performance. For example, a subordinate who feels that he or she has been unfairly criticised may become angry.

Similarly, insensitive negative feedback may arouse feelings of anxiety or despair. If high levels of emotion are aroused, such reactions will make it much more difficult to have a constructive discussion with the subordinate. People who are experiencing intense adverse emotions are much less likely to listen to what the manager has to say, are less capable of analysing issues logically, and are more likely to raise objections and present counter-arguments.

Obviously, then, it makes sense to avoid using insensitive words and phrases which are likely to arouse or aggravate adverse emotional reactions. Yet this may be more difficult than it appears, as we may use such words and phrases without realising we are doing so. It is all too easy to assume that our interpretation of events is entirely accurate and thus words such as 'carelessness', 'mistakes', 'interference', 'failure', 'faults', 'corner-cutting', 'weaknesses' and so on are merely factual descriptions of the subordinate's behaviour and personality. However, the subordinate may have different views and skilful questioning may reveal that he or she was not as much at fault as appeared at first sight. Furthermore, even if the remarks were justified, more neutral terminology could lead to a more constructive discussion of the issues concerned and this could be well worth sacrificing the satisfaction of being 'right'. Indeed, it appears that skilled negotiators even avoid using positive descriptions of themselves that could irritate the other party by implying that they do not possess these characteristics. For example, describing oneself as fair and reasonable has the implication that the other party is *un*fair and *un*reasonable.[7]

Another way in which the manager may increase the intensity of negative emotions in interactions with subordinates, without necessarily meaning to, is by negative mood matching. This occurs when negative emotions expressed by the subordinate arouse a similar emotional reaction on the part of the manager. Thus the manager reacts to the subordinate's anger, anxiety or depression by becoming angry, anxious or depressed. For example:

SUBORDINATE: The situation seems hopeless. Nothing I have tried has worked. I can't see any way out.

MANAGER (despairingly): No, neither can I.

Expressed in cold print, this may seem unrealistic. Nevertheless, in our training sessions on handling emotions, such exchanges have taken place on several occasions.

Rather than matching the subordinate's mood, which will tend to intensify it, the manager should try to behave in the manner that he or she would prefer the subordinate to adopt. Providing such a 'model' increases the likelihood that the subordinate's behaviour will become more like the manager's, rather than the other way around.

Care must be taken, however, not to go to the opposite extreme. For example, it has been shown that whilst people in a moderately good mood prefer the company of happy people, depressed people prefer to meet and get acquainted with unfortunate, unhappy people.[8] Thus attempting to cheer up a depressed person by behaving in a jolly manner is more likely to alienate him or her than have the desired effect. We might also prefer someone who is angry to be calm and logical, but behaving in a calm, logical and obviously patient manner toward someone who is angry may simply be infuriating. The appropriate behaviour when faced with someone who is expressing negative emotions is to show concern, without either exhibiting the same emotion oneself or acting in such a way that one appears to be denying it. Ways of showing such concern will be discussed in a later section.

It is also worth noting that an individual's mood affects his or her perception of events. Given a message which includes both positive and negative elements, happy people are more influenced by the positive parts and unhappy people by the negative parts. Similarly, happy people tend to give very charitable, benevolent descriptions of their acquaintances, whereas angry people give uncharitable and over-critical descriptions of their friends.[9] This has two implications for the manager. First, the subordinate's descriptions of other people and events are likely to be biased in the direction of his or her mood and this must be taken into account when evaluating the implications of what they are saying. The subordinate is unlikely to believe this, however, and thus overtly suggesting that he or she is exaggerating is likely to be extremely counterproductive. Secondly, the subordinate's mood will influence how he or she perceives the manager's behaviour in an interaction. Thus depressed subordinates are likely to interpret the manager's comments as being more negative than they really are and not hear positive comments, whilst an angry subordinate is more likely to perceive neutral or mildly critical comments as being antagonistic or threatening. This means that with emotional subordinates even more care has to be taken in the choice of words or phrases that might exacerbate emotional reactions.

No matter how careful the manager may be, however, he or she may still inadvertently arouse adverse emotional reactions or have to respond to emotional reactions caused by other factors that are unrelated to the manager's behaviour in an interaction. If such negative emotional reactions do occur, how can they best be handled? To some extent, this depends upon the type of emotion, its intensity and the complexity of its causes.

A variety of methods can be used to dissipate anger when it occurs at low or moderate intensity and the reasons for it are relatively straightforward. If the anger has occurred because the subordinate has not fully understood the circumstances involved, then an *explanation* of the true situation may serve to resolve the situation. If the subordinate has a reasonable case and there is an obvious and equitable solution, then the manager can *promise* to do something to resolve the problem. If the manager is in some way responsible for the subordinate's anger, then a firm and sincere *apology* may dissipate the anger, particularly if combined with a constructive discussion of ways of avoiding similar problems in future. For example:

I really am very sorry about that. I must make sure it doesn't happen again. How do you think we can arrange things differently next time so that the problem doesn't arise?

People who are anxious about something tend to overestimate both the likelihood of an unpleasant event occurring and how unpleasant it would be if it did occur.[10] They also tend to feel that if the event did occur, they would be unable to cope with it. Thus *factual statements* concerning actual probabilities and severity of problems, *positive feedback* concerning the individual's past record in coping with difficult situations and *promises* of help in solving the problem may assist in alleviating low or moderate anxiety. As already noted, *self-disclosure* may also help the subordinate to feel that he or she is not unique or alone in experiencing such problems. For example:

SUBORDINATE: I'm rather worried by the rumours about redundancies I've been hearing recently.

MANAGER: As everybody knows, the company is going through a difficult time at the moment, but I would think it very unlikely that there would be redundancies in our department. In any case, with your track record, you would be one of the last people we would want to lose.

SUBORDINATE: It's still worrying though. If I were made redundant, I don't know what I would do.

MANAGER: Well, I still don't think it's likely, but if the worst came to the worst and you were made redundant, you would receive quite a large redundancy payment which would keep you going whilst you looked for another job. I can understand your concern. I was made redundant about twelve years ago, and I thought it was the end of the world. But I did get another job and quite a good one at that as it turns out. I'm not saying it was a pleasant experience, but I came out of it all right in the end, and with your qualifications and experience, I'm sure you would too.

In some respects, the characteristics of depression are the opposite of those of anxiety. The anxious person overestimates the likelihood of unpleasant things happening, whereas the depressed person feels that he or she is already in an unpleasant situation and underestimates the likelihood of things getting better. In addition, depressed people often blame themselves for the things which have gone wrong in their lives.[11] Thus, criticism or even sensitive negative feedback is both unnecessary and likely to make them feel even more depressed. What the manager has to do is to find some way of convincing the subordinate that the situation is not as bad as it appears. Again, if the subordinate is only moderately depressed, this may be done by giving *factual information* about future prospects, *praising* the subordinate's past successes in overcoming difficulties and making *promises* to take action which will improve the situation.

It must be stressed, however, that the above recommendations are appropriate only in the case of emotions of low or moderate intensity. If the emotion is of high intensity, none of the above methods may work. If a subordinate is very angry, then explanations may be regarded as inadequate 'excuses', apologies may be seen as insincere or brushed aside as irrelevant, and promises may be mistrusted or rejected as too little and too late. Even their perceived inadequacy simply provides the subordinate with additional targets against which to express his or her anger, thus making him or her more angry rather than less. In the case of extremely anxious or depressed subordinates, attempts at reassurance in the form of factual statements, promises, praise, positive feedback, self-disclosure and so on simply will not be accepted. The subordinate will either be so preoccupied with their own concerns that they will not listen or they will regard any reassurances as unrealistic attempts to cheer them up. What then can be done? We would recommend that intense adverse emotional reactions should be tackled in three stages. First, the subordinate should be given the opportunity to express and dissipate the emotion or emotions; then the manager should make sure that he or she has a thorough understanding of the cause of the emotions; and only at this stage should an attempt be made to resolve the underlying problem or problems.

Diffusing intense emotions presents a difficult problem. In many cases, one cannot afford to agree with a highly emotional person's perception of the situation because this is often distorted, as we have already seen. Conversely, disagreeing with a highly emotional person is likely to intensify the emotion in the case of anger or be disregarded in the case of anxiety or despair. Ignoring the problem or refusing to allow the subordinate to talk about it will not make the problem go away and could adversely affect the manager's long-term relationship with the subordinate. What is needed, therefore, is a neutral response that both expresses concern and encourages the subordinate to talk about his or her emotions, without committing the manager to any particular viewpoint. This can be achieved by using the *reflective*.

The reflective reflects back the emotional contents of what the other person is saying in a concerned and non-evaluative way. It usually takes the form of a statement, but is often said in a mildly questioning tone of voice, as if checking the accuracy of one's perceptions. For example:

SUBORDINATE: That's typical. I try to do my job and all you can do is criticise me for some minor infringement of company regulations. That's the final straw. From now on, you can worry about maintenance problems. If the machine breaks down and we have to wait two months for spares, that's your problem, not mine. I don't see why I should worry. No one else does!

MANAGER: You seem to be very upset about this.

SUBORDINATE: Of course, I'm upset. I do my best for the company. I get no thanks when things go right, but as soon as I ignore one petty rule, I get criticised out of all proportion.

MANAGER: You feel that you don't get enough recognition for the work that you do.

SUBORDINATE: No, I don't. You look at other people. They do the bare minimum. If a machine breaks down, they just call in maintenance. They don't care how long it takes to put it right. I try to run things efficiently. I try to be prepared for emergencies and what happens. Instead of thanking me for all the extra work I put in, all you can do is criticise.

MANAGER: And you find that demoralising because it seems unfair.

SUBORDINATE: Yes, it does. I think the company should give more recognition to the people who have the company's interests at heart. And support. Why didn't you back me when I put forward my proposal to change the maintenance procedures?

MANAGER: You think that would have helped.

SUBORDINATE: Yes, it would. Look if we could approach one of the fitters direct, instead of filling in forms in triplicate justifying every little minor job, we might be able to . . .

Presented as they are here, without any indication of the way in which they are said, such reflectives may appear artificial or even trivial. It may also appear that encouraging people to talk about their emotions in this way would result in them becoming even more emotional. However, the reverse is the case. The subordinate cannot argue against the manager's views because the manager isn't expressing any. The manager not only responds non-evaluatively to the subordinate's comments, but also resists being drawn into expressing his or her views in response to questions from the subordinate. These too should be reflected back, as shown in the manager's final contribution in the above example. Thus by doing no more than simply reflecting back the emotional content of what the subordinate is saying, the manager is, in effect, encouraging the subordinate to explain and justify the emotion. In order to explain his or her position, the subordinate has to use reason, and the more reason is used, the less easy it is to remain emotional. Reason gradually takes over and the emotion dissipates. This probably works faster and more effectively with anger, but even in the case of anxiety and despair, people are likely to feel better having been given the opportunity to unburden themselves of their problems.

At this stage, once the subordinate has returned to a more stable emotional state, the manager can then move to other techniques in an attempt to resolve the underlying problem. It may well be that the manager has gained a good understanding of the problem through the use of reflectives. In the above example, the initial cause of the anger was being criticised for a 'minor infringement of company regulations', but further underlying causes, including lack of recognition for superior performance, lack of support and the irritation with what the subordinate regarded as petty rules, emerged as underlying factors in the course of the discussion. Nevertheless, it is worth moving to more direct questions in order to make sure that one has an understanding of what is the real problem. This is necessary for two reasons. First, the problem as it appears initially may have deeper, underlying causes. An adverse emotional reaction may be triggered by some trivial event, but the real causes may be much more complex. By the same token, subordinates may complain about relatively minor problems, either because they feel they cannot talk about the serious problems or as a way of initiating a discussion which will lead to the more serious worries in due course. Secondly, one emotion can hide another more fundamental one. A subordinate may appear to be angry, but underneath is actually anxious and hides this by an outward show of anger. In both cases, successfully dealing with the problem as it initially appears leaves more fundamental problems unresolved. Therefore use of the information-gathering questions and statements described earlier could lead to a better understanding of the real problem.

Having gained an understanding of the problem, the manager can then move on to an attempt to find a solution. This may involve using the methods discussed earlier for handling low or moderate levels of emotion or other methods to be discussed in Chapters 6 and 7. However, it is worth reiterating that until the emotion has been dissipated, there is little point in trying to find a rational solution to the problem because the subordinate is unlikely to be willing or able to discuss things rationally. The skilful use of reflectives can provide a particularly effective way of defusing such highly charged emotional situations and channelling the discussion towards a more rational examination of the problem.

Reflectives can also be used as a means of bringing out into the open feelings which are being expressed at a relatively low level, but still appear to be having an adverse effect on the interaction. For example:

You don't seem very enthusiastic about the idea.

I seem to sense a certain reluctance on your part.

I get the impression that you are rather annoyed about something.

By bringing such negative feelings out into the open, the manager may be able to solve the problem and eliminate the source of doubt, fear or irritation which would otherwise prevent a more constructive discussion from taking place.

Finally, it must be pointed out that the appropriate use of reflectives is probably the most difficult of all the techniques we have described in this chapter. It requires the following attributes:

1. A high level of listening and diagnostic skill to identify the other person's exact feelings and the reasons for them.
2. The ability to feed these back to the other person in a concerned way, without revealing one's own evaluation of the situation or person.
3. The ability to take personal criticism, or perhaps even abuse, without reacting to it defensively or emotionally.

Increasing positive emotions

In the previous section, we discussed ways of diminishing negative emotions. Obviously, many of these methods can also be used to increase positive emotions. For example, *praise* or *positive feedback* can make people feel more pleased with their successes, more proud of their accomplishments, more confident in their abilities, gratified that their contribution has been recognised and so on. Correspondingly, *promises* concerning outcomes which the subordinate would value may also make the subordinate feel happier about future prospects. Less obvious, perhaps, is the fact that reflectives can also be used to encourage someone to talk about their positive emotions. For example:

You must be very pleased about that.

So, everything worked out just as you planned it then?

Positive emotions can be enhanced by positive mood matching, just as negative ones are increased by negative mood matching.[12] Expression of pleasure, interest, excitement, and so on, when the other person expressed similar emotions is likely to result in the emotions being increased or experienced over a longer period of time. Conversely, responding in a neutral way to such expressions of positive emotions will almost certainly cause the emotion to decrease and may also give rise to negative emotions such as resentment.

Reducing positive emotions

So far we have been concerned with ways of influencing emotions in a positive direction. There may be times, however, when it would be beneficial for the subordinate to experience less positive feelings. If the subordinate falsely believes that he or she is doing well and has a good future with the organisation, it would be unfair to leave the subordinate in a state of ignorance about the true state of affairs if these are likely to lead to adverse consequences such as dismissal, poor salary increases, decreased promotion prospects and so on. It is also bad for the employing organisation, as the unfulfilled expectations are likely to lead to dissatisfaction, adverse effects on work performance and other forms of non-compliant behaviour.

High levels of positive emotion may also be inappropriate in certain types of problem-solving discussions. Positive moods are likely to be associated with enhanced creativity, but they are likely to inhibit performance on tasks which require analytic, detail-oriented strategies. In an experiment on performance appraisal, depressed subjects considered more information, assessed more facts, were more inclined to balance positive and negative points, and made more discrete judgements, whereas people who were elated tended to form sweeping global impressions.[13] So, if the manager wishes to have a discussion with a subordinate involving detailed analysis requiring considerable depth of thought, then a happy mood would be counterproductive. Obviously a deeply depressed subordinate would not be able to perform effectively either, so we are concerned with reducing positive emotions or bringing about low levels of negative emotions rather than engendering high levels of adverse emotion.

Various question-and-statement types we have already mentioned can be used to achieve this. The obvious ones are *criticism, negative feedback* and *threats* or *warnings*, but *reflectives* may also be used. Just as people find it difficult to be rational about something when they are experiencing high levels of negative emotion, they may find it difficult to concentrate on other things when they are experiencing a positive emotion. As noted in the previous section, the immediate effect of reflecting back positive feelings may be to enhance them. In the longer term, however, like negative emotions, expressing them will tend to diminish them somewhat. If someone desperately wishes to give some good news, express satisfaction with their achievements and so on, then it may be better to allow time for the positive emotions to burn themselves out, and encourage them to do so using reflectives, rather than to try to impose on the subordinate an abrupt change of mood. As we have noted before, using

Table 4.4 *Components for handling emotion, to enable the interaction to proceed on a rational basis*

Component	Appropriate use	Inappropriate use
Apologies e.g. 'First of all I must apologise for . . .' 'I'm *very* sorry, I didn't realise . . .'	When used confidently and constructively to eliminate a source of grievance which might inhibit rational discussion.	If too abject, off-hand or patronising.
Reflectives e.g. 'You seem upset about . . .' 'You feel it would be unfair to . . .' (i.e. reflecting back the *emotional* content of what is expressed).	To indicate, without evaluation, a concerned awareness of the subordinate's emotions or frustrations and to provide an opportunity to discharge these by letting the subordinate work through the problem(s).	If used evaluatively, reproachfully or disparagingly. Where manager cannot handle criticism or abuse. In situations of severe time constraint. For checking particular points of information or fact.

reflectives may seem time-consuming, but they are likely to achieve the desired effect much more quickly than trying to 'stop' the emotion by using other means.

Components for handling emotion not previously identified in relation to other purposes are summarised in Table 4.4. These are relatively few and have greatest relevance to the reduction of negative emotions. It is less easy to identify specific verbal components which are concerned with influencing emotions in other ways. We suspect that this is usually achieved using the components described in previous sections in a particular way, rather than by means of a separate set of components. Thus 'blood curdling' threats, 'generous' praise and 'fulsome' praise are obviously intended to produce a greater emotional response than would occur if the same things were said in a more matter of fact way. In the next chapter we will examine the significant role played by such nonverbal cues in the manager–subordinate interactions.

At the end of this chapter there are three sets of exercises. The first two are intended to allow managers to assess their ability to recognise different types of questions and statements and the situations in which their use is most appropriate. The third provides the opportunity to formulate appropriate reflectives, because we consider these to be the most difficult to use of the techniques described in this chapter.

Exercise 4.1
Recognising question-and-statement types

Types

Below are listed question-and-statement types.

Closed   Warning   Comparison   Advice   Hypothetical
Factual statement   Leading   Explanation   Multiple
Feedback   Bridge   Order   Lubricators   Self-disclosure
Open   Criticism   Probing   Evaluative statement
Reflective   Promise   Summary

Question/statement

Please classify each of the following questions/statements as one of the types listed above.

A. How do you think we can best respond to the company's
    latest safety initiative?   _____

B. The number of accidents in your department increased by
    5 per cent during the last quarter, whereas other
    departments showed no increase and in some cases a
    slight decline.   _____

C. You do keep the safety manual in an accessible place, don't you? _____

D. The accident record in your department simply isn't good enough. It's by far the worst in the whole company. _____

E. You feel frustrated because you can't get people to realise the importance of following safety regulations? _____

F. If something isn't done to improve the accident record in your department, I will have great difficulty in justifying an above average merit award in next year's appraisal. _____

G. How do you feel about your accident record? I mean, how many accidents were there in your department last year? Were there many which resulted in people having to take time off work and how long were they typically off for? _____

H. What seems to have emerged from the discussion so far is that the safety training is successful with the younger employees, but the older ones seem to be much more reluctant to adopt the new procedures. _____

I. I need the current accident figures by Monday at the latest if they are to be included in the company Safety Audit and it won't look good for the department if we are missing the data for the last quarter. _____

J. I believe that ensuring safe working practices is one of the manager's most important responsibilities. _____

K. Do you think that safety training is more effectively carried out in the workplace or the training department? _____

L. How many days were lost through accidents in your department last month? _____

M. I remember when one of my subordinates had a serious accident. I knew that I wasn't directly responsible – it wasn't something anyone could have foreseen – but I felt sick about it for a long time afterwards. It changed my attitude to safety. I suppose it's the reason why I always put so much emphasis on safety matters. _____

N. You will have the accident figures for your department on my desk at 9 o'clock on Monday morning without fail. _____

O. What precisely has he done which makes you say that he isn't sufficiently safety conscious? _____

P. The company is going to introduce random safety checks in all departments from the first of next month.   _____

Q. One of the ways you can make your subordinates more safety conscious is simply by turning up at random intervals and checking whether they are following the correct safety procedures.   _____

R. What would you do if you saw one of your subordinates breaking safety regulations?   _____

S. I see . . . yes . . . go on . . . mmm . . .   _____

T. If you will do your best to ensure that current safety procedures are followed for the remainder of the year, I will see what I can do to get the changes you suggest included in the new company Safety Manual.   _____

U. Having agreed what we need to do with respect to accident prevention, now let's move on to discuss the question of quality control.   _____

The answers to this exercise are given in Appendix III.

Exercise 4.2
Appropriate use of question-and-statement types

Which of the questions/statements from Exercise 4.1 would be most appropriate to use for the following purposes? For example, if you think that question C would be most appropriate for the purpose of 'Introducing a topic, encouraging the other person to talk and gathering information on a broad basis', then write C on the right-hand side of the page alongside the first item in the list below, and so on for each item.

Purpose   Question/statement

1. Introducing a topic, encouraging the other person to talk and gathering information on a broad basis.   _____

2. To influence someone's behaviour by giving your reasons for wanting them to behave in a certain way.   _____

3. Providing a smooth link between one topic and another.   _____

4. Getting the other person to explore and reveal his or her own needs, values, etc.   _____

5. Establishing specific facts which require only short answers. _____

6. Letting someone know your own beliefs and attitudes on certain subjects. _____

7. Providing a subordinate with non-evaluative information about the standard of his or her performance. _____

8. Giving a subordinate guidance on ways in which he or she could achieve certain objectives, where compliance is not essential and the subordinate is motivated to achieve the objectives. _____

9. Encouraging someone to continue talking and expand his or her views without interrupting his or her flow of words. _____

10. To dissipate an adverse emotional reaction by indicating non-evaluative concern without expressing your own views on the subject. _____

11. Getting a subordinate's acceptance of your view, usually in the form of compliance rather than commitment. _____

12. Making sure that a subordinate has a clear and unequivocal understanding of the behaviour which is expected of him or her in a situation where conformity is essential and he or she might not otherwise be forthcoming. _____

13. Making sure that a subordinate is aware that adverse consequences will follow unless action is taken to prevent them. _____

14. Getting the other person to think about previously unconsidered areas. _____

15. Motivating a subordinate to achieve an acceptable standard of performance on a task which he or she is reluctant to perform by indicating that it will or is likely to be rewarded. _____

16. Encouraging someone to give more precise and detailed information. _____

17. Reducing levels of depression or anxiety by helping someone to realise that he or she is not alone in having experienced the problem concerned and the emotional reaction to it. _____

18. Ensuring that details are not forgotten, and gaining commitment to an action plan. _____

19. Providing someone with information which he or she may need to make a decision or solve a problem without indicating the course of action he or she should take. _____

20. Letting a subordinate know that his or her behaviour or performance is unacceptable in some respect. _____

The answers to this exercise are given in Appendix III.

Exercise 4.3
Dealing with emotion and frustration

In dealing with expressions of frustration and emotion, there is a tendency for most people to attempt to solve the 'problem' for the emotional or frustrated individual. The intention is commendable but unfortunately it is rarely, if ever, successful. Attempts to solve the problem by using such things as premature advice ('What you need to do is . . .') or inappropriate self-disclosure ('I had similar problems when I first came here, but what I did was . . .') usually fail to do what is probably most required, to let the individual speak frankly about the problem. To do this requires the manager to try to see and understand the problem from the subordinate's own frame of reference. This usually results in the aggrieved person releasing his or her emotion or frustration and will eventually lead to a more rational problem-solving situation. The manager will be seen to be demonstrating an attempt at understanding by attending to, listening and verbally responding in such a way that shows interest and concern in the subordinate's problems.

Below are a number of statements, intended to express emotion or frustration, followed by a number of possible responses. Read the responses and decide which one is trying to indicate interest and concern and which one is a poor response. Try to give reasons for your decision (e.g. shows disrespect, premature advice, irrelevant self-disclosure, or shows concern and is likely to encourage the subordinate to comment further or talk frankly about it).

Example

'Sandra Smith has it in for me. Ever since I started this job she's been at me. I behave just like the other operators, but when something goes wrong she always checks what I was doing first.'

(a) 'Just try and ignore it. Don't go and do anything stupid or you might be in worse trouble.'

(Poor response because it gives premature advice and attempts to stop any further expression of emotion or frustration.)

(b) 'You feel she's being unfair to you and don't like it.'

(Good response because it reflects back the problem and is likely to elicit further comment.)

(c) 'You say she's always at you. Have you done something to upset her?'

(Poor response because it is expressing disbelief in what has been said – it is judgemental.)

(d) 'We all get problems like this at times and it makes life that bit more difficult. If you stay cool, she'll stop eventually. Now have you finished that special assignment?'

(Poor response because it is placating, shows inappropriate sympathy, gives premature advice and attempts to change the subject.)

Now try the following examples for yourself:

1. 'I feel just like a slave around here. I was employed as a shorthand typist and yet I'm expected to make tea and coffee, do the shopping and stay around during the lunchtime and at hometime in case something needs doing at short notice. Last night I didn't get home until nearly 7 o'clock.'
   (a) 'I'm sorry about last night. Did you have something special on?'
   (b) 'I understand how you feel but often it's not anyone's fault, expecially if there's an urgent order to be completed.'
   (c) 'I'm sorry, but the person before you really liked getting involved and I assumed you would too.'
   (d) 'You resent being expected to do things which you don't think are part of your job.'
2. 'I don't know if it's me or not. Over the last two years we've hired a lot of young people. They're all polite to me, but that's about it. I can't seem to find out what makes them "tick". I don't understand them and I find it hard to establish any kind of relationship with them.'
   (a) 'You don't seem to know where the fault lies.'
   (b) 'You're having difficulty handling your subordinates.'
   (c) 'You feel somewhat isolated from them and it's puzzling you.'
   (d) 'What do you think I can do to help?
3. 'If it keeps on like this we'll go under. The stop stewards in my department are giving me hell. If I try to move people around there's an uproar. With the company the way it is and pressure on me to improve productivity, I've just got to have more leeway to run the department more efficiently.'

    (a) 'You're feeling under pressure from both management and shop stewards and its affecting your efforts to organise the work.'
    (b) 'Could you elaborate on that a little more?'
    (c) 'You've got to use more discipline. Take away their privileges if they don't do as you want them to.'
    (d) 'OK, it's hard on you but if we keep our heads we can work something out. Let's see if we can sort it out.'

For the last two examples, construct your own response:

4. 'I really find it hard to work for him. He's so inconsistent. I seem to be getting along fine, then for no apparent reason he blows up. I just don't know where I am with him.'
5. 'Do you know, I've really enjoyed working here for the past three months. The work's really interested me and I get a lot of satisfaction out of doing it.'

The answers to this exercise are given in Appendix IV.

Notes and references

1. J. T. Dillon (1990), *The Practice of Questioning*, Routledge.
2. P. L. Wright (1989), 'Motivation and job satisfaction', in C. Molander (ed.) *Human Resource Management*, Chartwell-Bratt.
3. D. G. Pruitt (1981), *Negotiation Behaviour*, Academic Press.
4. D. Hosking and S. Fineman (1990), 'Organizing processes', *Journal of Management Studies*, **27**, 583–604.
5. S. Fineman (1991), 'Organising and emotion', contribution to the conference, *Towards a New Theory of Organisations*, University of Keele, April.
6. O. Hargie, C. Saunders and D. Dickson (1987), *Social Skills in Interpersonal Communication*, 2nd edn, Routledge.
7. N. Rackham and J. Carlysle (1978), 'The effective negotiator, part 1: the behaviour of successful negotiators', *Journal of European Industrial Training*, **2**, (6), 6–11.
8. See G. H. Bower (1991), 'Mood congruity and social judgements', in J. P. Forgas (ed.), *Emotional and Social Judgements*, Pergamon.
9. *Ibid.*
10. E. B. Foa and M. J. Kozak (1991), 'Emotional processing theory: research and clinical implications for anxiety disorders', in J. D. Safran and L. S. Greenberg (eds), *Emotion, Psychotherapy and Change*, Guilford.
11. M. Kovaks and A. T. Beck (1979), 'Cognitive-affective processes in depression', in C. E. Izard (ed.), *Emotions in Personality and Psychotherapy*, Plenum; P. Gilbert (1992), *Counselling for Depression*, Sage.

12. J. D. Safran and L. S. Greenberg (1991), 'Affective change processes: a synthesis and critical analysis', in Safran and Greenberg, *op. cit.*
13. See N. Schwarz and H. Bless (1991), 'Happy and mindless, but sad and smart? The impact of affective states on analytical reasoning', in Forgas, *op. cit.*

CHAPTER 5

Nonverbal components of manager–subordinate interactions

Introduction

Face-to-face communication is very much a multichannel process. We not only hear the words said, but also register the other person's tone of voice, facial expression, body posture, gestures, proximity and so on. Such nonverbal cues may act to supplement, modify, contradict, or even replace the actual words spoken. The extent to which people rely on nonverbal cues to interpret what is being said depends to some extent on what is being communicated. The actual words spoken are more important cues to meaning when communicating factual information. However, nonverbal cues are more important than verbal as sources of information about emotions, attitudes, and relationships between people, particularly when verbal and nonverbal cues conflict.[1]

To illustrate this point, let's consider some examples:

That's interesting.

Would you go and see Jones in Duplicating and make sure that copies of my report will be ready for this afternoon's meeting.

I'm sorry about that. I must make sure it doesn't happen again.

Each of these apparently straightforward messages can mean entirely different things to the recipient according to the way it is expressed.

For example, the impact of the statement 'That's interesting' is likely to be enhanced if it is said in a lively tone of voice, with an animated expression, whilst leaning forward and looking the person in the eye. On the other hand, the same statement said in a flat tone of voice, with a neutral expression, whilst leaning back and staring out of the window, presents a contradictory message. The words express interest, but the nonverbal cues 'say' the opposite, and as we have already noted, it is the nonverbal cues which are more likely to be believed.

The second and third examples illustrate the way in which nonverbal cues can indicate such things as friendliness and relative status or power in interactions between people. The 'request' to go and see Jones in Duplicating could be said with a pleasant smile, leaning forward, touching the person's arm, as when asking a friend a favour, or in a harsh, domineering tone of voice, with aggressive facial expression and body posture, making it the equivalent of an order, and an unpleasant one at that, or in a pleading tone of voice, with abject facial expression and body posture, turning it into a humble request.

Similarly, the apology in the third example could be said in at least three different ways:

1. In a low tone, with eyes cast down, an unhappy facial expression, hunched shoulders and fidgeting hands.
2. In a clear, firm tone of voice, with direct eye contract, an interested facial expression, squared shoulders, leaning slightly forward, and slightly clenched hands.
3. In a slightly irritable tone of voice, looking over the other person's shoulder, with a disinterested facial expression, relaxed body posture, leaning slightly backward, and with a negligent wave of the hand.

The first is likely to be seen as an abject apology by someone of lower status or power, pleading not to be punished. The second will probably be regarded as a sincere expression of regret and a credible commitment to rectify the situation. The third is more likely to be seen as someone of superior status or power attempting to get rid of a 'trivial' problem by making an insincere expression of regret and a promise which probably would not be kept.

These examples illustrate two of the main problems which may arise in handling nonverbal cues. First, managers may not realise that they are sending contradictory nonverbal messages alongside their intended verbal ones, and thus reducing or even negating their impact. Secondly, they may not realise that by varying their nonverbal cues, they can sometimes change the 'tone' of what they are saying to beneficial effect. For example, they may be able to change an order into a request, which may be more acceptable to the subordinate but no less compelling, or apologise to a subordinate without appearing to demean themselves or running the risk of loss of authority.

A third problem, not illustrated above, is that of failing to observe nonverbal cues from the subordinate, and we will return to this later.

It will be apparent that nonverbal communication can take many different forms. Virtually anything a human being does could, under some circumstances, communicate something to an observer. Potentially, therefore, nonverbal communication could cover all human behaviour except for the spoken and written word.[2] In Table 5.1, we list some of the main nonverbal cues which may communicate something of significance in manager–subordinate interactions. Although the list is by no means exhaustive, it does give some indication of the wide variety of different behaviours which can be included under the heading of nonverbal communication.

What is communicated by such nonverbal cues also varies widely. They can

Table 5.1 *Nonverbal components in manager–subordinate interactions*

Type of nonverbal cue	Examples
Facial	
Facial expression	smiles, raised eyebrows, wrinkled forehead, wide open eyes, tightly closed mouth
Direction of gaze	direct eye contact, downcast eyes
Vocal	
Acoustic	pitch, loudness
Voice qualities	nasal, raspy
Speech tempo and rhythm	drawling, staccato
Pauses and hesitations	periods of silence before or during verbal messages
Vocalisations	'um', 'er', 'ah'
Physical	
Head movement	nodding, shaking
Gestures	movements of the hands and arms, such as clenching the fist, making 'chopping' motions with the hand.
Postures	hand on hips, arms crossed, leaning forward or backward, hunched shoulders
Posture shifts	changing one's position in a chair, crossing and uncrossing one's arms or legs
Continuous movements	swinging one's foot, playing with a pencil
Self-manipulation	scratching one's arm, rubbing one's chin
Distance between people	too close, comfortable, too far
Body orientation	face to face with another person, at an angle
Touch	touching someone's hand, putting an arm round someone's shoulders

express primary emotions and other feelings such as liking, friendliness and warmth. They can indicate people's status or power, how confident they feel and whether they are telling the truth or not. They help to regulate interactions between people, by letting the participants know when someone wishes to speak, hand over the speaker's role to someone else, continue listening, and so on. They can reflect the complexity of the verbal message the person is attempting to communicate and his or her difficulty in expressing it. Finally, in a limited number of cases, nonverbal signals can act as a substitute for explicitly verbal messages. For example, a nod can replace 'yes', a shake of the head can stand for 'no', and a shrug of the shoulders for 'I don't know'.

However, nonverbal cues do vary considerably in the extent to which they provide a *reliable* means of communication. In other words, some forms of nonverbal behaviour represent the same thing relatively consistently, whilst others may represent different things in different situations or when performed by different individuals. For example, certain facial expressions represent particular emotions with a high degree of consistency, even across different cultures.[3] On the other hand, the meaning of body movements is much more variable. Activities such as scratching the back of one's hand or swinging one's foot may be a sign of nervousness in one person whilst another may perform them habitually irrespective of his or her emotional state. According to Dittman, 'With few exceptions, we cannot look at a person's movements and know definitely what they mean in body language.'[4]

Even when ambiguous, nonverbal cues can still serve a useful function. They can act as warning lights, telling us that there may be something which is worth checking out or exploring in more detail. To make good use of nonverbal cues for this purpose, it is necessary to have a good understanding of what nonverbal cues can or, in some cases, usually mean and, of course, to have noticed the cues in question in the first place. Let us now, therefore, examine in more detail some of the main areas in which any understanding of nonverbal communication might help managers to interact more effectively with subordinates and others within organisations.

Areas of nonverbal communication

Substitutes for verbal messages

As noted previously, even in people without hearing or speaking difficulties, there are a few nonverbal signals which can act as a substitute for verbal messages. Examples include a nod for 'yes', a shake of the head for 'no' and shrugging the shoulders for 'I don't know'. They can, of course, also accompany such verbal messages, but they are comprehensible on their own. Even these relatively explicit signs can have different meanings according to the context. For example, nodding one's head whilst someone else is talking can be the equivalent of 'M-hm', 'I see', and so on. Similarly, the head shake performed continuously whilst saying something complimentary (e.g. 'There was really beautiful photography in that movie') can indicate a positive attitude rather than a negative one.[5] Nevertheless these do not constitute serious sources of ambiguity, as the meaning can be deduced from context, just as we can deduce the meaning of similar sounding words, such as 'bough' and 'bow' from their verbal context.

Emotions

A wide variety of nonverbal cues may provide information about the emotions being experienced by the person exhibiting them. In general, facial expressions provide more precise information concerning emotions than other nonverbal cues, but this is not invariably the case. For example, it has been found that anxiety can be judged more accurately on the basis of vocal cues alone than by using facial expressions, posture and gesture combined.[6] Much less is known about the relationship between physical cues, such as posture and gesture, and specific emotions, and it has been suggested that the face carries information about what emotion is being experienced whereas the body carries information about its intensity.[7] None the less there is evidence that certain body postures are associated with interest and boredom, as we shall see.

It must be recognised, however, that people vary considerably in the extent to which they display their emotions and the circumstances in which they display them. Some people may show their emotions readily whilst others may block the expression of particular emotions (e.g. anger), or, in extreme cases, may be poker-faced, never revealing in their faces how they feel. Also, some people may block the expression of an emotion in one situation – for example, never allowing themselves to show anger in front of customers or superiors – but allow themselves to show the same emotion in other situations. Moreover it is, of course, possible to fake emotions we do not feel (e.g. 'Thank you for a *lovely* dinner party, Mrs Jones, it was *most* enjoyable!') and people vary in the extent to which they can do this convincingly. Therefore, whilst nonverbal cues *may* provide accurate information concerning emotions, two reservations need to be noted: the fact that someone is not displaying emotion is not necessarily a sign that he or she is not experiencing it; and the fact that someone is displaying emotion need not necessarily indicate that he or she is *genuinely* experiencing it.

Bearing these reservations in mind, then, let us now review the nonverbal cues associated with the commonly identified emotions.

Interest

Interest may be shown in the face by several different cues, which may occur separately or in combination. These include raised eyebrows, brows drawn together but neither raised nor sharply lowered, eyes focused on or following the person or object of interest, softly opened mouth and pursed lips (see Figure 5.1).[8] Body postures associated with interest are leaning forward and drawing the legs back whilst sitting[9] (see Figure 5.2).

Boredom

The facial cues associated with boredom seem not to have been studied.[10] However, the vocal cues associated with boredom include speaking more slowly and softly in a voice which is lower pitched and shows a relatively narrow pitch range.[11] Body postures associated with boredom include lowering the head, tilting it to one side, turning the head away, supporting the head on one hand, leaning back and stretching out the legs (see Figure 5.3).[12]

Figure 5.1 *The facial expression of interest*

Source: P. E. Bull (1983), *Body Movement and Interpersonal Communications*, reprinted by permission of John Wiley & Sons, Ltd.

Figure 5.2 *Posture of interest*

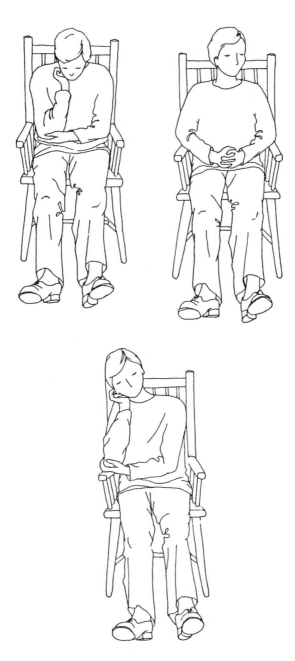

Source: P. E. Bull (1983), *Body Movement and Interpersonal Communications*, reprinted by permission of John Wiley & Sons, Ltd.

Figure 5.3 *Postures of boredom*

Figure 5.4 *The facial expression of surprise*

Surprise

When surprised, the eyebrows are raised so that they are curved and high. This creates wrinkles across the forehead and gives the eyes a large, rounded appearance. The whites of the eyes are seen above the iris and often below as well. The jaw drops and the mouth is opened in an oval shape (see Figure 5.4).

Happiness

Happiness or joy is expressed through smiling and laughter. The smile is easy to recognise. The corners of the mouth pull back and slightly upward, the cheeks rise, the eyes narrow slightly and wrinkles radiate from the corners of the eyes and run from the nose to just beyond the corners of the mouth. In a more intense smile, the lips may be parted and the teeth exposed (see Figure 5.5).

However, there are also smiles which do not indicate happiness. These include the phoney smile, where nothing much is felt but an attempt is made to appear as if positive feelings are felt and the masking smile, where an attempt is made to conceal a strong negative emotion by appearing to feel positive.[13] Sometimes people may succeed in producing a false smile which is indistinguishable from a felt smile, but the false smile often differs from the genuine smile in a number of ways. For instance, there is usually no sign of raised cheeks or wrinkles at the corners of the eyes, although these may occur if the false smile is an extremely intense one. False smiles are also likely to be asymmetrical, to

Figure 5.5 *The facial expression of happiness*

appear earlier or later than would be called for by the situation, to be more abrupt in both onset and offset than genuine smiles and to last longer. In the case of masking smiles, there may also be signs of the negative emotion which the smile is intended to hide, making them less likely to be convincing than the phoney smile.

The reverse of the false smile is the dampened smile, where the person actually does feel positive emotions but attempts to appear as if those feelings are less intense than they actually are. For example, we may wish to avoid showing amusement overtly in order to avoid hurting a friend's feelings or annoying a superior. In the case of the dampened smile, the lips are pressed, the lower lip pushed up and the corners of the lips tightened. The same cues may also occur in conjunction with the masking smile when the person is attempting to conceal very strong negative emotions.[14]

With respect to vocal cues, happiness is associated with speaking louder and more quickly in a voice which is both higher pitched and shows greater variability in pitch than normal.

Sadness
In sadness, the inner corners of the eyebrows are drawn upward and together, while the eyes are slightly narrowed and the corners of the mouth are pulled downward. The lips may tremble and sometimes the chin is pushed forward and quivers (see Figure 5.6). In the case of intense sadness (distress), tears and

Figure 5.6 *The facial expression of sadness*

audible crying may also occur. Decreased eye contact also occurs in sorrow, despair or sadness.[15]

With respect to vocal cues, sadness is associated with speaking more slowly and softly, in a low voice that shows relatively small variability in pitch. Longer silent pauses also occur.[16] According to Scherer the same vocal cues are present in grief as in sadness.[17] Similarly, Izard states that the predominant expression on the face of someone suffering grief is that of sadness.[18] However, he suggests that other emotions may also be present including feelings of guilt, anger and fear.

Anger
In the full expression of anger, the eyebrows are lowered and drawn together, pulling the skin of the forehead tight, creating vertical furrows or ridges between the inner corners of the eyebrows and causing a bulge on or slightly above the nasal root. The eyes appear narrow and hard and stare at the source of annoyance or anger. The mouth takes on a squarish or rectangular shape. The upper and lower lips become thin parallel lines and may protrude slightly, whilst the corners of the mouth give up their normally soft curve for a hard angular appearance (see Figure 5.7). Taken together, these signs represent the full, innate expression of anger seen in young infants. In adults, however, it tends to be seen only in intense, spontaneous anger. As children grow up, they learn to suppress many of the signs of anger. The frown becomes less intense, staring is

Figure 5.7 *The facial expression of anger*

avoided altogether or the gaze shifted from time to time, and the square mouth and bared teeth are replaced by a tightly closed mouth, clenched jaws and compressed lips. This means that one may have to look for more subtle cues in order to identify anger in adults. Unfortunately, many of these more subtle cues can also indicate emotions other than anger. For example, frowning, staring and clenching the jaws a little may be signs of interest or concentration. Izard, therefore, suggests that the more the expression of anger or any other emotion is modified, the more you have to know about the individual and the situation to make the correct guess as to what emotion is felt.[19]

According to Scherer, anger is associated with speaking more quickly in a voice which is louder, higher pitched and shows a wider pitch range and greater pitch variability than normal.[20] Similarly, Siegman found that angry male interviewees spoke more loudly, more quickly and interrupted their interviewers more often.[21] However, these characteristics only occurred in the case of overt anger. In the case of covert or hidden anger, the speech style was generally in the opposite direction from that associated with overt anger, with interviewees speaking more slowly, less loudly and with significantly less interruptions.

Disgust
In the full expression of disgust, the eyebrows are drawn down and together, the nose wrinkled, the cheeks are raised, the upper lip pulled up, the lower lip pulled downward and the tongue pushed forward (see Figure 5.8). In adults, however, the full expression of disgust may be masked or we may, consciously

Figure 5.8 *The facial expression of disgust*

or unconsciously, use only one component of the expression, such as raising the upper lip or wrinkling the nose, to express disgust.

Contempt
Several nonverbal cues may signal contempt, including standing tall, lifting or cocking the head upward at an angle, a lifted brow, a lifted corner of the upper lip and tightened mouth corners (see Figure 5.9). A sneer may also indicate contempt and Izard believes that the tightened corner of the mouth may be a learned modification of this expression.[22]

With respect to vocal cues, contempt is associated with speaking louder and more slowly in a voice which is lower in pitch but also has a relatively wide pitch range.

Fear
In the full expression of fear, the eyebrows are lifted and slightly pulled together creating deeper wrinkles in the middle of the forehead than at the sides, the eyes are opened wide and sometimes the upper lids are raised showing the whites of the eyes between the eyelid and the pupil, the corners of the mouth are retracted straight back and the mouth is usually slightly open (see Figure 5.10). As with anger, however, people learn to mask or disguise their feelings of fear, and therefore its full expression is rarely seen, appearing only under the most intense stimulation or in unguarded moments.[23] Vocal cues of fear include speaking louder and more quickly, in a voice which is higher pitched and has a wider pitch range and greater pitch variability.

Figure 5.9 *The facial expression of contempt*

Figure 5.10 *The facial expression of fear*

Anxiety

Izard regards anxiety as a blend of other emotions, rather than a primary emotion in its own right.[24] Thus the predominant emotion in anxiety is fear, but sadness, shame, guilt and anger may also be present. Izard suggests that individuals may differ in the relative importance of the various emotions in anxiety. Thus to understand someone's anxiety and help him or her overcome it requires an understanding of the various different emotions involved in that particular person's case.

The vocal cues of anxiety include superfluous repetition of one or more words, incomplete sentences, reconstructing sentences, omission of a whole word or part of a word, slips of the tongue, stuttering and incoherent sounds.[25] Contradictory findings have been found with respect to the pace of speech. In some studies, anxiety has been found to be associated with long silent pauses and a general slowing down of speech, whilst in others the reverse pattern has been found. It has been hypothesised that mild and moderate levels of anxiety tend to accelerate speech, but very high levels of anxiety are associated with slower speech and more pauses. Siegman suggests that some highly anxious people may in fact deliberately slow down their speech in order to cover up their anxiety and use longer silent pauses to plan what they are going to say, thus reducing the speech disturbances noted earlier.[26]

Shame

In shame, the gaze is averted and the face turned away, usually by turning the head to the side and downward. Blushing commonly occurs and there may also be a tendency to curl up and make the body appear smaller (see Figure 5.11). In adults, these expressions are often modified and may reveal themselves simply by a downward glance or the person may hold his or her head high, in effect substituting the look of contempt for the look of shame.[27]

Liking, friendliness and warmth

Apart from the primary emotions so far discussed, a variety of nonverbal cues may also indicate liking, friendliness or warmth towards another person. These include nodding, smiling, greater eye contact, leaning forward, standing or sitting closer to the other person, standing or sitting facing the other person, a relaxed body posture and an open body position, with arms and legs uncrossed.[28] The evidence with respect to touching is mixed. Touching is often a sign of friendship and can increase liking.[29] However, it can also be seen as a prerogative of the socially powerful.[30] For example, a boss is more likely to put his or her arm round a subordinate's shoulder than vice versa. Thus, bosses who touch subordinates in an attempt to demonstrate closeness, as Blanchard and Johnson recommend, may not have the effect they intend.[31] Their behaviour may be regarded as a show of dominance or an invasion of privacy by a manager taking advantage of his or her position.

Figure 5.11 *The facial expression of shame*

It is, of course, possible to 'overdo' any of the cues of liking, friendliness and warmth (e.g. by standing too close or staring fixedly), in which case they may become unpleasant or embarrassing. If it is impossible to retreat physically from the situation, the other person is then likely to take measures to reduce the level of intimacy, such as decreased eye contact, turning away, leaning back, looking down, shading the eyes, narrowing the eyes and so on. Self-manipulative behaviours, such as scratching the head, are also likely to occur.[32]

It is also worth noting that the effect of cues associated with liking can vary with the circumstances. For example, liking affects how people react to the nonverbal behaviour of others. Whilst it may be pleasant to be close to someone we like, we tend to be more comfortable at a greater distance from someone we dislike.

Status, power and dominance

There are numerous nonverbal signals which indicate which of two or more people has the higher status, has more power or is more dominant. An important one is the amount of time people spend looking at each other during conversation. In conversations between equals, the proportion of time which people spend looking at their partners is greater when listening than when they themselves are speaking. However, dominant people spend less time looking at the other person whilst he or she is speaking than do deferent people. This may be because high-status or controlling individuals do not feel as strongly the need to comply with the social norm of appearing to pay attention to other people whilst they are talking.[33]

Patterns of gaze during conversations also influence other people's assessment of the relative power of the people involved. People who look more whilst speaking and less whilst listening are seen as being more powerful, whereas those who look less whilst speaking and more whilst listening are seen as less powerful.[34]

With regard to vocal cues, dominant people tend to talk more loudly and to interrupt more.[35] Lower-status people, on the other hand, respond more quickly when talking to higher-status people, but there are more pauses whilst they are talking,[36] perhaps because they are searching for the right thing to say.

As already noted, touching may be an indication of dominance. In one study, the toucher was perceived not only as being higher in status and dominance, but also as more aggressive, more confident and more independent. The recipient, on the other hand, was seen as lower in status and dominance and less aggressive, confident and independent following the touch.[37]

Finally, seating arrangements may indicate something about the relationship between the people involved in an interaction. People were asked how they would sit at a table with another person in different social situations. In competitive situations, the vast majority of people chose to sit opposite each other, whereas in co-operative situations, more people chose to sit at the same side of the table. When the situation was described as simply involving a conversation, the most popular seating arrangement was diagonally across the table.[38] It seems likely, therefore, that if people are of different power or status, sitting on the opposite side of a desk will enhance differences between them, whereas sitting across the corner, on the same side, or even away from the desk will minimise the effects of power or status differences on the interaction.

Confidence

Nonverbal cues of confidence include high levels of eye contact, greater use of gestures, lower levels of self-manipulation (e.g., scratching), and faster and louder speech with fewer pauses. If pitch and volume are too divergent from normal, however, the speaker may be evaluated more negatively. These cues may also enhance the speaker's credibility and thus increase his or her ability to persuade other people.[39]

Deception

We have already noted on several occasions that nonverbal cues may sometimes give a more accurate indication of people's feelings than what they are actually saying. We have also noted that people sometimes attempt to hide their feelings, either by not exhibiting the relevant nonverbal cues or by exhibiting the nonverbal cues of emotions they are not actually experiencing. Detecting deception by means of observing nonverbal cues is thus in some senses a competition, with one party attempting to appear convincing and the other attempting to identify whether the nonverbal cues support or in some way contradict the verbal message. This conflict of interests can produce unexpected and even contradictory effects. For example, people believe that lack of eye contact in others makes them less credible, but when asked to lie or conceal information, people will *increase* eye contact,[40] thus producing the opposite effect.

In general, the face is a relatively poor source of information about deception, perhaps because people realise that others pay particular attention to it and therefore make a greater effort to control their facial expressions when lying. Pupil dilation and blinking, which are more difficult to control than other facial cues, are associated with deception. There are also fewer changes in facial expression, perhaps due to the attempt to monitor and control one's expressions when being deceptive. However, levels of smiling and eye contact are not significantly different from normal.[41] Several studies have shown that people are less able to detect deception from seeing the face alone than from seeing the body alone. One study also showed that observers actually rated deceptive responses *more* positively when they saw the face alone, but honest responses more positively when judging from the body alone. Specific bodily cues which have been found to be associated with deception include more self-manipulation (e.g. scratching), decreased use of illustrative hand movements and either more or fewer movements of the legs and feet than usual.[42]

Tone of voice has also been found to be a more trustworthy indicator of deception than facial expression. Vocal cues associated with deception include higher pitch, increased speech errors, speech hesitation, negative statements, irrelevant information and over-generalised statements (those including such terms as 'every', 'all', 'none', 'nobody', and so on), shorter responses and more indirect speech.[43]

Although we have presented the general picture with respect to the cues to deception, there are numerous variations. Deception can produce different effects depending on the circumstances and on who is doing the deceiving. Some examples are as follows:

Subjects who were high and low in Machiavellianism were induced to cheat in an experimental study and then interrogated afterwards. Part of the way through the interrogation, they were accused of cheating. Low Machiavellian subjects decreased eye contact during the first part of the interrogation and decreased their eye contact still further when accused of cheating. High Machiavellian subjects decreased their eye contact less than the low Machiavellian subjects during the first part of the interrogation and actually increased their level of eye contact when accused of cheating.[44]

In another experiment where subjects were induced to cheat and interviewed afterwards, low-anxious subjects exhibited more facial pleasantness in the deceptive than the honest situation, whereas high-anxious subjects showed more facial pleasantness in the honest situation.[45]

Subjects given little opportunity to plan when being deceptive take longer to reply and speak more slowly, whereas those given the opportunity to rehearse their answers reply and speak more quickly.[46]

In an experiment on deception skills, extroverts were more successful than introverts at controlling their speech patterns (reaction times, silent pauses and speech rate) so that they were nearly the same when lying and telling the truth. As might be expected, subjects with better acting skills also tended to have speech patterns which were similar when lying and telling the truth.[47]

What these studies show is that, whilst some nonverbal cues may typically be associated with lying, some people may be able to appear honest whilst lying, whilst others may 'overshoot' and go to the opposite extreme. Thus, in the case of certain nonverbal cues, deviations from the norm in either direction may be suspicious. Appearing too planned, rehearsed or lacking in spontaneity, or trying to be too persuasive, presenting a too slick or exaggerated performance may also be signs of deception.[48]

As in other areas, the nonverbal cues associated with deception are far from infallible indicators. Again, therefore, the most useful action when suspicions are aroused is to use the appropriate types of questions and statements to elicit the required information. Particularly useful here are precise, well-directed probing questions. One of the reasons why certain nonverbal cues occur in association with deception is thought to be the fact that lying usually requires more concentration than telling the truth. The liar has to make up responses and make sure that they are plausible and consistent. Precise probing questions, such as 'What made you decide not to consult the Personnel Manager?' will make the other person have to think harder and a series of good probing questions may take him or her beyond areas which have been prepared, thus making it more difficult to lie convincingly. In an experimental study by Cody, Marston and Foster, for example, it was found that liars found it particularly difficult to improvise specific details, such as times and places, when giving spontaneous answers to unexpected questions.[49]

Such questioning need not be aggressive or brutal. The power of a good probing question is often in the content of the question, rather than the way in which it is said, providing that the questioner insists, however gently, on it being answered. Contrary to the way interrogators are portrayed in films and on television, expert interrogators among both the police and private detectives say that a patient, calm, quietly persistent, non-judgemental approach is more likely to arrive at the truth in the long run.[50] In the working environment, such an approach has another advantage. The manager may have to continue working with the other person after the interview is over, whereas the police interrogator or private detective may never see him or her again.

Regulation of verbal communication

An important class of nonverbal cues, known as 'regulators', serves the function of regulating and integrating the exchange of verbal information in an interaction. These regulators, according to Ekman and Friesen, 'tell the speaker to continue, repeat, elaborate, hurry up, become more interesting, less salacious, give the other a chance to talk, etc. They can tell the listener to pay special attention, to wait just a minute more to talk, etc.'[51] Rosenfeld gives examples of nonverbal cues which might fulfil each of the above functions – silent attention or periodic nods, a cocking of the head whilst cupping the ear, a puzzled expression, rapid head nods, yawning, opening the mouth, raising a hand, tapping the listener with a finger and raising the hand to signal wait.[52] As virtually any category of nonverbal behaviour can act as a regulator in some circumstances, however, this list could be extended almost indefinitely.

None the less it is possible to identify some of the primary nonverbal cues which help to produce a smooth and orderly exchange of information between people in conversations or discussions.[53] Such cues commonly occur at the junctures which mark the end of a segment of speech. At this point, the speaker may invite one of two types of response from the listener. The speaker may seek brief confirmation that the listener is attending, understands or agrees with what the speaker is saying. Of course, the speaker could obtain this information by asking explicit questions, such as 'Does this make sense from your point of view?' and 'You do agree, don't you?', but to do so continually would break up the flow of what the speaker is saying and there is also the danger that the other person will respond at length, which the speaker might not want at that point. Under these circumstances, feedback may be solicited using nonverbal cues, such as pausing and looking towards the listener when completing a segment of speech. Positive feedback, such as nods, smiles, saying 'mm-hmm', 'uh-huh', 'I see' or 'that's true' and so on, serve to reassure the speaker that he or she is communicating successfully and can safely continue with what he or she is saying. On the other hand, lack of response from the listener or negative feedback, such as shaking the head, frowns or puzzled looks, are likely to be unsettling to the speaker, who may either stop speaking or repeat, elaborate or modify his or her comments to make them more comprehensible or acceptable.

The other type of response which the speaker may invite from the listener is a longer contribution in which the listener takes over the speaking role. There are several nonverbal cues which indicate that the speaker wishes, or at least is willing, to relinquish the speaking role to the other person in the discussion. These include pausing after a segment of speech, rising or falling pitch at the end of a segment of speech, grammatical completion of a segment of speech, drawl on the final or stressed syllable of a segment of speech, termination of a hand gesture or relaxation of a tense hand position, and certain stereotyped expressions, such as 'and so on' or 'you know', especially if accompanied by a drop in pitch or loudness.

These cues, in effect, provide the listener with an opportunity to take over the speaking role. However, it is not obligatory for the listener to do so. He or she may simply give the brief signals of attention, understanding or agreement noted earlier or remain silent. Conversely, listeners may attempt to claim the speaking role even though the speaker has not indicated that he or she wishes to relinquish it. The two main nonverbal cues that the listener wishes to take over the speaking role are turning away from the speaker and beginning a hand gesture after having both hands at rest. If such cues are acknowledged by the speaker, then a smooth exchange of speaking roles can take place. Conversely, cues that the speaker does not wish to relinquish the speaking role include looking or turning away from the other person at the end of a segment of speech, reducing silent pauses, filling pauses with 'ahs' and 'ums',[54] and a hand gesture that is maintained or not returned to rest during a pause. The latter has been found to be particularly effective in preventing the listener from taking over the speaking role, even after he or she has signalled a wish to do so.

The nonverbal cues we have discussed do not, of course, invariably produce an orderly flow of information in conversations. People may not notice each others' nonverbal cues or interpret them incorrectly. As such cues are often low level and ambiguous, they are likely to be subject to the kinds of perceptual distortion discussed in Chapter 3. Alternatively, the speaker and listener may disagree about when they should change roles, and thus deliberately ignore clear signals from the other person. According to the type of cue being misunderstood or disregarded, this will lead to unwanted and embarrassing silences or to interruptions or simultaneous speech.

Difficulty of expressing verbal messages

A number of nonverbal cues provide indications that the speaker is having difficulty in expressing what he or she wishes to say. Speech becomes more hesitant, with longer pauses before speaking, longer and more frequent silent pauses during speech, greater use of 'ahs' and 'ums', and other types of speech disturbance.[55] Eye contact also tends to decrease, the more difficulty the person has in expressing verbal messages. The tendency to look at the other person in a conversation less whilst talking than whilst listening is thought to be an example of this phenomenon. As Fehr and Exline point out, 'a speaker must not only labor to produce coherent speech, but also, to the extent that he or she monitors a listener, process ongoing feedback provided by the listener's displays. At times this feedback may overload or distract the speaker, necessitating gaze aversion (feedback inhibition) in order to maintain a fluent stream of conversation.'[56]

Variations in nonverbal behaviour

In our account of nonverbal behaviour and communication, we have only been able to give a very broad outline of what has been typically found, largely based on studies of majority group populations in Britain and North America. In some cases, such as facial cues of certain primary emotions, the meaning of nonverbal cues appears to be universal. In other cases, however, patterns of nonverbal behaviour may differ according to the individual's gender, age, race, social class, personality, nationality and cultural background. Some examples are as follows:

> Extroverts not only tend to sit closer to others than introverts, but also tend to choose positions allowing greater eye contact.[57]

> Arabs and Mediterranean people and in some cases Latin Americans prefer closer speaking distances than British, North European and North American people.[58]

> Women tend to smile and gaze at others more than men and to approach others more closely. Women are also better at decoding nonverbal cues than men.[59]

> In the USA, it has been found that blacks gaze at the other persons in conversations less than whites do. It has also been suggested that this tendency is most marked when interacting with a superior or authority figure, where blacks gaze less as a sign of respect. Black children, for example, are socialized to lower their eyes when an older person or teacher is talking to them. In contrast, white children are told to 'Look me in the eye when I'm talking to you!' and several studies have shown that white eye gaze tends to increase in the presence of higher status individuals.[60]

It is impossible to provide a comprehensive account of all the ways in which nonverbal behaviour differs between individuals and groups in the space of a single chapter. However, detailed reviews can be found in Heslin and Patterson,[61] Hall,[62] Halberstadt,[63] and in individual chapters in Siegman and Feldstein.[64]

Implications for manager–subordinate interaction

The implications of nonverbal communication for manager–subordinate interactions can be examined under two main headings. First, there are the nonverbal cues which the manager consciously or unconsciously sends to subordinates and the way subordinates are likely to respond to them. Secondly, there is the extent to which the manager notices and correctly interprets the nonverbal cues exhibited by subordinates.

Nonverbal cues exhibited by the manager

From the point of view of the manager's own behaviour, the main implications are as follows:

1.   It is important to display appropriate nonverbal cues, whilst both speaking and listening. Inconsistency between verbal and nonverbal messages whilst speaking is likely to be interpreted as insincerity or deception, and it is the nonverbal message which is more likely to be believed. Conversely, lack of nonverbal responses whilst listening may deprive the other person of feedback concerning the manager's feelings about what is being said. In some cases, where the manager wishes to reserve judgement, this could be an advantage. In others, however, lack of feedback can be disconcerting or demoralising to the other person. For example, if a manager reacts impassively when told what the subordinate considers to be important, exciting or encouraging news, the subordinate may feel that the manager is not interested and dry up or feel resentment that his or her concerns or achievements are not being given the attention they deserve. Of course, it may well be that the manager actually experiences the appropriate emotions or attitudes, such as enthusiasm, warmth, attention and so on, but is simply not *displaying* them. However, if they cannot be observed, the other person may assume that they are not there. As Hall puts it 'Being a nice person' is not a skill, but success at showing others you are a nice person and doing so convincingly does reflect a skill.[65] The same might be said for showing that one is a determined, ruthless, aggressive person who will stand no nonsense, and doing so convincingly.

2.   The facial expressions which express primary emotions appear to be innate in most cases. Thus it is not a question of knowing *how* to express these emotions by means of facial cues, but is simply a matter of displaying them appropriately.

3.   An appearance of friendliness, warmth and attention can be enhanced by a variety of cues, such as smiling, greater eye contact, standing or sitting closer, and so on, or decreased by, for example, smiling less, giving less eye contact, standing or sitting further away. Because of individual differences, it is impossible to give generally applicable ideal frequencies or distances with respect to such cues. 'Overdoing' signs of friendliness, warmth and attention to the extent that they become uncomfortable, however, is likely to produce characteristic 'retreat' behaviours, such as avoiding eye contact, leaning back, and so forth. Providing managers are aware of such responses, therefore they can modify their own behaviour accordingly, so that an acceptable balance can be achieved.

4.   When interacting with someone from a different culture, however, it may be very important to know whether there are any significant differences in patterns of nonverbal behaviour. As Halberstadt observes 'In nonverbal

communication, differences between ourselves and others are not often consciously noted, but are incorporated into our assessments of those others and into our evaluations of our interactions with them. In these situations a form of self-serving bias tends to surface; we tend to think that if all has not gone well, then there must be something wrong with the other person. After all, we were on our best behaviour. Although we all know that "people are different", we rarely incorporate that concept into our implicit understanding of nonverbal communication."[66] Lack of understanding of differences in patterns of nonverbal behaviour may have adverse effects in two ways. First, we may draw incorrect conclusions about other people's behaviour. For example, we may mistakenly regard someone who looks at us more than we are used to as being aggressive and one who looks less as being 'shifty', when these behaviours simply reflect different cultural norms. Secondly, our own nonverbal cues may be misinterpreted or inadvertently give offence. Furthermore, we may not realise that this has happened and need to take steps to rectify the situation, or if the offence is very great, there may be little we can do to rectify the situation. For example, an American was seeking to develop a business relationship with a prominent Javanese at a cocktail party in Java and all seemed to be going well. However, it took nearly six months to arrange another meeting. He finally learned that he had unwittingly humiliated the Javanese at the cocktail party by momentarily placing his arm on the shoulder of the Javanese in the presence of other people, an almost unpardonable breach of traditional Javanese etiquette. A graceful apology mended this breach to some extent, but a truly cordial business relationship never did develop.[67]

5.   The outward signs of differences in status and power can be manipulated in a number of ways. Managers can indicate that they wish to minimise the effect of status and power differences in an interaction by talking more softly, not interrupting, looking more at subordinates whilst the subordinates are talking, glancing away more whilst they themselves are talking, and arranging seating positions so that chairs are on the same side of the table or diagonally across the corner of the table. Such nonverbal cues would be appropriate in situations where the manager wishes to show concern, gather information in a considerate way or solve problems participatively. Conversely, the manager may wish to emphasise differences in rank in some situations, such as a disciplinary interview. In this case, speaking louder, interrupting when the subordinate strays from the point at issue, increased eye contact whilst the manager is talking, decreased eye contact whilst the subordinate is talking and a seating arrangement with chairs on opposite sides of the table would be more appropriate.

6.   Finally, there exist a variety of cues which managers can use to indicate whether they wish subordinates to speak or to listen to what the manager has to say. In many respects, it is the former which require more attention. In our experience, most managers seem to have little difficulty in indicating that they

wish to continue speaking or to take over the speaking role. In any case, even if their nonverbal signals are unclear or the subordinate chooses to ignore them, the manager can always fall back on an explicit verbal message such as, 'If I may interject' or 'No, you can have your turn later; for the moment I am going to have my say.'

On the other hand, the manager who does not display the nonverbal cues of attention and interest when attempting to gather information may find that the subordinate gives shorter and shorter answers and perhaps dries up altogether. Worse still, the manager may not realise what effect his or her nonverbal cues are having, and attribute the lack of the response to the other person being taciturn, unwilling to talk, and so on. This situation can be rectified by asking the appropriate questions, such as open, probing or comparison questions, and following them with nonverbal cues such as nodding, smiling, leaning forward, eye contact and so on. Also important is the ability to tolerate silence. A pause is sometimes a sign that the other person wishes to relinquish the speaking role. On the other hand, pauses may be a sign that the person is having difficulty in phrasing what he or she wishes to say and such pauses occur more frequently when people of lower status are speaking to people of higher status. It seems likely, therefore, that these two factors will provide the manager with greater opportunities to take over the speaking role, which may at times lead to useful information being lost.

Care also needs to be taken in the use of interruptions. In some cases, an interruption may be appropriate. A subordinate may be providing irrelevant information at great length or very general information without significant details, leading the discussion further and further away from the key issues. In these circumstances, a polite interruption, followed by a relevant probing question to elicit the information required, can be very useful. On the other hand, there is always the danger that the manager will interrupt just as the subordinate is about to say something significant, thus losing important information and perhaps also annoying the subordinate at the same time. In most cases, therefore, it would seem better to err in the direction of patience when deciding whether to interrupt or not.

Perhaps more common than the outright interruption is overlapping speech, where the manager begins to speak just as the subordinate is apparently coming to the end of what he or she is saying. An overlap of a few words may seem trivial, but if done consistently, this can have several adverse effects. It can irritate the other person. Because it is difficult to talk and listen effectively at the same time, it may prevent the manager from picking up relevant information. Finally, it deprives the manager of thinking time. As a result of overlapping speech, the interaction often speeds up, with the manager's contributions being made more quickly and therefore less thoughtfully. Conversely, waiting until pauses occur between speech not only allows subordinates to finish what they are saying, but also gives managers the time needed to develop more effective questions and statements.

Interpretation of nonverbal cues exhibited by the subordinate

It is much less easy to give managers precise guidance on the interpretation of subordinates' nonverbal cues. As we have pointed out several times, nonverbal cues are inherently ambiguous. Some, like the facial expressions of primary emotion may be universal, but as we have seen, even these can be masked, disguised or faked. Others vary according to age, personality, gender, social class, nationality, cultural background and so on. Yet others may be purely individual mannerisms and mean anything at all depending on the circumstances.

Unless they represent very salient, spontaneous reactions, therefore, it may be difficult to ascribe precise meanings to nonverbal cues with any degree of certainty. Often they merely indicate that something *might* be happening, rather than that something specific and identifiable *is* happening. So, in many cases it may be unwise to draw firm conclusions on the basis of nonverbal cues alone. As we suggested with respect to the performance improvement checklist in Chapter 2, it might be better to treat this information as the basis for hunches or hypotheses which need to be checked out by the skilful use of questions and statements. For example, taking steps to deflect someone's anger will probably only be effective if they actually are angry. In the case of emotions, using reflectives expressed with a degree of tentativeness, such as 'I get the feeling that something I have said may have upset you', may encourage people to talk about their feelings and reveal what emotions, or combination of emotions, they are experiencing. Given the ambiguity of nonverbal cues, the answer might be 'Oh no, it's just that I have suddenly got cramp in my foot.' If so, nothing is lost. On the other hand, such a question might bring out into the open, and defuse, a feeling of resentment which might otherwise have had an adverse effect on the remainder of the interaction.

Similar considerations apply with respect to the nonverbal cues which indicate whether the subordinate wishes to take over, keep or relinquish the speaking role. Ignoring such cues can lead to continual interruptions, embarrassing silences, loss of information and frustration or resentment on the part of subordinates who feel that they have not been given a fair opportunity to state their case. Where the subordinate wishes to take over the speaking role, this can be encouraged, where appropriate, using the nonverbal cues described earlier. Where such cues occur at a low level, however, they can be checked out using an explicit question, such as 'Is there something you wanted to say here?' or 'Was there something you wanted to add?' Again, the answer may be 'No', but equally the question may elicit useful information from a subordinate who was unsure whether to come in or to comment further at that point.

To respond effectively to nonverbal cues, however, it is necessary to notice them in the first place. Thus the question of attention is vitally important and a number of factors significantly reduce the likelihood that nonverbal cues will be observed let alone correctly interpreted. First, they are often very brief. Izard states that most adult facial expressions last only from approximately half a second to four seconds.[68] Secondly, because people often mask their feelings, nonverbal cues often occur at a very low level, such as slight inflections in the tone of voice or small changes in facial expression. Thirdly, managers may have little attention to spare for the observation of nonverbal cues because they are simultaneously planning their own contribution to the discussion. Dittman notes with respect to body movements, for example, that 'By far the greater majority of movements . . . serve more as cues from which we make inferences. If all the cues add up right, our guesses from these messages can be very good ones, but usually, we don't have time for much inferring if we are to keep up with the conversation and, because of the way our perceptual apparatus works, our attention in conversations is drawn to decoding the speech.'[69] Furthermore, the more difficult the manager finds it to express what he or she wishes to say, the more likely they are to turn away from the other person in order to concentrate,[70] thus further reducing nonverbal feedback at the time it is most needed.

Lastly, as noted in Chapter 3, low level cues are particularly susceptible to being distorted in the direction of the perceiver's needs and expectations. Thus the manager may see and hear what he or she want or expects to see and hear, rather than what is actually happening. An example of this occurred in one of the author's training sessions. The discussion between manager and 'subordinate' in a role-played interview went as follows:

MANAGER: You would like to go on a human relations course, wouldn't you?
(*a leading question, said with enthusiasm*)

SUBORDINATE: Well, er yes . . . if you say so. (*said hesitantly, in a low voice, with a slight shrug of the shoulders*)

MANAGER: Good. I'm glad you agree. I'll fix that up. Now, another thing I wanted to talk to you about is . . .

When asked afterwards whether he thought the subordinate was enthusiastic about the human relations course, the manager said that he thought he was. He was then asked to listen to a tape recording of the above passage and asked whether he still thought the subordinate was enthusiastic. The manager said 'No, he isn't, is he? It's obvious when you listen to it isn't it? I can't understand how I missed it at the time.' Part of the answer was undoubtedly lack of attention. The manager was busily thinking about the next topic he wished to raise and was only half listening to the subordinate. In addition, however, the manager expected the subordinate to agree, and also wanted him to agree, because that would solve one of the manager's problems. The scene was thus ideally set, by the manager himself, to miss important nonverbal cues that were more revealing of the subordinate's true feelings than the actual words spoken.

For all these reasons, therefore, unless managers make a conscious effort to pay more attention to nonverbal cues and their meaning, checking this out if necessary with further questions, then important information may be lost. It is worth noting that we are not suggesting that managers should become good at reading nonverbal cues simply because this will enable them to be more considerate in their behaviour towards their subordinates. This aim may be laudable in itself, but it is by no means the whole story. We are suggesting that understanding nonverbal cues will help managers to gather information which will help them to become more *effective* managers. In fact, there is some evidence that people with a more task-oriented style of leadership tend to be better at decoding nonverbal cues than people with a more socio-emotional style of leadership.[71]

However, it must be recognised that the development of the skills of expressing and interpreting nonverbal cues is by no means as easy as it may seem. Skills are learned through practice with feedback. Unfortunately, the opportunity to obtain feedback concerning nonverbal skills is much more limited than it is with verbal communication. If one passes the salt instead of the pepper because one has misinterpreted a verbal cue, one is likely to receive explicit feedback, such as 'No, I wanted the pepper.' However, if one misinterprets a nonverbal signal, an explicit verbal correction is less likely to occur. Indeed, it has been found that there is virtually no relationship between self-ratings of decoding skills and actual ability to decode nonverbal cues. On the other hand, a positive relationship has been found between people's rating of their ability to express nonverbal cues and their actual ability to do so. Depaulo and Rosenthal suggest that feedback may be an important factor here.[72] When we express ourselves emotionally, we receive more immediate and more obtrusive feedback than when we read the emotional expressions of others. Even so, it is probably much easier to monitor what one is saying verbally and, if necessary, correct it, than it is to monitor and correct the *way* one is saying it (e.g. tone of voice, body posture). It is one thing to realise that the way one has said something has not had the effect one would have liked, but quite another to know precisely what one should do to put it right. The question of feedback in the acquisition of nonverbal cues will be taken up again in Chapter 8.

Exercise 5.1
Identification of nonverbal cues

Identify the probable meaning of each group of nonverbal cues in the following two 'interviews'.

Interview 1

Questions and statements	Accompanying nonverbal cues
MANAGER: Come in. Sit down.	(a) Smiling, leaning forward, relaxed posture, high level of eye contact. Gestures towards chair alongside his/her desk.

SUBORDINATE: I got your note. What did you want to see me about?

M: I wanted to talk to you about the quarterly output figures.

S: Oh, They've been released have they? I didn't realise they were out yet. What do they show?

M: Yes, they've just been released and they show that productivity in your section is down by 10 per cent.

S: Oh, I had a feeling they would be down, but not by that much.

M: So, what are you going to do to rectify the situation?

S: Well, the main problem has been an increase in the number of rejects. So I will have to put greater emphasis on quality inspection. I think there are two things I can do. I will give one of my subordinates special responsibility for quality inspection throughout the production cycle and I will call all the operatives together, explain the vital importance of maintaining quality standards, and provide special training where necessary.

(b) Raised eyebrows, high level of eye contact, leaning forward with legs drawn back under chair.

(c) Leaning back, tilting head to one side and supporting it in one hand, stretching out legs, speaking slowly in a quiet, low-pitched voice with narrow pitch range.

(d) Quick, slightly lop-sided smile, which disappears rather abruptly.

(e) Inner corners of the eyebrows drawn upwards and together, eyes slightly narrowed and corners of mouth pulled downward; speaking slowly and softly in a low voice, with unvarying pitch and occasional silent pauses.

(f) Eyebrows raised, creating wrinkles across the forehead and giving the eyes a large rounded appearance.

(g) High level of eye contact, speaking relatively quickly and loudly, with no pauses; gestures whilst speaking.

(h) At the end of each segment of speech, looks away, fills any pauses with 'ahs' and 'ums', and makes hand gesture which is not returned to rest.

(i) Whilst subordinate is talking, manager nods, smiles and says such things as 'yes' and 'Uh huh'.

M: Ok. Give that a try, and if you have any problems, come back and see me. You've always been one of our better managers, so I'm sure this is just a minor hiccup and we'll soon see you back among the higher performers again.

S: Thank you very much. I'm glad you still have confidence in me. it's very reassuring.

(j) Fall in pitch and loudness at end of statement; drawl on final or stressed syllable; termination of hand gesture or relaxation of tense hand position.

(k) Smiles, causing wrinkles to radiate from the corners of the eyes, whilst speaking at a fast pace in a voice which is louder, higher pitched and more variable in pitch than usual.

Interview 2

Questions and Statements

Accompanying Nonverbal Cues

MANAGER: Come in. Sit down.

(a) Unsmiling, sitting upright, high level of eye contact, loud voice. Indicates chair on opposite side of desk.

SUBORDINATE: I got your note, your message. What was it . . . what did you want to see . . . to see me about?

(b) Speaking quickly, stuttering occasionally.

M: I wanted to talk to you about the quarterly output figures.

(c) Sitting upright, with head at an ángle, lifting an eyebrow and the corner of the upper lip.

S: Oh, they've been released have they? I didn't realise . . . realise they were out yet. What do they . . . show?

(d) Speaking slowly, with silent pauses.

M: Yes, they've just been released and they show that productivity in your section is down by 10 per cent.

(e) Eyebrows drawn down and together, nose wrinkled, cheeks raised, upper lip pulled upward and lower lip pulled downward.

S: Oh, I had a feeling they would be down, but not by that much.

(f) Gaze averted, face turned away, shoulders hunched.

M: So, what are you going to do to rectify the situation?

(g) Stares at subordinate; eyes appear narrow and hard; eyebrows are lowered and drawn together causing vertical furrows between the inner corners of the eyebrows: mouth takes on a squarish, rectangular shape; speaks quickly, in a loud, high-pitched voice which shows greater pitch range and variability than usual.

s: Well, the main problem has been an increase in the number of rejects. So I will have to put greater emphasis on quality inspection. I think there are two things I can do. I will give one of my subordinates special responsibility for quality inspection throughout the production cycle and I will call all the operatives together, explain the vital importance of maintaining quality standards, and provide special training where necessary.

(h) Low level of eye contact: pauses before speaking, then speech hesitant with frequent silent pauses and use of 'ahs' and 'ums'.

(i) Whilst subordinate is talking, manager turns away from subordinate and begins hand gesture after having both hands at rest.

m: Ok. Give that a try, and if you have any problems, come back and see me. You've always been one of our better managers, so I'm sure this is just a minor hiccup and we'll soon see you back among the high performers again.

(j) High level of eye contact, but blinks more frequently, speaking in a voice which is higher pitched than normal, whilst alternatively scratching the back of hand and rubbing an ear.

s: Thank you very much. I'm glad you still have confidence in me. It's very reassuring.

(k) Speaking slowly and quietly. Mouth tightly closed, with clenched jaws and compressed lips when finished speaking.

The answers to this exercise are given in Appendix V.

Notes and references

1. J. K. Burgoon, (1985), 'Nonverbal signals', in M. L. Knapp and G. R. Miller (eds), *Handbook of Interpersonal Communication*, Sage.
2. For a detailed review of research in this area, see A. W. Siegman and S. Feldstein (eds) (1987), *Nonverbal Behavior and Communication*, 2nd edn, Erlbaum.
3. A. J. Fridlund, P. Ekman and H. Oster (1987), 'Facial expressions of emotion: review of literature, 1970–1983', in Siegman and Feldstein, *op. cit.*

4. A. T. Dittman (1987), 'The role of body movement in communication', in Siegman and Feldstein, *op. cit.*, 60.
5. *Ibid.*
6. K. L. Burns and E. G. Beier (1973), 'Significance of vocal and visual channels in the decoding of emotional meaning', *Journal of Communication*, **23**, 118–30.
7. P. Ekman (1965), 'Differential communication of affect by head and body cues', *Journal of Personality and Social Psychology*, **2**, 726–35.
8. Descriptions of the facial cues to emotion in this section are based on the following sources except where otherwise noted: C. E. Izard (1991), *The Psychology of Emotions*, Plenum; P. Ekman and W. V. Friesen (1975), *Unmasking the Face*, Prentice Hall.
9. P. E. Bull (1983), *Body Movement and Interpersonal Communication*, Wiley.
10. P. E. Bull (1987), *Posture and Gesture*, Pergamon.
11. Descriptions of the vocal cues to emotion in this section except where otherwise noted, are based on: K. R. Scherer (1981), 'Speech and emotional states', in J. K. Darby (ed.), *Speech Evaluation in Psychiatry*, Grune and Stratton.
12. Bull, *op. cit.*, n. 9.
13. P. Ekman and W. V. Friesen (1982), 'Felt, false and miserable smiles', *Journal of Nonverbal Behavior*, **6**, 238–52.
14. *Ibid.*
15. See B. J. Fehr and R. V. Exline (1987), 'Social visual interaction', in Siegman and Feldstein, *op. cit.*, n. 2.
16. A. W. Siegman (1987), 'The telltale voice: nonverbal messages of vocal communication', in Siegman and Feldstein, *op. cit.*
17. Scherer, *op. cit.*
18. Izard, *op. cit.*
19. *Ibid.*
20. Scherer, *op. cit.*
21. A. W. Siegman (1985), 'Expressive correlates of affective states and traits', in A. W. Siegman and S. Feldstein (eds), *Multichannel Integrations of Nonverbal Behavior*, Erlbaum.
22. Izard, *op. cit.*
23. *Ibid.*
24. *Ibid.*
25. Siegman, *op. cit.*, n. 16.
26. Siegman, *op. cit.*, n. 16.
27. Izard, *op. cit.*
28. P. A. Anderson (1985), 'Nonverbal immediacy in interpersonal communication', in Siegman and Feldstein, *op. cit.*, n. 21.
29. *Ibid.*
30. N. M. Henley (1977), *Body Politics: Power, sex and nonverbal communication*, Prentice Hall.

31. K. Blanchard and S. Johnson (1982), *The One Minute Manager*, Morrow.
32. M. Argyle and J. Dean (1965), 'Eye contact, distance and affiliation', *Sociometry*, **28**, 289–304.
33. Fehr and Exline, *op. cit.*
34. J. F. Dovidio and S. L. Ellyson (1982), 'Decoding visual dominance: attributions of power based on relative percentages of looking while speaking and looking while listening', *Social Psychology Quarterly*, **45**, 106–13.
35. Siegman, *op. cit.*, n. 16.
36. B. Pope and A. W. Siegman (1972), 'Relationship and behavior in the initial interview', in A. W. Siegman and B. Pope (eds), *Studies in Dyadic Communication*, Pergamon.
37. B. Major and R. Heslin (1982), 'Perceptions of cross-sex and same-sex reciprocal touch: it is better to give than to receive', *Journal of Nonverbal Behavior*, **6**, 148–62.
38. R. Sommer (1965), 'Further studies of small group ecology', *Sociometry*, **28**, 337–48; M. Cook (1970), 'Experiments on orientation and proxemics', *Human Relations*, **23**, 61–76.
39. See M. L. Patterson (1983), *Nonverbal Behavior: A functional perspective*, Springer-Verlag.
40. Fehr and Exline, *op. cit.*
41. M. Zuckerman and R. E. Driver (1985), 'Telling lies: verbal and nonverbal correlates of deception', in Siegman and Feldstein, *op. cit.*, n. 21.
42. Bull, *op. cit.*, n. 9.
43. Zuckerman and Driver, *op. cit.*
44. R. V. Exline, J. Thibaut, C. B. Hickey and P. Gumpert (1970), 'Visual interaction in relation to Machiavellianism and an unethical act', in R. Christie and F. L. Geis (eds), *Studies in Machiavellianism*, Academic Press.
45. A. Mehrabian (1972), *Nonverbal Communication*, Aldine–Atherton.
46. Zuckerman and Driver, *op. cit.*
47. A. W. Siegman and M. A. Reynolds (1983), 'Self-monitoring and speech in feigned and unfeigned lying', *Journal of Personality and Social Psychology*, **45**, 1325–33.
48. Zuckerman and Driver, *op. cit.*
49. M. J. Cody, P. J. Marston and M. Foster (1984), 'Deception: paralinguistic and verbal leakage', in R. N. Bostrom and B. H. Westley (eds), *Communication Yearbook 8*, Sage.
50. J. T. Dillon (1990), *The Practice of Questioning*, Routledge.
51. P. Ekman and W. V. Friesen (1969), 'The repertoire of nonverbal behavior: categories, origins, usage, and coding', *Semiotica*, **1**, 49–98, esp. 82.
52. H. M. Rosenfeld (1987), 'Conversational control functions of nonverbal behavior', in Siegman and Feldstein, *op cit.*, n. 2.
53. The remainder of this section is based on the following sources, except

where otherwise noted: S. Duncan and D. W. Fiske (1977), *Face-to-Face Interaction: Research methods and theory*, Erlbaum; H. M. Rosenfeld (1987), 'Conversational control functions of nonverbal behavior', in Siegman and Feldstein, *op. cit.*, n. 2.

54. Siegman, *op. cit.*, n. 16.
55. *Ibid.*
56. Fehr and Exline, *op. cit.*, 259.
57. M. Cook (1970), 'Experiments on orientation and proxemics', *Human Relations*, **23**, 61–76.
58. M. L. Patterson and J. A. Edinger (1987), 'A functional analysis of space in social interaction', in Siegman and Feldstein, *op. cit.*, n. 2.
59. J. A. Hall (1985), 'Male and female nonverbal behavior', in Siegman and Feldstein, *op. cit.*, n. 21.
60. A. G. Halberstadt (1985), 'Race, sociometric status, and nonverbal behavior', in Siegman and Feldstein, *op. cit.*, n. 21.
61. R. Heslin and M. L. Patterson (1982), *Nonverbal behavior and social psychology*, Plenum.
62. Hall, *op. cit.*
63. Halberstadt, *op. cit.*
64. Siegman and Feldstein, *op. cit.*, n. 2.
65. J. A. Hall (1979), 'Gender, gender roles, and nonverbal communication skills', in R. Rosenthal (ed.), *Skill in Nonverbal Communication*, Oelgeschlager, Gunn and Hain, 33.
66. Halberstadt, *op. cit.*, 227–8.
67. E. T. Hall and W. F. Whyte (1960), 'Intercultural communication: a guide to men of action', *Human Organization*, **19**, 5–12.
68. Izard, *op. cit.*
69. Dittman, *op. cit.*, 50.
70. Fehr and Exline, *op. cit.*
71. Hall, *op. cit.*, n. 43.
72. B. M. DePaulo and R. Rosenthal (1979), 'Ambiance, discrepancy and deception and nonverbal communication', in Rosenthal, *op. cit.*

CHAPTER 6

Structuring interactions with subordinates

Introduction

In short interactions with subordinates, the questions and statements described in Chapter 4 may be used singly. For example, a closed question may elicit the precise piece of information required, or an order may be obeyed instantly, without any further interaction being necessary. Usually, however, manager–subordinate interactions are more complex than such simple one-component exchanges. Even if the manager simply says 'Thank you' on receiving the information, or when the subordinate signals compliance, then two components are being used in sequence, closed question then recognition, or order then recognition, and we can see the beginnings of an interaction structure. In longer interactions, the discussion may cover several different topics, each of which consists of a number of different components, sequenced in different ways.

This provides us with two ways of looking at the structure of manager–subordinate interactions. There is the way in which particular components follow each other in sequence and, in longer interactions, the way in which the interaction as a whole, and the topics covered within it, are introduced, sequenced, resolved, and so on.

Sequences of components

We will examine sequences of components first. Consider the following examples:

MANAGER:	I see from the latest production figures that output was down last month. Do you have any ideas why that should be?	Open question
SUBORDINATE:	Well, we had some problems with absenteeism, but I think the main problem was machine breakdown.	
MANAGER:	That was a serious problem last month?	Restatement

SUBORDINATE:	Yes, we would have easily reached production targets if it hadn't been for that.	
MANAGER:	How many hours did we lose altogether?	Closed question
SUBORDINATE:	About five or six hours. I don't have the exact figures with me, but about that.	
MANAGER:	Was it the same machine or different ones?	Comparison
SUBORDINATE:	The same one. The new automatic baler.	
MANAGER:	Is there any particular reason why that one should be causing problems?	Probe
SUBORDINATE:	Not really. It's an excellent machine. We tested it thoroughly before we bought it . . .. There is one thing though . . .	
MANAGER:	Mmmm . . .	Lubricator
SUBORDINATE:	Well, if the automatic baler breaks down, the whole department grinds to a halt and everyone has to wait until it's repaired. With the others, we can shift people around and keep production going, but with the automatic baler everyone gets a break.	
MANAGER:	So you think it might be the operators?	Closed question
SUBORDINATE:	Well I can't prove it, but I'm beginning to think it might be.	
MANAGER:	Well that is certainly something which needs to be looked into. Over the next month I think you should keep a close eye on that machine. Check whether there is any sabotage or whether there is any reason why that particular machine should cause us problems. Let me know what you find at the next production meeting, or earlier if you come up with something significant.	Order
SUBORDINATE:	Right, I'll do that.	
MANAGER:	OK, that's one reason for the fall-off in output. Any others? You said something earlier about absenteeism . . .	Bridge Open

Another manager might tackle the problem as follows:

MANAGER:	I see from the latest production figures that output was down last month. You realise how serious this is, don't you?	Leading question
SUBORDINATE:	Well, yes I do. I'm always conscious of . . .	
MANAGER:	So what are you going to do about it?	Probe
SUBORDINATE:	Well, I'm keeping a close eye on things. One of the problems we've had is with machine breakdown. We lost a lot of time through machine breakdown last month.	
MANAGER:	That shouldn't happen. With proper maintenance schedules, those machines should run virtually non-stop. You do realise how important proper maintenance is, don't you?	Leading question
SUBORDINATE:	Yes, I . . .	
MANAGER:	And you are keeping to the official maintenance procedures, I take it?	Leading question
SUBORDINATE:	Oh yes, definitely.	
MANAGER:	Good. Well I want you to keep a particularly close eye on these machines over the next month. Check each machine thoroughly and make sure that correct maintenance procedures are being followed. And I'll expect a big improvement next week, all right?	Order
SUBORDINATE:	(*dubiously*) Yes, all right, I'll do that . . . but there is one other thing . . .	
MANAGER:	Good. And another thing. Absenteeism was high again last month. You can't expect to run an efficient department when half your staff don't turn up, can you?	Leading question

These two examples illustrate a number of factors which may influence what is achieved in such interactions between managers and subordinates.

The components employed

The first example illustrates the use of a variety of components – probes, comparison questions, closed questions – in order to elicit more precise information after an initial open question. The open question allowed the subordinate to state what he or she thought was the most important problem in general terms, whilst each successive question brings the manager closer to the key problem until it is finally identified. The key point is that the manager did not know what this key problem was before the introduction started, and therefore this sequence was necessary in order to discover the key question he or she should ask. In an ideal world, of course, the subordinate would immediately realise what was the key information the manager required and volunteer it straight away, rendering the use of skilful questioning unnecessary. In the real world, however, subordinates are often, rightly or wrongly, reluctant to give their bosses the particular piece of information which might be useful to them. It might be because they do not realise that it would be useful or because they are afraid it will be used against them or, as in this case, because the subordinate is not yet sufficiently sure of his or her facts. In such cases, skilful questioning techniques may be essential to gain the information required.

In the second example, an inappropriate sequence of components is used leading to a much less satisfactory conclusion. There is little variety in the components used. The continual use of leading questions results in the manager simply confirming his or her own prejudices rather than learning anything new. One probing question is used which could, in another context, be useful. However, it is sprung on the subordinate suddenly. This does not allow the subordinate the opportunity to gather his or her thoughts and the information obtained is less useful than it might have been.

Purposeful sequences of components

So far we have been assuming that the decision about the next component to be used in a sequence is made spontaneously as the interaction progresses. In many cases this will be so. However, there also exist, whether by design or habit, sequences of components which typically follow the same pattern. This is akin to the driver who will have to make spontaneous responses to particular driving situations, but will also have a repertoire of habitual sequences of responses, such as those involved in changing gear, making turns and so on. In the context of manager–subordinate interactions, we have called such purposeful sequences of components *gambits*. Some are well known interviewing techniques discussed in the literature, others debating tricks, and still others may be habitual ways of interacting with other people which the manager has developed over the years and now uses without realising. Some examples are as follows.

The funnel technique

The funnel technique has a variety of uses. It was initially developed as a means of gathering information.[1] It allows an interviewer to home in on some specific piece of information when he or she initially lacks sufficient background information to ask the precise question required. It consists of an open question to begin with, followed by a narrowing series of probes or other more precise questions and ending with a closed question or summary (see Figure 6.1). The information gained from each question is used to phrase the next one more precisely until the interviewer is able to ask for the specific piece of information required.

Apart from being used simply to gather information, the funnel technique can be used to define a problem. Broadly speaking, the first example given at the beginning of this chapter provides an illustration of the use of the funnel technique for this purpose. Lacking detailed information about the causes of the fall in production, the manager could not have known at the beginning of the discussion that he or she needed to ask about the role of the operators in the breakdown. The manager is only able to ask a specific closed question on this issue because he or she had gradually narrowed down to it through the preceding sequence of questions.

In this example, the funnel technique is used solely as a means of defining the problem. Having pinpointed the possible cause of drop in production, the manager then suggests what should be done to remedy the situation. However, the funnel technique can also be used as a means of helping subordinates to arrive at their own solutions to problems. Like the information-gathering funnel, the problem-solving funnel begins with an open question. For example:

How do you think we might tackle this problem? *or*

If this situation were to happen again, what might you do differently?

This is then followed by probing questions, such as:

How do you think you might do that?   *or*

Can you think of any drawbacks to that approach?

Comparison and hypothetical questions might also be used. For example:

What are the relative merits of having a maintenance contract with the manufacturers and using our own maintenance department?

If there was a breakdown over the weekend, would that cause any special problems?

This sequence of questions should ultimately lead to a summary of the actions to

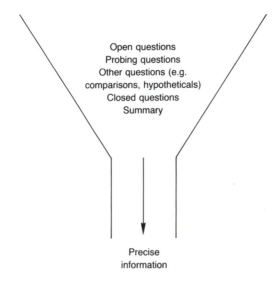

Open questions
Probing questions
Other questions (e.g.
comparisons, hypotheticals)
Closed questions
Summary

Precise
information

Figure 6.1 *The funnel sequence*

be taken to solve the problem or of the further work which needs to be done to solve it. For example:

So we are agreed then. At the next departmental meeting I will propose that we should enter into a maintenance contract with the baling machine manufacturers.

I think we have got as far as we can on this. What I want you to do is to bring precise figures on the relative cost of internal and external maintenance to our next meeting and we will decide where we will go from there.

Using the funnel technique in this way, first to identify the causes of a problem and then to derive a solution to it, forms what has been termed a 'double funnel' (see Figure 6.2).[2] It must be noted that when using the funnel technique, either to define or derive solutions to problems, the manager may need to provide as well as gather information. The subordinate will only be able to arrive at a good solution to the problem if he or she has the necessary information, and the manager may have additional information about the causes of the problem or about the feasibility and acceptability of potential solutions. Thus, in addition to asking appropriate questions, the manager may also need to provide appropriate information on these matters in the form of factual statements, self-disclosure, evaluative statements and feedback.

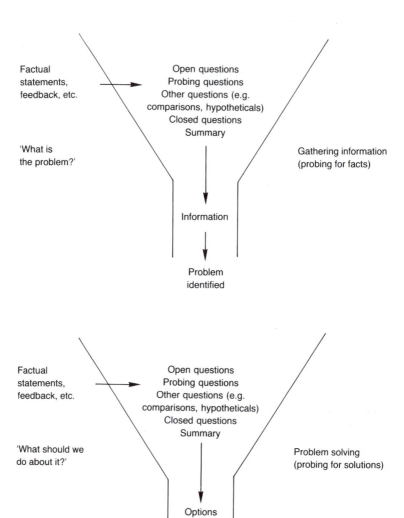

Factual
statements,
feedback, etc.

Open questions
Probing questions
Other questions (e.g.
comparisons, hypotheticals)
Closed questions
Summary

'What is
the problem?'

Gathering information
(probing for facts)

Information

Problem
identified

Factual
statements,
feedback, etc.

Open questions
Probing questions
Other questions (e.g.
comparisons, hypotheticals)
Closed questions
Summary

'What should we
do about it?'

Problem solving
(probing for solutions)

Options

Agreed
solution(s)

Figure 6.2 *The double funnel*

The inverted funnel

At times it can be useful to reverse the order of the questions in a 'funnel' and start with a narrow question before moving to progressively more open ones. This is known as the 'inverted funnel'.[3] An initial closed question can be used to establish very quickly whether an area is worth probing further or which area should be probed further. For example:

> Are you interested in promotion?
>
> What kind of job would interest you?
>
> What attracts you to that type of job?
>
> What additional skills do you think you would need to develop in order to perform that job well?

Alternatively, if the answer to the initial closed question is 'No', then the manager might ask:

> In that case, is there anything else which might interest you as far as your future career in the company is concerned?
>
> What could we do to make your present job more satisfying?

The tunnel sequence

The tunnel sequence consists of a series of questions of the same degree of openness.[4] Often, they are a series of closed questions. For example:

> How many staff report directly to you?
>
> What grades are they?
>
> Are they all full-time?
>
> How many are part-time?

The sequence could also be a series of narrow probes. For example:

> What exactly did you say to the shop steward?
>
> What did she reply?
>
> No, what were the exact words that you used?
>
> What was her response to that?

The advantage of this technique is that it can elicit a large amount of specific information in a short time. This may be useful in order to make a decision or provide the basis for further discussion. It can be particularly useful as a means of pinning someone down to specific factual information when he or she is attempting to evade an issue by talking generalities. The latter example above provides an illustration of this use. The major potential disadvantage of the tunnel sequence is that the unvarying question style may not give the other person an opportunity to elaborate. Thus important background information which might put the factual information in an entirely different light could be lost.

Hammering the point home

This is a gambit which is used to ensure that a subordinate has 'got the point'. It consists of a series of orders, requests, pieces of advice or explanations, interspersed with leading questions, such as 'You do understand, don't you?' In other words, the manager ensures that a clear-cut conclusion is reached and understood by the subordinate by restating the same conclusion several times in different ways. Sometimes this may be necessary, but if the manager still continues once the subordinate has understood, then he or she is likely to become irritated and resentful. Thus correctly identifying the point at which to stop requires considerable skill, particularly in the interpretation of nonverbal cues.

Trap setting

Trap setting represents an attempt to get a subordinate to provide, without realising it, information which will prove conclusively that he or she is wrong, has made a mistake, or is at fault in some way. When 'successful', it commonly consists of a series of leading questions, eliciting compliant responses, until the trap is sprung with a triumphant leading criticism, such as 'So, you admit you simply weren't thinking when you . . .'

In our experience, however, trap setting is rarely, if ever, successful in the long term. If the subordinate falls into the trap, it is likely to cause resentment and may also be damaging to his or her self-esteem, neither of which are particularly effective ways of motivating an improvement in performance. Furthermore, having fallen into a trap once, most subordinates will become wary of falling for the same trick twice. Even within the space of a half-hour interview, we have observed interviewees refuse to give the expected answers to leading questions, having been caught by a trap-setting gambit. Requests for clarification are common, such as 'I'm not sure what you mean' or 'Are you thinking of a specific example?' or 'That all depends'. In other words, the subordinate sees the trap coming and examines it from all angles, but resolutely refuses to fall into it. Needless to say, this does not result in a constructive discussion.

Praise before blame

A widely held managerial aphorism is that praise should always be given before blame. As with many of such maxims, the notion has some validity. If both the praise and the blame are done skilfully and appropriate weight given to the praise in relation to the blame, then the subordinate may be more willing to accept criticism because his or her 'good points' have also been recognised. However, it would be unwise to assume that this gambit will always have the desired effect. It can fail, and fail badly if used unskilfully. This is particularly likely to happen if the praise is brief and general (e.g. 'Overall, your performance is reasonably good'), whilst the criticism is lengthy and detailed. We are not saying that praise and criticism should always be *equally* lengthy and detailed. This could be difficult to achieve if there is a complex performance problem which needs to be addressed. At the same time, it is important to make sure that the praiseworthy aspects of performance are reviewed at some length and in some detail before proceeding to the criticism. Even then, the gambit may fail if it is used in a relatively mechanistic manner. To the subordinate, the saying 'Always give praise before blame' may translate as 'Watch out! Blame always follows praise!' If the manager continually praised a subordinate and then hit him over the head with a rolled-up newspaper, the subordinate would undoubtedly get ready to duck whenever he was praised. Much the same thing is likely to happen with blame. If it always follows praise, then the praise may become a source of anxiety rather than pleasure.

Blame before praise
The aim of this gambit is to bring home to a subordinate the need to improve his or her performance by pointing out his or her deficiencies, and then, having gained the subordinate's agreement to an improvement plan, build up his or her confidence and commitment by the lavish use of praise. Managers who have used this gambit on our training courses have commonly said that they did so because they felt that the subordinate needed 'taking down a peg or two' before he or she would accept the need for an improvement in performance. In our experience, this is a high-risk strategy. The subordinate may become so angry or demoralised by the initial criticism that the manager either does not have the opportunity to get round to the praise or the subordinate does not respond to it positively if it is used. Even in disciplinary interviews, where there is a valid need to bring home to the subordinate the importance of improving his or her performance, the technique is still a risky one. The danger here, however, is that the lavish praise at the end may help the subordinate to feel better, but may also wrongly give the impression that his or her poor performance was not such a serious problem after all.

Causal analysis
This is a gambit used by the authors to minimise the risk of adverse emotional reactions to attempts to improve performance. It is a way of getting someone to recognise how he or she might do something better next time, without going through the stage of pointing out limitations in current performance, and in particular without using emotive words, such as 'faults', 'shortcomings', 'went wrong', and so on. Typically, it consists of a series of open questions and

probes, followed by recognition and/or advice, depending on the individual's ability to solve his or her own problems. For example:

> When you did X, what effect did that have?
>
> Was that the effect you wanted?
>
> In that case, can you think of any way in which you might have handled things differently to produce the effect you wanted?

followed by:

> That's a good idea, why don't you try that next time?   *or*
>
> And another way of tackling the problem would be to . . .   *or*
>
> Well, one way of tackling the problem would be to . . .

This gambit has a number of advantages as a means of identifying a solution to a performance problem. By avoiding criticism or blame, it is less likely to arouse negative reactions. Done skilfully, it not only identifies a solution to the problem, but also provides the subordinate with an opportunity to practise his or her problem-solving skills. If the subordinate does arrive at an acceptable solution to the problem, he or she is more likely to be committed to it than to an imposed solution. Finally, even if the subordinate is unable to come up with a solution, then any suggestions made by the manager are more likely to be accepted, because the subordinate has at least been consulted first. Indeed, if the subordinate is unable to think of a solution, he or she may ask the manager what he or she thinks would be the best thing to do.

Where we have seen this gambit fail, it has often been associated with the manner in which it was carried out. If the manager already has a solution in mind towards which he or she is leading the subordinate, even though actual leading questions are not being used, then causal analysis has a certain similarity with trap setting. Done well, it can still be a useful coaching device for relatively inexperienced subordinates. Done badly, perhaps with excessive signs of patience and interest, it can appear condescending and patronising, thus causing resentment at being treated like a school-child.

The pace of the interaction

One factor which influences the quality of the information gathered and the quality of decisions made is the pace of the interaction. By this we mean not only the speed with which the manager and/or subordinate speak, but also, and more crucially, the speed with which their respective contributions follow each other. In the second example, at the beginning of the chapter, on several occasions the manager did not allow the subordinate to finish his or her responses before asking another question or introducing another topic. Excessive pace in an interaction has a number of adverse effects:

1. It denies the subordinate time to give a reasoned, relevant reply.
2. It denies the manager the time to understand the implications of what the subordinate is saying.
3. It denies the manager the time to phrase the right question or statement which will produce the response which he or she wants.

Managers are, of course, very busy most of the time. Mintzberg,[5] for example, talks of 'much work at unrelenting pace'. Paradoxically, a slower pace of interaction may achieve the same or better results more quickly. The shorter the time available, the more essential it is not to waste time by asking irrelevant questions or making irrelevant statements which do not achieve the desired results. It may take longer to select just the right question, but it is more likely to solve the problem and do so in less time than six rapid-fire but inappropriate questions.

A number of devices can be used to slow an interaction down and thus provide thinking time.

Allow silence

Many people seem to find silence disturbing. They cannot think precisely what they should say next, so rather than say nothing, they say the first thing which comes into their head, which may not further the aims of the interaction at all. On the other hand, silence need not be embarrassing providing the person using it is doing so purposefully. In this case, it is not a sign of inadequacy, but the skilful use of time to achieve a more desirable outcome. It can then become even more disturbing to the other person, however, particularly if he or she has just said something tendentious or asked a pointed question. The ensuing silence may put pressure on him or her to say something, either modifying or elaborating on what he or she has just said.

Labelling

If silence would cause unwanted tension in the interaction, this can be avoided by making explicit what is happening. The manager can quite simply say, 'Wait a minute. Let's think about this for a moment.' Having overtly labelled silence as a pause for thought seems to make it much less threatening to both parties.

Restatement

Another useful device for obtaining thinking time, providing it is not overused, is to restate or paraphrase what the other person has just said. This throws the conversational ball back into the other person's court, and whilst he or she is talking, the manager can be thinking of his or her next contribution to the discussion. An illustration occurs in the first example at the beginning of the chapter, where the manager says in response to the subordinate's comment about machine breakdown, 'That was a serious problem last month?' Used appropriately, such restatements can also signal that the manager is listening or act as an open question signifying 'Tell me more about that.' However, they are not infallible – the subordinate may simply answer 'Yes' – and would become very tedious if overused.

Listening

An important influence on the structure of, and outcomes from, an interaction is the extent to which the manager actually listens to what the subordinate is saying. This applies both to the words themselves and to the nonverbal cues of enthusiasm, doubt, acceptance and rejection, and so on. As noted in Chapter 5 observation of visual cues, such as facial expression, body posture and gestures can also provide important information concerning the subordinate's feelings. Just as it is important for the manager's nonverbal cues to be consistent with the verbal message if he or she is to be convincing, a lack of correspondence between what the subordinate is saying and the accompanying nonverbal cues may be a sign that he or she is not convinced, and further discussion is necessary.

Several instances of listening and not listening are included in the examples at the beginning of this chapter. As noted above, the first manager's use of restatement – if used with the appropriate nonverbal cues – is a sign that he or she is listening, as is the use of lubricators later and the reintroduction of absenteeism into the discussion after the subordinate's earlier comment. In the second example, the manager does not 'hear' the subordinate's doubts about routine maintenance being the solution to the problem and continually interrupts, thus depriving him- or herself of the opportunity to listen. Both the manager and the subordinate had 'another thing' which they wanted to talk about at the end of the extract. However, the manager did not give him- or herself the opportunity to discover what the subordinate's point was, and it may have been important.

Acquiring listening skills is not an easy task. Simply trying harder or concentrating may not provide an effective solution to the problem of not listening if the manager is actually doing something which is preventing him or her from hearing and recognising the implications of what is being said. It will be necessary instead to discover the causes of the problem and to identify what the manager needs to do differently in order to listen more effectively.

One cause of not listening is preconceived ideas. The manager believes that he or she already knows the facts or the solution to a problem and therefore does not need to listen to what the subordinate has to say. This may occur because the manager has already made up his or her mind before the interaction began. Methods of reducing the effects of such preconceived ideas are discussed in the next chapter. Alternatively, the manager may assume that he or she has understood what the subordinate has to say after hearing only part of it and then stop listening, often waiting impatiently for the subordinate to finish so that he or she can have his or her own say.

A second cause of not listening, which sometimes occurs in conjunction with the first, is planning what one is going to say next before the other person has finished speaking. This may occur because the manager is simply more interested in getting his or her point across than listening to the subordinate. Sometimes, however, it occurs because the manager is concerned that he or she will not know what to say when the subordinate stops talking and an embarrassing silence may then occur. Whatever the cause, the result is the same. Human beings are not equipped to listen and to plan their own contribution simultaneously and if they try to do both at the same time listening inevitably suffers.

One way of avoiding such mental rehearsal is to think about how one might briefly restate what is being said instead of thinking about the next question one might ask. This has two effects: first, it encourages listening, because it is impossible to make an accurate restatement without listening to what is being said; secondly, it means that the manager need never fear not knowing what to say next. In most cases, the restatement will not actually be needed. Having concentrated on what the other person is saying, the next question or statement will usually come to mind quite naturally. However, if it does not, the manager always has the restatement to fall back on.

Reaching a conclusion

Although the two interactions described at the beginning of this chapter differ in a number of ways, they do have one thing in common. Both reach a conclusion. The conclusion may be less relevant in the second example because of the manager's inferior questioning and listening skills, but the subordinate does at least clearly understand what the manager thinks he or she should do next. In some cases, however, the opposite problem may arise. The manager may handle the interaction skilfully until the final stages, and then fail to achieve his or her objectives because he or she does not bring it to a successful conclusion.

This is not to say that *all* interactions between managers and subordinates should lead to clearly identified conclusions. Some interactions may take place simply for the enjoyment of the interaction itself, such as the discussion of a recent sporting event or an amusing incident which took place in another department. Such interactions may serve a useful function, in that they will probably help to develop or maintain a closer working relationship between the manager and subordinate, but little will be lost if they do not lead to clear-cut conclusions. Even in the case of work interactions, the manager may not always feel that arriving at clearly identified conclusions is justified. It may not be tactful, confidential information may be involved, other people may need to be informed first, indirect methods of influence may have a greater probability of success, and so on.

Whilst such reasons may be valid in some instances, care must be taken not to use them as an excuse for ducking issues. In many cases, the interaction will not have been a success from the manager's point of view unless clear and agreed conclusions are reached. Moreover the manager cannot be *sure* that clear and agreed conclusions have been reached unless they are explicitly stated. The subordinate *may* have intuitively come to exactly the same conclusions as the manager without them being explicitly stated, but unless this is checked out, there is always the possibility that the subordinate's perceptions, and later, memory, of them differ significantly from the manager's. It is worth considering, therefore, what can be regarded as bringing an interaction to a successful conclusion and how this might be achieved.

To some extent, this will depend on the purpose of the interaction. If the purpose of an interaction is to gather information, it can be regarded as having been brought to a successful conclusion when the manager has collected all the information which can contribute towards making a good decision. If the manager fails to do this, and realises it, he or she can, of course, re-open the discussion at a later date and ask further questions. However, this is time-consuming at the least and could also be irritating or undiplomatic. For example, the question of availability for transfer raised once could be casual interest, but raised twice could cause unwanted speculation or uncertainty. It is therefore usually more effective and certainly more elegant to obtain all the relevant information the first time the issue is raised.

Various techniques can be used to increase the likelihood of doing so. If the issue is sufficiently important or delicate, it can be useful to identify the key information required to make a good decision before the interaction takes place and then ask oneself before closing the discussion, 'Do I have the information necessary to make a good decision now?' A summary is also a useful device. After a wide-ranging discussion, it is often difficult to remember all the details which have emerged and the manager may assume that he or she has more precise information than is actually the case. Pausing to summarise out loud gives the manager the opportunity to review the adequacy of the information he or she has gathered. If there is little to summarise or the conclusions are vague or important information is missing, then obviously further information-gathering is required. The summary also gives the subordinate the opportunity to review the information he or she has provided and correct any misapprehensions or provide additional information missing from the summary, should this be necessary. Lastly, the manager can follow the summary by specifically asking the subordinate whether he or she has any further information; for example, 'Does that cover everything?' or 'Is there anything you want to add?'

If the purpose of the interaction is to give information, then it can be regarded as having been brought to a successful conclusion when the subordinate has assimilated and understood all the information which the manager wishes to impart. There are a variety of ways of checking whether the information has been successfully transmitted. Simply asking the question, 'Do you understand?' may suffice, although care must be taken that the subordinate is not saying 'Yes' in order to avoid appearing stupid. Nonverbal cues can be observed whilst the information is being given to check whether the subordinate is showing signs of comprehension, acceptance, attention, puzzlement, rejection and so on. If the information is relatively complex, the manager can summarise the main points at the end. Alternatively, the manager may ask the subordinate to summarise. The latter has the advantage of providing an explicit check on how much the subordinate has remembered and understood. How it is perceived by the subordinate, however, will depend on the circumstances and the manner in which it is done. It could be seen as being helpful, but equally it could be regarded as patronising or arrogant. If the purpose of giving the information is to influence behaviour in a disciplinary interview, this may not be a problem. In other situations, it could alienate the subordinate concerned if used inappropriately. This question will be taken up in the next chapter when we come to examine different approaches to interactions and their likely effects on subordinate responses.

If the purpose of the interaction is to influence the subordinate's behaviour, then it can be regarded as being brought to a successful conclusion if precise actions are agreed which will result in an improvement in the subordinate's performance to which manager and subordinate are committed. These may be actions to be taken by either the subordinate or the manager, or both. For example, the manager might conclude, 'Over the next four weeks, I want you to check the maintenance records of the automatic baler to see whether there is any pattern and keep a close eye on its current performance. In the meantime, I will check with our other factories to see whether they have had any problems with the same machine.'

One reason why a manager may fail to arrive at a high-quality solution to a performance problem is that he or she did not collect all the information necessary to do so before reaching a conclusion. Equally, however, managers may skilfully collect the information but fail to use it to reach a clear-cut conclusion. Such interactions not only leave problems unresolved, but are also likely to leave the subordinate with a feeling that interactions with the manager concerned are a waste of time – a 'non-event' – because they never achieve anything.

Again, therefore, it is a useful exercise to conclude the discussion of each problem area with a summary of what is to be done about it. Of course, it would be naïve to assume that all problems *can* be solved, but even failure to solve a problem is worth summarising in order to establish between manager and subordinate exactly where they have got to and what is to be done next; for example, shelve it until a later meeting, refer it elsewhere, collect more information, bring someone else into the decision-making process, and so on.

As with information-gathering, if it is difficult to find anything to summarise or the solution lacks precision, then obviously the discussion has not come to a satisfactory conclusion. Furthermore, the discipline of making a summary will also focus the manager's mind during the preceding discussion, because he or she will realise that in order to be able to make an adequate summary at the end, he or she will have to use the necessary interpersonal skills in order to arrive at an adequate solution in the first place.

In addition to summarising the main points arising from the discussion, it may be worth checking at the end how the subordinate feels about any conclusions reached. The subordinate may not be in any doubt about *what* has been decided, but could still feel resentful, anxious or in some way dissatisfied about the decision or the way in which it was made. It is all too easy to ignore feelings in the drive to find a solution to a pressing work problem, but they can make a substantial difference to how committed the subordinate is to putting it into practice. Thus, however irritating it may be to discover that a subordinate still has reservations about what appears to be a perfectly reasonable decision, it is better to find out what they are and deal with them before they have adverse effects on his or her performance rather than after.

Stipulating criteria of success is more difficult when the primary purpose of the interaction is handling emotion. Broadly speaking, attempts to handle emotion can be regarded as successful if the manager influences the subordinate's emotions in the direction intended and this has the longer-term effects the manager wished to achieve. Thus a manager may wish to make a subordinate worried about the quality of his or her performance in order to motivate the subordinate to improve it. This attempt can be regarded as a failure in one sense if the subordinate does not become worried, perhaps because the manager did not put over the message convincingly enough. Equally, it is a failure if the anxiety aroused causes the subordinate's performance to become worse rather than better. Consequently, a knowledge of how emotions affect people's behaviour and how the particular subordinate in question is likely to respond is important when attempting to arouse negative emotions in an attempt to motivate subordinates. The same reprimand, delivered in exactly the same way, may motivate one subordinate to do better, completely demoralise another, arouse bitter resentment in a third, and so on.

For a manager wishing to reduce adverse emotions, the initial criterion of success is that the subordinate is less angry, anxious, depressed and so on by the end of the interaction, but this 'success' will be of little lasting value if the adverse emotions recur soon afterwards. As we suggested in Chapter 4, when faced with adverse emotions, it is important to gain an understanding of the emotion or emotions and allow them to be expressed before trying to reach a solution of the problem or problems that have caused the emotions in the first place. At this point, having permitted or encouraged the subordinate to express the emotions, it is then important to try to find some way of changing the situation so that they do not arise with the same severity again. In many cases, this will involve changing the subordinate's working environment; in other instances the problem may lie outside work or in an inability on the part of the subordinate to cope with the 'normal' stresses of working life. As suggested in Chapter 2, expert counselling may be appropriate in such cases.

Overall structure

We now turn to the longer interactions between manager and subordinate which may cover several issues within the same interaction. The question of structure arises here in relation to the way in which these issues are sequenced and related to each other, and the way the interaction as a whole is introduced and concluded. Consider the following interactions.

Example A
The manager (Ellen) calls her subordinate (Dan) into her office and tells him that she is concerned about his department's production figures for last month. She explains why she is concerned. There has been a complaint about late delivery, higher production figures have been achieved in the past, and she has had advance warning of a big sales drive which will require a stockpile of finished articles to meet the hoped for dramatic increase in demand. She establishes that there are three main problem areas which have contributed in varying degrees to the lower production figures. These are machine breakdown, absenteeism and occasional shortages of raw materials. Each of these is discussed in turn, establishing precisely what the problem is, what its causes are and what can be done to prevent it happening again, or at least minimise its effects. Ellen then summarises the agreed actions and both of them leave the meeting knowing exactly what they are going to do to tackle the problem.

Example B
The manager (Colin) calls his subordinate (George) into his office and tells him that he is concerned about his department's production figures. Colin begins by asking why so much time has been lost through machine breakdown and gathers some information on this question. He suggests that lack of routine maintenance may be the problem, but George argues that the main problem is absenteeism because this necessitates putting people on machines which they are not used to. The problem of absenteeism is discussed, but no clear-cut conclusions reached. Colin then queries why production has been delayed by shortage of raw materials and George points out that forward planning is difficult because of the unpredictable nature of machine breakdowns. Colin returns to the question of routine maintenance, but George points out that recommended practices are already being followed. The discussion continues in this manner with the three main issues being raised and discussed, but dropped before any conclusion is reached. The meeting closes with Colin telling George that he will have to do something about falling production rates because there is a big sales push coming and they will need all the stocks they can build up. George agrees that something will have to be done, but leaves the meeting with no clear idea of what it is.

Example C

The manager (Bill) calls his subordinate (Mary) into his office and tells her he is concerned about her department's production figures. Mary says she is very pleased to talk about the problem because she is worried too. Bill says that he has identified a number of things which he feels are contributory factors and which he would like to discuss in turn, beginning with machine breakdown. Mary replies, with some emphasis, that her main problem is the supply of raw materials, and in particular suppliers who do not live up to delivery promises no matter how many times they are reminded. She is told that they will come to that later, but first they will deal with machine breakdown. Mary replies that solving the machine breakdown problem will not make much difference if they do not have the raw materials anyway. Bill insists that they will get to raw materials problem in good time, but first they will deal with the question of machine breakdown. For a moment they glare at each other in silence, but Mary then slumps in her chair and says, 'OK, if that's the way you want it.' For some time afterwards she makes little contribution to the discussion and is grudgingly acquiescent when Bill makes suggestions about what she should do to solve the machine breakdown and absenteeism problems. She brightens somewhat when the discussion finally gets round to the raw material problem and makes a number of useful contributions. Bill summarises what they have agreed and Mary leaves the meeting in a slightly happier frame of mind than she was after the first five minutes, when she was within an inch of telling him what he could do with his job and his machines. However, she is by no means convinced that Bill's suggestions on the machine breakdown and absenteeism problems will have any useful effect at all.

These examples illustrate some of the advantages and disadvantages inherent in different ways of structuring manager–subordinate interactions. These interactions vary in the extent to which the manager establishes an *organised* structure for the interaction. An organised structure, as we would define it, is one which consists of a logical sequence of discrete sections, each of which deals with a single important topic. Ideally, each section will reach an agreed conclusion, and the topic will not be raised again until the final summary. If this happens, then the final summary should be relatively straightforward, simply a repetition of the points agreed at the end of each section to remind both manager and subordinate of the main conclusions they have reached. If full agreement has not been established earlier, then disagreements are likely to arise at the summary stage, extending the interaction, perhaps causing friction, and certainly reducing the clarity of the conclusions. Example A is an illustration of a successful interaction using an organised structure.

At the opposite extreme is Example B, which is an interaction with a *diffuse* structure. That is, one in which the topics covered take the form of a number of themes, which occur and recur throughout the interaction, interwoven with each other. There are situations where such a structure might be effective. For example, if the manager is trying to defuse a highly charged emotional situation by allowing the subordinate to talk him- or herself out, then the manager will simply respond (with reflectives, restatements and lubricators) to the subordinate's comments rather than attempt to impose his or her own structure on to the interaction. For most purposes, however, a diffuse structure is likely to suffer the major drawback that each issue is dropped before agreement is reached about what should be done about it. Each time it is raised again involves some going over old ground, and the end result is often a long interaction with no clear-cut conclusions.

An interaction structure can either be developed during or before an interaction. If there is not time to plan the interaction beforehand or the manager does not know all the ramifications of the problem to be discussed then the structure can be developed at the beginning of the interaction. For example, the interaction might begin in the following way.

Example D

MANAGER: As you know, I'm worried about the recent fall in output in your department, Dan, and I think we should work out a joint plan of campaign to deal with the problem.

SUBORDINATE: OK.

MANAGER: Now, there are two major contributory factors I can identify – machine breakdown and raw material supply. I think we need to have a very close look at both these questions. Is there any other factor which you would identify?

SUBORDINATE: Absenteeism. That's a big problem.

MANAGER: Anything else?

SUBORDINATE: No, I think those are the main three.

MANAGER: Very well, we'll deal with each in turn. Where would you like to start?

SUBORDINATE: Absenteeism. That's my biggest headache.

MANAGER: OK, we'll start with that and then go on to machine breakdown and raw materials supply. So, tell me about the problems you've been having with absenteeism.

If the manager knows beforehand that an interaction is to take place on some particular topic, and the topic is important enough to warrant it, then advance planning can be very useful. The plan might consist of a list of the main topics the manager wishes to raise, the key points to be raised within each topic, and some hypotheses concerning possible outcomes or conclusions of the interaction. The manager equipped with such a plan will be in a much better position to select and perform individual components of the interaction skilfully than one who is also attempting to structure the interaction as a whole at the same time.

Whilst a plan may be useful, however, rigid adherence to it can be disastrous.

Even the most well-thought-out plan may turn out to be inappropriate because of something which happens in the course of the discussion. It may be that the subordinate finds some particular issue extremely sensitive and is obviously very uneasy about discussing it further. The manager will then have to decide whether more is to be gained by proceeding with the issue immediately or leaving it until some later occasion when both have had time to think it over. The subordinate may also have some burning issue that is dominating his or her thoughts at the moment which is preventing him or her from concentrating on other things until it is cleared up. Again, the manager will have to decide whether more is to be gained by sticking to the original plan or changing it to accommodate the subordinate's priorities. Much will depend upon how relevant the issue is which the subordinate wishes to discuss, how flexible or compliant the subordinate is, and how important he or she feels the issue is. If it is simply a matter of changing the order in which issues are discussed, then there is a strong argument for doing so. A subordinate who is highly concerned about one particular topic may simply not attend to the discussion properly until that issue is dealt with, and the value of much of the earlier discussion will then be lost. Example C is an illustration of what can happen when a plan is too rigidly adhered to in the face of changing circumstances. Nevertheless a plan can still be useful even if it is changed by force of circumstance. It can be used as a checklist. The manager can tick or cross off items on the list, whatever the order in which they are dealt with. A glance at the list will show those issues still remaining, and the manager can then restructure the remainder of the interaction much more easily than would be possible if he or she had no plan at all.

A similar point is made by Rackham and Carlisle[6] in their study of the factors involved in effective negotiation. They found that less successful or 'average' negotiators placed heavy reliance on *sequence planning*. That is, their plans were based on the assumption that they would discuss a number of issues in a certain order, each linked with and leading to the next. They would frequently verbalise a potential negotiation in terms like 'First I'll bring up A, then lead to B, and after that I'll cover C and finally go on to D.' Rackham and Carlisle point out that in order to succeed, sequence planning requires the consent and co-operation of the other party to the negotiation, and often this is not forthcoming. By contrast, successful negotiators were more likely to use *issue planning*. In other words, they tended to plan around each individual issue in a way that was independent of any sequence. They were careful not to draw sequence links between a series of issues, and would consider issue C, for example, as if issues A, B and D did not exist.

One further point is worth making about the way in which manager–subordinate interactions are structured. The structure used need not bear any relationship to the manager's 'leadership style'. A manager using an organised structure could be 'democratic' or 'participative', in that he or she allows the subordinate a large say in defining the structure. Example D provides an illustration of this process. Alternatively, the manager may develop his or her own structure and impose this on the subordinate irrespective of his or her wishes. Example C provides an illustration of this more authoritarian approach. By the same token, a manager using a diffuse structure may be democratically deferring to the subordinate's wishes or autocratically criticising the subordinate on a number of unrelated issues as they come to mind. Given that it is possible to perform the same style in such radically different ways, it is hardly surprising that the research literature provides little evidence of any consistent relationship between leadership styles and performance.[7]

Exercise 6.1
Structuring interactions

Provide short answers to the following questions:

1. What form does the sequence of questions take when using the funnel technique?
2. What are the main purposes for which the funnel technique can be used?
3. What form does the 'double funnel' take?
4. What other components, apart from those used to gather information, may be required when using the funnel technique and under what circumstances?
5. What form does the sequence of questions in the 'inverted funnel' take?
6. What purposes can the inverted funnel be used for?
7. What form does the 'tunnel' sequence of questions take?
8. What are the main purposes for which the tunnel sequence can be used?
9. What is the main potential disadvantage of the tunnel sequence?
10. What components are typically used in the gambit 'hammering the point home'?
11. What is the main dilemma faced by the manager in using the gambit 'hammering the point home'?
12. What are the main disadvantages of 'trap setting'?
13. What pitfalls need to be avoided when using the gambit 'praise before blame'?
14. What are the main disadvantages of the gambit 'blame before praise'?
15. What are the main potential advantages of 'causal analysis' as a means of identifying a solution to a performance problem?
16. Under what circumstances might causal analysis fail to achieve its objectives?
17. What are the main disadvantages of an interaction conducted at a high pace?

18. What devices can be used to slow down an interaction in order to provide the manager with more time to think?
19. What steps can be taken to improve listening during an interaction?
20. What are the main advantages of giving a summary at the end of an interaction?
21. What advantage is there in asking the subordinate to give a summary at the end of an interaction?
22. What other actions might the manager take at the end of an interaction to increase the probability of reaching a successful conclusion?
23. What are the advantages of ensuring that an interaction has an organised structure.?
24. What disadvantage may occur if an interaction is too rigidly structured?
25. What steps can be taken to reduce the potential adverse effects of an organised interaction structure?
26. Under what circumstances would it be more appropriate to employ a diffuse structure in an interaction?

The answers to this exercise are given in Appendix VI.

Notes and references

1. R. L. Kahn and C. F. Cannell (1957), *The Dynamics of Interviewing: Theory, techniques and cases*, Wiley.
2. We are grateful to Bob Parkinson for suggesting this concept to us.
3. Kahn and Cannell, *op. cit.*
4. J. Hays (1991), *Interpersonal Skills: Goal-directed behaviour at work*, Harper-Collins.
5. H. Mintzberg (1980), *The Nature of Managerial Work*, Prentice Hall, p. 29.
6. N. Rackham and J. Carlisle (1978), 'The effective negotiator, part 2: planning for negotiations', *Journal of European Industrial Training*, **2** (7), 2–5.
7. G. A. Yukl (1980), *Leadership in Organizations*, 2nd edn, Prentice Hall.

CHAPTER 7

Approaches to manager–subordinate interactions

Introduction

In previous chapters we have described the range of verbal and nonverbal components which a manager can use in an interaction with a subordinate, and the different ways in which such interactions can be structured. However, it is extremely unlikely that a manager will use all these in any one interaction. Those actually used will depend in part upon the reactions of the subordinate. For example, the subordinate may provide information readily or be evasive, respond willingly to attempts to influence his or her behaviour or resist them, become angry, enthusiastic or apathetic, or so on. This will influence what the manager says and does to a greater or lesser degree, which, in turn, can vary from simply asking a question another way or restating an order more firmly to restructuring the whole interaction because the subordinate is not responding as expected.

Another influence on the components used in an interaction and the way it is structured is the manager's preferences with respect to the kind of interaction he or she wishes to have with the subordinate. Two factors are important here: first, the extent to which the manager is prepared to allow the subordinate to influence the content of the interaction and the decisions which are reached; secondly, the extent to which the manager wishes to conduct the interaction in a warm, friendly manner or one which is cold and businesslike, emphasising differences in status and authority. Both elements will influence the manager's general approach to the interaction and therefore the verbal and nonverbal components and ways of structuring the interaction which he or she chooses to use. As noted in Chapter 1, this aspect of leadership has been the primary concern of leadership theorists for many years. Much has been written about the relative merits of the democratic, autocractic, participative, authoritarian, person-centred, task-oriented, considerate, and many other leadership styles. None the less this approach to leadership theory has a significant drawback from our point of view. The theorists do not describe in any detail how to perform these various leadership styles or what skills are needed to perform them well. There is, however, one writer who has addressed this problem, not as a leadership theorist, but in relation to performance appraisal interviewing – Norman Maier.

Maier suggests that there are three types of appraisal interview, which he calls the Tell and Sell, the Tell and Listen and the Problem Solving.[1] Essentially, these are different methods of giving subordinates feedback about past performance and/or establishing plans for future performance improvement. Maier makes the important point that successful appraisal interviewing depends both on selecting the right method and on having the necessary skills. Two interviewers might use the same method but achieve different results because one was more skilled. Equally, two interviewers with the same level of skill could achieve different results because one had chosen a superior method to the other. Maier does not claim, however, that any one type of interview is superior to the others in all circumstances. Rather he suggests that each method has its own advantages and limitations, depending on the objectives the manager wishes to achieve, the employee's age and experience, the way in which the employee is likely to react to the approach, and so on. He therefore not only describes each type of appraisal interview, but also indicates the skills which will be required to perform them successfully, and the circumstances in which their use would be appropriate and inappropriate. Furthermore it appeared to us that the use of Maier's three approaches need not be restricted to the formal appraisal interview; they could equally well be used as general techniques for the day-to-day management of staff.

We consequently decided to take Maier's work on appraisal interviewing, rather than leadership theory, as the starting point for our analysis of the different ways in which managers can approach interactions with their subordinates. As might be expected, however, it required some further development in a number of areas before it could provide a comprehensive framework for the analysis of leadership skills at this level.

Purpose of the interaction

Because they were described within the context of appraisal interviewing, Maier's three approaches were originally envisaged as means of providing feedback about past performance and establishing plans for performance improvement. These are, of course, important aspects of day-to-day management. They are activities which can, and ideally should, be carried out whenever a performance problem or an opportunity for performance improvement arises. Thus any of Maier's three approaches can be used for these purposes in informal interactions throughout the year, as well as in formal appraisal interviews.

However, interactions which take place in the course of day-to-day management of staff may also have several other purposes. The manager is likely to have a wide variety of information, apart from feedback about performance, which could help the subordinate to do his or her job more effectively. Similarly, the manager will have a wide variety of other problems, apart from the subordinate's work performance, with which the subordinate may be able to help, either by providing relevant information or suggesting alternative solutions. Conversely, the subordinate may ask for the manager's help in solving a personal problem or demand action to resolve a grievance. Whilst Maier's three approaches were not originally intended for such purposes it would be possible to use one or more of them in each of these types of interaction. This function, however, would require considerable broadening of their scope. Furthermore, they may not represent the most appropriate approach in all circumstances.

Range of approaches and associated components

Maier describes only three types of appraisal interview. It is possible, though, to identify three other approaches which could be used either in appraisals or in other interactions between manager and subordinate. These we will call the Tell, the Ask and Tell and the Ask and Listen approaches. Moreover Maier indicates the skills required for his approaches only in very general terms. For example, he says that the Tell and Listen approach requires the skills of active listening, use of pauses, and reflecting and summarising feelings, but he does not indicate in any detail the questions and statements the manager would need to use either to influence behaviour or gather information. We feel that for purposes of skills development it is important to draw out such links between different approaches and the components which are required for their effective use. Our full list of approaches and their associated components is therefore as follows.

The Tell approach

Using the Tell approach, the manager simply informs the subordinate of his or her decision without first asking the subordinate for any opinions and without giving any specific reasons, arguments or other inducements for accepting it. The obvious component of this approach is the order, but requests, suggestions or advice may also be used (e.g. 'I must ask you to . . .', or 'I would strongly advise you not to . . .').

The successful use of the Tell approach relies heavily on the manager's ability to make correct decisions without checking them out with the subordinate and the subordinate's willingness to accept these decisions without question. Under certain conditions, both these requirements may be fulfilled. The manager is more likely to be able to make the right decision without consulting the subordinate in the following circumstances:

1. When the decision is simple, and the solution self-evident.
2. When the manager is an expert, and respected as such by the subordinate.
3. When there is an emergency, and the subordinate recognises that there is no time for detailed discussion or explanation.

The manager can also increase the probability of having made the right decision in the first place by thoroughly checking his or her facts and examining alternative interpretations or solutions.

Conditions which are likely to increase acceptability of the Tell approach to the subordinate (but not necessarily the validity of the decision) include the following:

1. An organisational climate in which giving orders is an accepted norm (e.g. the armed forces and emergency services).
2. Compliant subordinates who accept, or even prefer, an 'authoritarian' style.
3. Where the manager has high reward and/or punishment power, and is known to use this to reinforce his or her decisions.
4. Where the manager has much higher status in the organisation than the subordinate.

The main advantage of the Tell approach is that it saves time when rapid decisions have to be made. It can also be useful when other methods of behavioural influence have been used and resulted in irreconcilable differences of opinion. If the manager is convinced that his or her viewpoint is correct, then the Tell approach can be used to curtail further fruitless argument. In some cases, it may even be preferable to the subordinate to have an issue settled in this way, particularly if he or she has come to the conclusion that further discussion would be a waste of time because it would inevitably lead to the same decision whatever arguments were put forward.

The Tell approach may also appear to be a very convenient general technique for the management of people. It saves managers all the time and effort required to explain their decisions to their subordinates, find out what motivates them, examine alternative viewpoints, and so on. Yet for most purposes, the Tell approach has a number of serious drawbacks. Subordinates who do not know why they are doing something are much less able to react adaptively to unforeseen circumstances. Many will be less motivated to perform well if they do not understand the reasons for what they are doing. They may resent the manager simply telling them what to do, and either object openly or respond with reluctant compliance. Finally, the subordinates may have useful information or alternative suggestions which could have helped the manager to make a better decision in the first place.

We also suspect that it may be very tempting to underestimate the importance of these factors. It would be pleasant indeed to be able to believe that we can reach good decisions without needing help from other people, particularly subordinates, and that our subordinates hold us in such respect that they would be only too willing to implement our decisions without questions. Most of us no doubt have, at one time or another, encountered managers who believed this about themselves – and were quite wrong! The result is poor-quality decisions, grudgingly implemented and sometimes deliberately sabotaged. Unfortunately, being sure that one is right is no guarantee that one actually is, or that one's subordinates will be equally convinced. Except in an emergency or as a last resort, therefore, it appears more effective to use one of the other approaches.

The Tell and Sell approach

Using the Tell and Sell approach, the manager informs the subordinate of his or her decision, and then attempts to persuade the subordinate to accept it by pointing out its advantages, personal or organisational. Typically, this approach involves the use of orders, requests, advice or suggestions, followed by explanations, threats or promises. Other components commonly used are leading questions, evaluative statements, praise, criticism, inhibitors and summaries. Leading questions are used in an attempt to get the subordinate to express overt acceptance of the manager's viewpoint. Evaluative statements are used to indicate what the manager regards as admirable, useful, unacceptable, and so on. Praise is used in an attempt to get the subordinate in a 'good mood' so that he or she will be more prepared to listen to what the manager will have to say. Criticism is used to bring home to subordinates their responsibility for past failures and the need for future performance improvement. In a well-organised Tell and Sell, summaries will be used to draw together and emphasise the main points which the manager wishes to put across. The subordinate's role in all this is intended to be relatively passive. He or she is intended to listen attentively to what the manager has to say and then agree, preferably enthusiastically, with the manager's viewpoint, plans for future action, and so forth. If the subordinate attempts to contribute more, therefore, inhibitors are likely to be used in an attempt to prevent the subordinate from speaking and allow the manager to retain the speaking role. The gambit 'hammering the point home' might also be used as part of the Tell and Sell approach.

The main advantage of the Tell and Sell approach is that it can be brief and to the point, getting a relatively simple message across clearly and unequivocally. It can be useful with relatively inexperienced members of staff who have not yet had time to develop ideas of their own or with subordinates who prefer to be told, rather than be involved in participative decision making. It is also the most appropriate approach for disciplinary interviews where both the improvement in performance which is required, and the consequences of not achieving it within a certain time, need to be spelled out in detail.

Like the Tell approach, the effective use of Tell and Sell relies upon the ability of the manager to make the right decision in the first place. At the same time, with the Tell and Sell, the manager must also be sure that the subordinate will 'buy' whatever is being sold. This requires a good understanding of human motivation in general and also the particular needs of the subordinate in question. If the manager is able to identify inducements which are highly important to the subordinate and 'tie' their attainment to acceptance of the decision, then the result can be a highly motivated subordinate who knows precisely what he or she is expected to do.

Used inappropriately, the approach has two main limitations. First, it inhibits independent judgement. The subordinate may have useful contributions to make to the matter being discussed and this will not emerge as long as the manager adheres to a Tell and Sell approach. Also, allowing the subordinate to put forward his or her ideas, whether or not these are finally accepted, provides the manager with an opportunity to assess the subordinate's knowledge and judgement, and develop the subordinate's decision-making skills by giving feedback and guidance, evaluating alternative suggestions, and so on. Secondly, the Tell and Sell approach may not have the intended motivational effect with all subordinates. Some may simply not like to be told. Others may not like what they are told on a particular occasion or the way they are told it, or they may be indifferent to the inducements being offered. If the manager persists with the Tell and Sell approach under these circumstances, the interaction is likely to develop in one of two ways. The subordinate may express his or her disagreement overtly, resulting in a time-consuming and perhaps acrimonious argument. Alternatively, the subordinate may hide his or her disagreement and overtly accept the manager's decision, knowing that this is the quickest way of escaping from a potentially unpleasant situation. As a result, the subordinate has no commitment to the decision and it will be implemented with little enthusiasm, if at all. Worse still, if the manager is poor at reading nonverbal cues, he or she may not even realise that the interaction has failed to attain its intended objectives.

Tell and Listen

Using the Tell and Listen approach, the manager informs the subordinate of his or her decision, and then asks for the subordinate's views about it. Like the Tell and Sell approach, the manager typically begins the interaction using orders, requests, advice or suggestions, perhaps combined with evaluative statements, praise and criticism, but then in the 'listen' phase employs information-gathering components such as open questions, comparisons, hypotheticals, lubricators, and so on. Among the gambits, 'hammering the point home' may be used in the Tell phase and 'trap setting' during the Listen phase.

The advantage of this approach is that it can lead to decreased defensiveness and high levels of motivation on the part of some subordinates because they feel that their views have been taken into account. If the subordinates do express their views honestly, and this depends largely upon the manager's manner, the manager will not leave the interaction with a false impression of the subordinate's commitment. In addition, if the manager actually does take the subordinate's views into account, this may allow a better decision to be reached than if the manager took the decision on his or her own.

On the other hand, unless the outcomes of the interaction are well summarised at the end, there is a danger that their impact may be dissipated during the Listen phase. Thus the interaction may produce no clear-cut conclusions. There is also a danger that the subordinates may produce information or alternative suggestions during the Listen phase which totally invalidates what they have been told earlier, rendering the Tell phase a complete waste of time. Finally, past experience may tell the subordinate that the manager never really listens during the Listen phase or becomes annoyed if disagreement is expressed. The subordinate may therefore simply agree from expediency, leaving the manager with the false impression that his or her views have been accepted.

Ask and Tell

Using the Ask and Tell approach, the manager first obtains information from the subordinate concerning some problem area and then tells the subordinate what he or she has decided. The approach involves the initial use of information-gathering components, such as open questions, probes, hypotheticals, lubricators, restatements, and so on, followed by orders, requests, advice, suggestions or leading questions, and perhaps also evaluative statements, threats and promises to 'sell' the decision if necessary. Gambits such as the 'funnel technique', 'trap setting' and 'hammering the point home' may also be used.

There are several advantages to this approach. First, the information obtained from the subordinate during the preliminary Ask phase may enable the manager to reach a better decision than could otherwise have been achieved. The key to the approach is the fact that the manager gathers this information before revealing his or her own views. This means that subordinates are more likely to express honest opinions and feelings about the subject in question, rather than simply tell the manager what they think he or she wishes to hear. Furthermore, it makes it easier for the manager to revise an initial decision, on the basis of the subordinate's comments, without appearing to yield to pressure from the subordinate.

Secondly, the approach can produce higher levels of commitment to the decision on the part of the subordinate. Some subordinates may respond more favourably simply because they appreciate being consulted before the decision is made. Furthermore the manager can use the Ask phase to gauge how the subordinate feels about the subject, and is therefore in a much better position to select a way of telling and, if necessary, selling the decision which is likely to be acceptable to the subordinate. Lastly, the approach may, under certain circumstances, represent a quicker way of reaching a decision with a subordinate. Although time is required to obtain the subordinate's views in the first place, this may be less time-consuming than telling the subordinate first, only to discover that the subordinate has information which shows the manager's views to be mistaken or irrelevant to the real problem.

Potential limitations of the Ask and Tell approach include the following.

Firstly, even though the subordinate has been consulted beforehand, he or she may still not like the decision the manager has reached. The same problem could, of course, also occur with any of the variants of the Tell approach which we have already described. The particular problem with the Ask and Tell approach is that the subordinate may reveal his or her preferences quite strongly in the Ask phase, only to find the manager deciding that, on balance, some other solution is more appropriate. Some subordinates may feel more prepared to accept the decision because they have been consulted; others may not. Because the manager has asked their opinion and then 'ignored' it, some may in fact be more resentful than if they had never been asked in the first place.

Secondly, there is the question of the 'ownership' of the decision. Whilst the subordinate may have provided information which helped the manager to make the decision, the manager still made the decision itself and told the subordinate what it was. Even if the subordinate agrees with the decision, there is the possibility that he or she might be more committed to it if involved in actually making the decision rather than simply providing information which helped the manager to make it.

The Problem Solving approach

The Problem Solving approach is quite different from those we have previously discussed. The manager does not tell the subordinate what he or she has decided. Instead, they work as a team in order to identify the solution to a common problem. Ideally, status differences should be minimised so that each can provide information, suggest solutions, evaluate the other's contribution, propose alternative ways of tackling the problem, build on the other's ideas, and so on. A wide variety of verbal components is appropriate when using this approach. Any of the information-gathering components can be used to encourage the subordinate to contribute information, ideas, potential solutions, and so forth. Providing information, using components such as factual statements and feedback, may be needed to ensure that the subordinate has the necessary information to make an effective contribution. Behavioural influence components, such as advice, suggestions, promises and explanations, are also relevant, although orders, threats, criticism and leading questions should be avoided as these will tend to have an inhibiting effect. Techniques for handling emotion such as apologies and reflectives may be required when tackling sensitive problems in order to defuse any adverse emotional reactions which might otherwise render rational problem solving impossible. The 'double funnel' and 'causal analysis' can be used to draw out the subordinate's ideas. In particular, causal analysis can provide a useful way of analysing sensitive performance problems without arousing adverse emotional reactions.

Used in appropriate circumstances, the Problem Solving approach can have considerable benefits. It encourages the generation of new ideas and the discovery of novel solutions to problems. It is forward looking, and thus avoids the necessity of evaluating the subordinate or the subordinate's past performance and the resentment which can arise when past mistakes are criticised. The whole emphasis is on finding solutions to problems, and it is therefore likely to lead to clear-cut conclusions concerning the ways in which the problem can be avoided in the future. This in itself is likely to be motivational as far as the subordinate is concerned, and the fact that the solution is at least in part the subordinate's own may further increase commitment to it. In addition, use of the Problem Solving approach gives the subordinate the opportunity to practise problem-solving skills and receive feedback and guidance from the manager, which can enhance the development of these skills.

Inevitably, however, there are also situations in which the Problem Solving approach may not be appropriate. If the subordinate is young and inexperienced then he or she may not have any ideas concerning the ways in which the problem can be solved. Indeed, if participation in problem solving is invited in a way which suggests that the new subordinate *should* have sufficient knowledge to contribute ideas, this could even arouse anxiety. As we have already noted, some older and more experienced employees may prefer to be told rather than invited to participate. They may take the view that the manager receives extra pay and status for making decisions, so why should the manager expect them to do his or her job as well? Alternatively, the manager may know from past experience that, when invited to participate in problem solving, the subordinate comes up with impractical or organisationally unacceptable ideas and becomes resentful and unco-operative when these are not accepted. Thus the subordinate will have to be told eventually, if the problem is serious enough, and it would be better to start with a Tell, rather than raise false expectations that his or her views are likely to influence the decision.

The Problem Solving approach is also inappropriate when the manager has little room for manoeuvre with respect to the decision to be made. The manager may be constrained by orders from his or her boss, or have come to the conclusion that only one solution is possible on the basis of his or her own analysis of the situation. It would still be possible to use the Problem Solving approach to give an illusion of participation and, nevertheless, arrive at the manager's decision by pointing out flaws in each of the subordinate's suggestions until only the manager's solution remains. Ultimately, however, this is counterproductive, as the subordinate is almost certain to realise what is happening eventually, and become extremely resentful concerning both the dishonesty and the waste of his or her time involved.

The Ask and Listen approach

Using the Ask and Listen approach, the manager asks the subordinate about some problem area and listens to the replies without advancing opinions. This can be an appropriate technique in two main situations. First, it can be used to gather information which may help the manager to make a later decision. For example, the manager may wish to obtain the subordinate's views about a possible transfer some time in the future or obtain data and opinions about equipment performance in order to plan future purchasing policy. In other words, the decision cannot be made immediately, involves other people within the organisation, or is an inappropriate one for someone at the subordinate's level. Thus the best the manager can do is to assure the subordinate that his or her views will be taken into account and, where appropriate, that he or she will be informed of the decision as soon as possible. When using the Ask and Listen approach for this purpose, all the information-gathering components would be relevant, as would the 'funnel technique'.

Secondly, the other main use of the Ask and Listen approach is to give the subordinate the opportunity to talk about a problem which is causing him or her concern. As we have already noted, there is little point in trying to get someone who is emotional to solve a problem rationally. In addition, suggesting solutions before obtaining all the facts is likely to be ineffective, as the subordinate may then produce additional information showing the solution to be impractical. The discussion can then degenerate into a series of solutions suggested by the manager, each of which the subordinate shows to be inadequate for one reason or another. If the manager genuinely wishes to help, therefore, it is better to encourage the subordinate to talk about the problem without suggesting solutions until the subordinate has calmed down and/or explained the situation in detail. This is an extremely difficult technique. It involves asking questions, listening carefully to the answers, and refusing to be drawn into premature attempts to provide answers to the problem. The main emphasis is upon information-gathering components, particularly those which will encourage the subordinate to talk at length. Inhibitors should be avoided, as should probes if the subordinate is discussing some sensitive area which could cause resentment or embarrassment. Apologies and reflectives and the sensitive use of self-disclosure may also be useful techniques for reducing adverse emotional reactions should these occur. Ultimately, it may emerge that the problem is simply not solvable. However, the manager has at least given the subordinate the opportunity to talk about it and this is often comforting in itself. If, on the other hand, it appears that the problem may be solvable, then the manager can switch to one of the other approaches in an attempt to achieve a solution.

The Ask and Listen approach is, of course, inappropriate when there is a work problem to resolve which requires action on the part of the subordinate. Collecting information may be a necessary first step towards the solution of the problem, but it is only the first step. To ensure that the problem is solved rather than merely discussed, a clearly defined plan of action must be drawn up and the subordinate's commitment to it obtained. For this purpose, the Problem Solving approach or one of the Tell approaches would be more appropriate.

The various approaches we have discussed in this section are summarised in

Table 7.1. A brief description of their main advantages and disadvantages and a listing of the verbal components they typically employ are included in the table.

Consideration

The approaches we discussed in the previous section differ mainly with respect to the amount of influence which the manager is prepared to allow the subordinate to have over the content of an interaction and the decisions which are reached in it. There is another way, however, in which managers' approaches to interactions can vary. This is in the extent to which they show consideration for the subordinate's feelings and needs. Thus it would be possible to carry out each of the six approaches in a warm, friendly and concerned manner or in a harsh, cold and uncaring fashion. Note that we are not here concerned with the feelings of the manager, but his or her behaviour. The manager may have a high concern for the feelings and needs of subordinates but fail to show consideration in the interaction. It is the extent to which consideration is shown and its effect on the interaction with which we are concerned.

Both verbal and nonverbal cues are relevant here. As we have indicated, there is a range of questions and statements which can be used in any one type of interaction. In each case, however, it is possible to select alternative questions and statements which show greater or less consideration. For example, when using one of the various Tell approaches, it is possible to employ orders backed up with threats or to employ advice or requests supported by explanations. It may be that in reality the subordinate has no more freedom to disregard the advice or request than the order, but the effect on the subordinate's feelings and future behaviour could be quite different. Similarly, information gathering in the Tell and Listen, Ask and Tell and Ask and Listen approaches can be carried out using open questions, and others that encourage the subordinate to talk freely, or using probes, closed questions and leading questions, which could turn the interaction into an interrogation rather than a discussion.[2]

Even more important are the nonverbal cues. As we showed in Chapter 5, it is possible to show greater friendliness and minimise differences in status and power by such things as smiling, talking more softly, standing or sitting closer to the subordinate, sitting at the same side of the table or across the corner, not interrupting, looking towards the subordinate more when he or she speaks, looking less when one speaks oneself, and so on. Conversely, looking stern, talking loudly, interrupting, standing or sitting, staring at subordinates whilst one is speaking oneself, looking away more when the subordinate is speaking, and so on, will emphasise differences in status and show less friendliness towards the subordinate.

We also pointed out in Chapter 5 that verbal and nonverbal messages need

Table 7.1 *Approaches to manager–subordinate interactions*

Approach	Description	Potential advantages	Potential disadvantages	Typical components
Tell	The manager tells the subordinate the decision, without asking his or her opinions or giving any specific inducements to accept it.	Saves time, particularly in emergencies. May be useful as a last resort, when other methods fail.	Useful information may be ignored. Subordinates may resent the approach and be reluctant to comply.	Orders, requests, suggestions, advice.
Tell and Sell	The manager tells the subordinate the decision, pointing out the advantages of compliance and/or disadvantages of non-compliance.	Can be brief and to the point, getting the message over in a clear, precise and unequivocal manner.	Inhibition of independent judgement, defensiveness, overt conflict or passive acceptance without motivation to change.	Orders, explanations, requests, praise, threats, promises, leading, evaluative statements, inhibitors, criticism, summaries.
Tell and Listen	The manager tells the subordinate the decision then allows expression of his or her thoughts or feelings about it.	Decreased defensiveness, more favourable attitude towards the manager. Less resistance to change may result.	Can develop into cosy chat with no clear-cut conclusions. Overt conflict or passive acceptance may still occur.	Orders, requests, evaluative statements, praise, criticism, *then* open, comparisons, hypotheticals, lubricators.

Ask and Tell	The manager asks the subordinate for his or her views on a problem before telling him or her the decision.	Solution is less likely to be irrelevant. The subordinate may be more motivated for having been consulted.	Subordinate may still feel his or her solution to be better and resent being told what to do.	Open, probes, comparisons, hypotheticals, lubricators, closed, restatements, summary, *then* orders, requests, leading, threats, promises, evaluative statements.
Problem Solving	The manager and subordinate analyse a problem together and attempt to find a mutually acceptable solution.	Generation of new ideas, development of clear-cut solutions, subordinate highly motivated.	Subordinate may lack ideas, produce impractical or organisationally unacceptable solutions, or be unwilling to participate.	Open, probes, comparisons, hypotheticals, lubricators, bridges, restatements, summaries, praise, advice, explanations, reflectives, factual statements
Ask and Listen	The manager asks the subordinate to talk about some problem area and listens attentively.	Subordinate may feel much better for having discussed the problem. Useful information may be gained.	The basic problem may remain unresolved.	Open, comparisons, hypotheticals, lubricators, reflectives, self-disclosure

not be consistent with each other. So the nonverbal cues which accompany an order could soften its impact making it appear more like a request. On the other hand, other nonverbal cues accompanying a request could signal that the subordinate is expected to comply without question. Nevertheless, the combination of verbal and nonverbal cues can make a marked difference to the manner in which a manager conducts an interaction with a subordinate. For example, an interaction in which the manager uses orders, probes and closed questions said in a cold, superior way will be entirely different from one in which advice and suggestions are said in a warm, friendly way, even though the amount of participation allowed in decision making might be the same in both cases.

Again, which approach is more appropriate will depend on the circumstances. Two main factors are involved: the likely response of the subordinate, and the extent to which compliance is essential. Consideration tends to produce more satisfied subordinates.[3] Thus, if the subordinate will supply the information required or comply with the manager's wishes when asked in a considerate manner, there seems little point in risking the negative consequences which can result from having dissatisfied subordinates by using a less considerate approach. The danger of using a considerate approach, however, is that the subordinate may feel that because the manager is behaving in a friendly manner, he or she is not serious in expecting compliance or will not react too unfavourably if the subordinate decides not to conform to the manager's wishes. For example, Burns found that tactfully given instructions from superiors were interpreted as information or advice by the recipient,[4] and Argyle points out that, for all its advantages, the persuasive-democratic style can be very misleading to those who are not used to it.[5] A less considerate approach is therefore appropriate when both the following conditions apply. First, compliance on the part of the subordinate is essential, either because there is an emergency and there is no time for polite niceties or because the manager has thought the problem through and come to the conclusion that there would be serious repercussions if the subordinate does not respond in a certain way. Secondly, past experience has shown that the subordinate does not respond when treated with consideration, and will only comply with the manager's wishes when the latter 'lays it on the line' in a cold and business like manner.

Changing approach during an interaction

So far, we have assumed for the sake of convenience that the manager will use the same approach throughout an interaction with a subordinate. This need not necessarily be the case, however. Sometimes a change in approach may be appropriate because the subordinate does not respond as expected. Suppose, for example, the subordinate responds to a Tell and Sell approach by indicating that he or she does not accept the manager's interpretation of the situation. The manager may then Tell and Sell more vigorously, which can have adverse consequences in some circumstances (see 'win–lose' syndrome later). Alternatively, the manager may decide to try a different approach (e.g. Ask and Listen or Problem Solving) in order to accommodate the subordinate's views. Managers may also change approach during an interaction because they feel that different approaches provide more appropriate ways of handling differing topics during an interaction. For example, they may tell where compliance is essential (e.g. conforming with safety regulations), but Ask and Listen with respect to a problem of mutual interest (e.g. coping with effects of late deliveries).

To be able to change approaches in this way requires a higher level of interpersonal skills than the mere mastery of each approach in isolation. In particular, it requires the sophisticated use of bridges, not only between topics, but also and simultaneously between approaches and the manner in which the interaction is conducted. If handled badly, such a transition could affect the interaction adversely. The subordinate may resent being asked at one moment, only to be told the next, because his or her responses were not what the manager wanted to hear. However, managers with greater interpersonal skills are likely to be more flexible, and have the ability to use a variety of different approaches within the same interaction, moving smoothly from one to the other.

Syndromes

The approaches which we have described represent the manager's intentions with respect to an interaction. Inevitably, things do not always work out as intended. For example, the manager may intend to Tell and Sell, but the subordinate may not listen to what the manager has to say and refuse to accept any of the manager's solutions. Faced with this kind of situation, the interpersonally skilled manager will be able to adapt his or her approach and/or the related verbal and nonverbal components, and thus still carry out a successful interaction. A less skilful manager, on the other hand, may find that an approach is not working, but fail to find a way of remedying the situation, resulting in an interaction which conspicuously fails to meet his or her objectives.

In our experience, approaches which go wrong often go wrong in very similar ways. Thus it is possible to identify certain recognisable types of interaction which occur when the approach selected by the manager fails to work as intended. We have called these 'failed interactions syndromes', their symptoms being the cluster of components and structural devices typically associated with them. Some of the syndromes which we have encountered in the course of interpersonal skills training are given below. In each case, we have described what we believe to be the underlying cause of the syndrome, its primary symptoms, and actions which can be taken to rectify the situation.

The preconceived ideas syndrome

Underlying cause
The manager has already decided what the facts of the case and the required solution(s) are before an interaction with a subordinate begins.

Major symptoms

- Leading questions (to gain compliance with preconceived ideas).
- Closed questions (to tidy up any major points of detail).
- Inhibitors (to prevent the subordinate from talking at length on 'irrelevant' matters).
- Not listening.
- Interrupting.
- Talking much more than the subordinate.

Remedial action
Syndrome level Treating information as hypothesis rather than fact.
Symptom level

- More open questions (to get subordinate talking).
- More lubricators (to keep subordinate talking).
- More restatements (to check understanding of points raised by the subordinate).
- Active listening (particularly listening and watching for nonverbal cues of agreement, disagreement, surprise, frustration, and so on, as well as the verbal content).

The recycling syndrome

Underlying cause
The manager has not thought through the ramifications of the problem areas before the discussion and feels that he or she needs more time to think, or is unwilling to face up to the emotional conflict which might arise if problem areas are probed too deeply.

Major symptoms

- The manager moves on to another topic before coming to an agreed conclusion concerning the topic under discussion.
- The manager periodically returns to the same topic or topics, interspersed with discussions of other subjects.
- The subordinate may reintroduce topics left unfinalised by the manager.
- Either (a) there is no summary of agreed future actions (because none exists); or (b) when the manager attempts to summarise, the subordinate objects that he or she never agreed to these actions.

Remedial action
Syndrome level

- Thinking likely problem areas through before the discussion.
- Being more prepared to face up to emotional conflict (a largely useless piece of advice unless backed up with training on *how* to do it at the technique level).
- Delaying closure on a topic until a full agreed solution is arrived at.

Symptom level

- More probes (to obtain detailed information about the problem area under discussion).
- More restatements (to ensure that the manager is sure he or she understands the subordinate's point of view).
- More tolerance of silence on part of manager (to allow subordinate 'thinking time' or force the latter to talk).
- More time spent on defining what the problem is.
- Greater participation by the subordinate in problem definition and solution.
- Use of causal analysis (as means of avoiding defensive reactions on part of subordinate).
- Use of funnel and double funnel to lead to specific outcomes.
- Practice in use of reflectives (to increase confidence in ability to handle emotional reactions should they arise).

The shopping-list syndrome

Underlying cause
The manager has decided that there are a number of key points to be covered and arranges them in a (to him or her) logical order. These points are then worked through in a mechanical fashion. Underlying this may be a lack of faith in his or her own skills, or a desire to cover too much ground in the time available, leading to a desire to have everything cut and dried beforehand.

Major symptoms

- The interaction moves at a relatively high speed covering a lot of points, none in any great depth.
- Multiples.
- Inhibitors (to prevent the subordinate deviating from the pre-arranged order).
- Interruptions (as above).
- Closed questions.
- Not listening.
- Premature closure on superficial solutions.
- Signs of frustration and/or non-acceptance on the part of the subordinate.

Remedial action

Syndrome level Treating plans as agendas, which are useful as guides or checklists, but which need not be rigidly adhered to.

Symptom level

- Asking the subordinate to suggest items for the agenda (e.g. 'Here is what I would like to talk about . . .. Is there anything else you think we should discuss in this meeting?').
- More open questions (to elicit the subordinate's views).
- Lubricators (to keep him/her talking).
- Active listening.
- Closure delaying techniques (e.g. 'Before we move on, is there anything else we should discuss on this subject?').
- Interim summaries with checks at end of each section (e.g. 'What we seem to have agreed so far is that . . .. Would you agree?').

The win–lose syndrome

Underlying causes

This type of interaction can arise for a number of reasons; for example:

1. The manager views interactions with subordinates as a contest which he or she is determined to win and encounters a subordinate who is unwilling to back down.
2. The manager wishes to have a constructive interaction in which he or she helps the subordinate to improve his or her performance, and believes that the first step is to get the subordinate to recognise and admit to his or her current failings. The subordinate refuses to do so, and the manager is afraid of losing face if he or she backs down, or gets annoyed with the 'unco-operative' subordinate, and an argument develops.

Major symptoms

- Emotional reactions on the part of both manager and subordinate.
- Neither is willing to accept the validity of the other's statements.
- A large number of critical statements.
- A little praise, and what there is is general and qualified (e.g. 'Overall, you have done quite well, but . . .').
- Closed questions and leading statements (e.g. 'You must realise that . . .').
- Interruptions.
- Inhibitors.
- Little use of requests, explanations and promises which, if used at all, rapidly decline when not accepted by the subordinate.
- A large number of orders and threats.
- Trap setting.

Remedial action

Syndrome level
Look for solutions which are win–win (i.e. will benefit both the manager and subordinate).

Symptom level

- More open questions, comparison, hypotheticals, lubricators, restatements, and so on (to gain an understanding of the subordinate's viewpoint).
- Active listening (as above).
- Greater use of detailed praise, explanations, requests, advice, and so forth.
- Replace criticism with causal analysis as a means of introducing the subject of performance improvement; employ double funnel.
- Use of reflectives, apologies as a means of handling emotional reactions if they arise.

Cosy chat syndrome

Underlying causes
The manager (a) does not believe the problem is sufficiently serious to merit much attention and is merely paying lip-service to it; or (b) feels he or she lacks skills to handle the interaction effectively, and probably fears an adverse reaction from the subordinate should he or she attempt to do so; or (c) wants to maintain an image of being a nice person.

Major symptoms

- Open questions with no follow through (e.g. 'How are things going in general?' . . . 'Everything alright?' . . . 'Good!').
- General praise.
- Vague promises.
- Rapid switch to more 'comfortable' topics, such as the weather, sport or office politics.

Remedial action
Syndrome level

- If the problem is genuinely not serious, none.
- If it is serious, attempt to influence the motivation of the manager (e.g. by carrying out a behavioural influence interview with the manager).

   or

- Provide interpersonal skills training for the manager.

Symptom level
Greater precision in use of all components.

The good information gatherer

Underlying cause
The manager has excellent information-gathering skills but, once having gathered the information, does nothing with it.

Major symptoms

- Skilful use of a wide variety of information-gathering components ('Tell me about it').
- Manager does not initiate any discussion of future actions to improve performance of the subordinate.
- Manager does not take up any attempts by subordinate to discuss ways of improving performance.

Remedial action
Syndrome level
Re-examination of objectives of discussion, to draw out the importance of emphasis on behavioural influence.

Symptom level

- Identification of possible areas of performance improvement and ways to achieve it, before the interaction.
- Use of information-gathering skills to identify areas where the subordinate feels he or she could improve his or her performance (e.g. 'What do you think you might have done differently?'); use of double funnel and causal analysis.
- Where the subordinate cannot solve his or her own problems, the use of behavioural influence components to persuade the subordinate to change his or her behaviour in the desired direction.
- Use of restatements and summaries to ensure agreement concerning performance problems and future courses of action.

The bought 'easy ride' syndrome

Underlying cause
The manager wishes to have as painless an interaction as possible, and therefore identifies what the subordinate wants and gives it to him or her unconditionally.

Major symptoms

- A large amount of recognition and general praise.
- Promises given as a 'gift'.
- No discussion of performance improvement.

Remedial action

Syndrome level

A recognition that increasing job satisfaction will not necessarily improve performance.

Symptom level

- Use of information-gathering skills to identify and agree areas where performance improvement could be achieved, and specific ways to achieve it.
- Where necessary, use of behavioural influence skills to obtain commitment to the ways for performance improvement.

The main use which we would envisage for these syndromes is in interpersonal skills training. Often, advice on how to improve interpersonal skills can be given in terms of components, the way the interaction is structured or the approach taken. For example, supposing a tutor wishes to give feedback to a leadership trainee who has just carried out a practice interaction which did not achieve its objectives. The interviewee asked many closed and leading questions, interrupted a great deal, did not listen to what the 'subordinate' had to say, and thus missed important information, resulting in mistaken or irrelevant conclusions being drawn. The tutor feels that the interaction could have been more productive had the manager used more open questions and probes, listened more closely to the subordinate, let the subordinate finish what he or she had to say, and taken the subordinate's views into account in deciding future courses of action. This is quite a lot to remember as a set of unrelated data. However, material is much easier to remember if it is both organised and meaningful, and the components used in an interaction, even a failed one, are often related in some way. In the case we have been discussing, for example, the trainee may have behaved as we have described because of a mistaken belief that he or she already knew the 'facts' of the case and what should be done to solve the problem, and therefore did not need to obtain any further information from the subordinate.

Thus the task of improving interpersonal skills can be tackled not only in terms of verbal and nonverbal components, but also as a syndrome ('preconceived ideas'). This has a number of advantages. First, it provides a unifying explanatory concept which will enable the trainee to remember and recognise the various undesirable symptoms more readily. Secondly, if the trainee understands the underlying problem, then this may assist the achievement of a solution. For example, the concept of treating data as hypotheses rather than established facts provides a rationale for the substitution of information-gathering components for those previously used. Not only will this help the manager to remember them, but he or she may also be led by this strategy to use other appropriate information-gathering components or gambits, in addition to those specifically mentioned by the tutor. Finally, and most importantly, understanding why the previous behaviour was inappropriate in a certain set of circumstances, and why another approach would be more successful, will enable the manager to be more skilful in selecting the right approach in future. Simply telling a trainee to stop using leading and closed questions and use more open questions and lubricators is not very good advice because he or she will undoubtedly encounter situations where closed and leading questions are appropriate, and open questions and lubricators are inappropriate (e.g. 'cosy chat' syndrome).

Conclusions

In this chapter we have looked at various ways of describing a manager's overall approach to an interaction with a subordinate. We have suggested that this can vary with respect to the amount of influence which the manager is prepared to allow the subordinate, and the consideration which the manager shows towards the subordinate during the interaction. Finally, we described some typical examples of unsuccessful interactions, and suggested ways in which they can be avoided or the situation rectified if they do occur.

We realise that by including 'approaches' in our model of the interpersonal skills of leadership, we are getting close to reintroducing the concept of leadership style which we criticised earlier. There is, however, an important difference. As we have already pointed out, leadership style theorists describe leadership behaviour only in very general terms. They do not identify the specific behaviours that are associated with any one style. The approaches described in this chapter, on the other hand, are closely associated with the use of certain verbal and nonverbal components and structural devices. These approaches are therefore in a sense merely a convenient shorthand way of referring to commonly occurring clusters of such components and structural devices.

Moreover our approach emphasises leadership as a skill, considering not only what leaders do, but how well they do it. As we noted in Chapter 1, we would regard the interpersonally skilled leader as one who:

1. has a wide variety of verbal components (question and statement types) at his or her disposal and is able to select the one most appropriate for the situation and particular purpose at hand, and perform it well, with the appropriate nonverbal cues;
2. is able to structure interactions effectively by linking these components into purposeful sequences which impel the interaction towards its objective(s); and
3. is able to develop an approach to the interaction that is appropriate to the objectives in question and the probable reactions of the subordinate.

In leadership training, the interactions between these levels are of particular importance. It is of little use attempting to change a manager's overall approach unless the component skills are also taught or in some way developed. It is all very well persuading an authoritarian manager that a Tell and Sell approach is not always appropriate and that he or she should use a more participative Problem Solving approach under certain circumstances. However, unless the manager knows and can use effectively the components of a participative approach (e.g. open questions, reflectives), he or she is unlikely to make a *good* participative manager. One may simply exchange an inappropriate style done well for an appropriate style poorly done, and it is anyone's guess which would be the more ineffective. Equally, however, attempting to improve leadership skills in terms of components alone also has its limitations. Without higher-level unifying concepts, trainees are reduced to learning an apparently random list of techniques, which is likely both to make the task more difficult and to reduce the motivation to learn. Concentration at any level of analysis, to the exclusion of others, is therefore likely to impair the effectiveness of leadership skills training.

In the next chapter we will examine the acquisition and development of leadership skills in more detail.

Exercise 7.1
Analysis of an interaction

This is an integrative exercise designed to provide an opportunity to review some of the main points concerning verbal leader behaviour from Chapters 4, 6 and 7. Analyse the interaction below between Bill Bean (administration manager) and Victor Ridsdale (office manager), one of Bill Bean's subordinates, in the following terms:

1. Classify the questions and statements used by the manager (BB), giving the name of each in the right-hand margin.
2. Make a brief note in the right-hand margin of anything that happened in the interaction which you think had a significant effect on what was achieved in the interaction or was a significant indication of what was achieved. This might be actions by the interviewer that had a beneficial or detrimental effect, or reactions on the part of the interviewee. A single word or brief phrase will suffice (e.g. 'Ignores Victor's comments' or 'Compliance!').
3. On a separate sheet(s) of paper:
   (a) comment on the structure of the interaction;
   (b) comment on the approach or approaches to the interaction taken by the manager;
   (c) summarise the main learning points for the manager, identifying as precisely as possible:
      (i) those things which were done well; and
      (ii) what the interviewer might do differently in future in order to become more effective in such interactions.

The numbers in the right–hand margin can be used to identify specific locations in the text where this would be useful.

Interaction

BB. Come in, Victor. Sit down. I thought we should have   001
a chat about how things have been going recently. You   002
probably know why.   003

VR. Well, er, no. Not really.   004

BB. Well, there have been a couple of incidents I think   005
we need to discuss. There's the question of   006
confidentiality for one. And another is the   007
complaints we have been getting about the information   008
which has been missing from the management information   009
system recently.   010

VR. Well, I've . . .   011

BB. But before we get to that, how are things generally?   012

VR. In what way?   013

BB. I mean, how are things in the office? Have you got   014
any problems with the staff? How are you getting   015
on with other departments? Are you happy with the   016
way things have been going recently?   017

VR. Well, naturally I wasn't very happy about not being   018
able to take the admin manager's job at Widnes, but   019
I don't think it has affected my work in any way.   020

BB. Mmm. You said at the time that you turned the job   021
down for personal reasons. If I'm not intruding,   022
could I ask you what the problem was?   023

VR. Oh, it was just the fact that the children are settled   024
and they've got some important exams coming up, and we   025
thought that we shouldn't disrupt them at this stage.   026

BB. So it was a conflict between accepting promotion and   027
the needs of the children?   028

VR. Exactly. And I felt that the needs of the children   029
had to come first. But that doesn't mean that I'm no   030
longer interested in promotion.   031

BB. But it does mean that it would have to be in the   032
Southampton area, at least for the time being?   033

VR. Yes, until the children are a bit older.   034

BB. Well, if you are looking for an admin manager's job,   035
you would have to wait for me to vacate my job.   036

Naturally, I'm interested in promotion too, but I 037
can't say when that is likely to happen. So, if you 038
are looking for promotion in the near future, it will 039
probably have to be in a different area. Are there 040
any other jobs at Southampton you might be interested 041
in? 042

VR. I haven't really thought. 043

BB. What is it that you most enjoy in your present job? 044

VR. The creative side. Developing systems. 045

BB. So, if we could find something which involved 046
developing new systems, say organisation and methods, 047
or something like that, you might be interested? 048

VR. (*noticeably brightening*) Well, yes, I would. 049

BB. OK. I'll talk to Personnel about whether there are 050
any jobs available in that kind of area and ask them 051
to keep me posted about any vacancies which come up. 052
In the meantime, you have a think in more detail about 053
the kind of job you are interested in, and we'll have 054
another discussion when we've had a chance to put a 055
few ideas together. How does that sound? 056

VR. Great. I'll look forward to that. 057

BB. But we still have to sort out your current 058
performance or you won't have any future career 059
prospects to look forward to. 060

VR. I'm not sure I understand. I haven't felt my 061
performance has been all that bad recently, except 062
perhaps for . . . 063

BB. Well, there was that business of letting out the 064
confidential information about the promotion of one 065
of the members of technical department. 066

VR. Yes. I'm really sorry about that. I thought what I 067
was doing was for the best, but it backfired on me. I 068
have really learned my lesson on that one, and I can 069
assure you that it won't happen again. I can only 070
apologise for any embarrassment that I might have 071
caused. 072

BB. Well, as long as you've learned your lesson, we'll say 073
no more about it. But that's not been your only 074
failing over the year. There were the complaints 075
about the missing information from the management 076
information system. 077

VR. I put some of the items back, like you said.   078

BB. Some, Victor?   079

VR. Well, most of them, but as you said earlier, we are   080
overloaded at times, and . . .   081

BB. Look, Victor, what do you think is the most important   082
aspect of your job?   083

VR. Saving money?   084

BB. Well, it is possible to put too much emphasis on   085
saving money, isn't it, Victor. After all, it was   086
trying to save money which got you into trouble   087
before, when you stopped the bonus payments for the   088
process workers.

VR. (*angrily*) Look, that wasn't altogether my fault.   089
You never gave me a chance to explain what happened.   090
Maybe I could have handled it better, but other   091
people made mistakes as well, and if everyone else   092
had done their job properly, there would have been no   093
need for me to get involved in the first place.   094

BB. You obviously feel upset about this.   095

VR. Yes, I do. I was acting in good faith, trying to do   096
my best for the company, and what happens. Something   097
goes wrong and Victor gets all the blame.   098

BB. Perhaps you should tell me your side of things.   099

VR. Well, what happened was, I was approached by the head   100
of the Wages section. He wanted advice on a note you   101
had initialled, authorising a bonus payment for six   102
process workers.   103

BB. Mmm. And why did he come to you?   104

VR. He'd tried to contact the Personnel manager, but he   105
was out, so he came to see me in case I knew anything   106
about it.   107

BB. And what exactly was the problem?   108

VR. The thing that was puzzling him was that although you   109
had initialled the note authorising double-time   110
payment, from the hours they had worked, they should   111
only have been paid time and a half. So it seemed   112
likely there had been a mistake somewhere. Of course,   113
it turned out later that it was a special rate which   114
had been negotiated for a one-off job, but I didn't   115
know that at the time.   116

BB. So what did you do? 117

VR. I advised him to delay payment until you got back. 118
I thought that if there had been a mistake, we would 119
never get the money back once it had been paid, so it 120
would be better to delay payment until you could sort 121
it out. 122

BB. Fine, I can see now why you did it. But what effect 123
did this have? 124

VR. Well, the process workers were upset and there was 125
nearly a walk-out. 126

BB. So what would have been worse for the company, losing 127
the money or having a strike? 128

VR. On balance, I suppose the strike. In the end, they 129
didn't go on strike, but if they had, it would have 130
cost the company a lot more money than the additional 131
bonus. I can see that now, but at the time, I didn't 132
see what else I could do. 133

BB. Well, was there anyone else you could have consulted, 134
apart from the Personnel manager? 135

VR. The process workers' boss, I suppose, or anyone else 136
in the Personnel department who might know what was 137
going on. 138

BB. Fine, so if a similar situation arose again, what 139
would you do differently? 140

VR. Think more about the consequences of my actions and 141
consult more before making a decision. 142

BB. That's it in a nutshell. You've got the point 143
exactly. Anything else you want to add? 144

VR. Well, if you could inform me about any special 145
bonuses or anything unusual which is likely to come up 146
when you are going to be away, that would be useful. 147

BB. Good idea. I'll make a note of that. So, let's get 148
back to the management information system. You 149
mentioned saving money as one of your primary 150
functions, but there is something more important than 151
that isn't there? 152

VR. Providing a service? 153

BB. Exactly. And we are not providing a service if the 154
managers we are supposed to keep informed complain 155
that they are not getting the information they need, 156
are we? 157

vr. Well, no, I suppose not. But I'm convinced they	*158*
don't use all the data. Some of it probably goes	*159*
straight into the bin.	*160*
bb. It may well do, Victor, but it's not your job to	*161*
decide what information the managers should want. If	*162*
you want to cut down on the amount of information you	*163*
distribute, you will have to consult the managers	*164*
first. Look, I think we can solve the problem quite	*165*
simply. Go round the managers you distribute the	*166*
information to. Find out what information they want	*167*
and what information they don't want. If there is any	*168*
information they don't want, you can eliminate it, but	*169*
if they say they do want it, it has to go in. That	*170*
way we should keep everyone happy. OK?	*171*
vr. Yes, I suppose I could do that.	*172*
bb. Good, I think that covers everything. I'm glad we've	*173*
had this chat. I think we have managed to get several	*174*
important matters sorted out. I don't want you to get	*175*
the wrong impression. I think that overall your	*176*
performance is quite good, but there have been these	*177*
one or two lapses recently which have been a little	*178*
worrying. However, if you can put into practice what	*179*
we have agreed in this meeting, make sure that there	*180*
are no further breaches of confidentiality, make sure	*181*
that the managers are getting the information they	*182*
need through the management information system, and	*183*
be a little less hasty in your decision making, then	*184*
I don't think we will have any problems in future.	*185*
And as I said, I will see Personnel about other	*186*
possible jobs which might interest you in the	*187*
Southampton area. OK?	*188*
vr. Yes. Thanks very much.	*189*
bb. Thanks for coming in, Victor. I think it's been a	*190*
very constructive discussion.	*191*

A model answer to this exercise is given in Appendix VII.

Notes and references

1. N. R. F. Maier (1958), 'Three types of appraisal interview', *Personnel*, **54**, 27–40.
2. Folger found that interviewees perceived closed questions as being more

dominant than open questions. See J. P. Folger (1980), 'The effects of vocal participation and questioning behavior on perceptions of dominance', *Social Behavior and Personality*, **2**, 203–7.
3. G. A. Yukl (1989), *Leadership in Organizations*, Prentice Hall.
4. T. Burns (1954), 'The directions of activity and communication in a departmental executive group: a quantitative study in a British engineering factory with a self-recording technique', *Human Relations*, **7**, 73–97.
5. M. Argyle (1975), *Bodily Communication*, Methuen.

CHAPTER 8

The acquisition and development of leadership skills

Introduction

Previous chapters have been concerned with developing an understanding of the interpersonal skills of leadership. In this chapter we shall concentrate upon the development of the skills themselves. Like other complex skills, interpersonal skills require *practice* to achieve a high level of performance.

However, practice is not in itself sufficient to produce an improvement in skilled performance. Feedback is also necessary. Without feedback the trainee cannot assess whether any further improvement in performance is desirable and, if so, what forms it should take. There are two main forms of feedback, intrinsic and extrinsic. Intrinsic feedback arises directly from the task itself; for example, asking a question and listening to the kind of response one receives. Extrinsic feedback, on the other hand, comes from some external source, such as a tutor, one's boss or colleagues. Extrinsic feedback is particularly important in the early stages of skills development, when the trainee may not be sure which aspects of performance he or she should be attending to, but intrinsic feedback becomes more important as the skill develops.[1]

Formal training courses, designed to provide practice with feedback and guidance from skilled tutors, represent one of the most effective ways of acquiring interpersonal skills, particularly in the early stages of skills development. In this chapter, though, we shall be concerned as much with the *self*-development of leadership skills as with their acquisition through formal training. To provide a framework for our discussion we shall first describe a model of manager–subordinate interactions, which identifies the key interpersonal variables involved and the relationships between them.

A model of manager–subordinate interactions

Figure 8.1 presents a model, setting out what we consider to be the interpersonal variables which strongly influence manager–subordinate interactions. It is intended to help both individual managers and tutors on formal training courses to analyse the processes involved in manager–subordinate

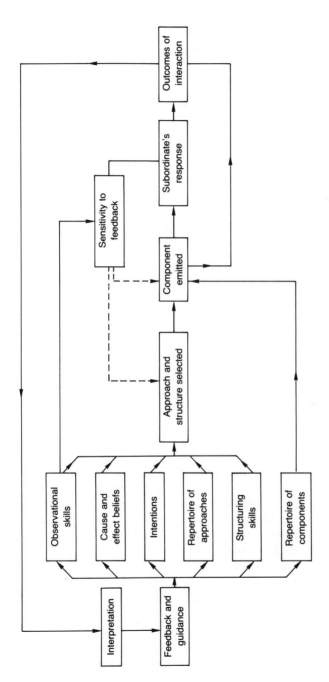

Figure 8.1 *Interaction and tutoring processes in manager–subordinate interactions*

interactions and to identify the specific aspects of the manager's behaviour which are tending to produce less satisfactory outcomes.

The model suggests that the behaviour of a manager in an interaction with a subordinate can be described in the following terms:

- The manager's general approach to the interaction (e.g. Ask and Listen, Tell and Sell, and so on).
- The way in which the manager structures the interaction (i.e. diffuse or organised).
- The actual verbal and nonverbal components used with such an approach/ structure (e.g. open questions, probes, orders).

The actual approach, structure and components selected by the manager will depend on a number of factors. The range of options open to the manager will be determined by his or her:

1. *Repertoire of approaches* The number of different approaches the manager is capable of utilising well.
2. *Structuring skills* The ability to develop an effective interaction structure, either before or during the interaction.
3. *Repertoire of components* The number of different components the manager is capable of utilising well.

Within the range of options available, the choice of approach, structure and components is likely further to be influenced by the manager's:

4. *Intentions* What the manager wishes to achieve from the interaction (e.g. gather information, solve a performance problem, listen to a grievance, deliver a reprimand).
5. *Cause-and-effect beliefs* The manager's expectations that using a particular approach, structure or type of component will lead the subordinate to respond in a certain way, thus producing certain outcomes, desirable or undesirable. An example of such a belief might be: 'If I tell subordinates exactly what is expected of them, and point out the rewards and punishment involved, they will know where they stand, and do as they are told.' Such beliefs may be conscious or unconscious, and clearly or vaguely articulated. One overriding belief which will influence the way the manager conducts the interaction is whether he or she believes there is only one correct way to conduct manager–subordinate interactions. Obviously, a manager who believes this is likely to have a narrow repertoire of approaches, structures and components.
6. *Observational skills* The manager's ability to interpret the subordinate's manner at the beginning of the interaction, particularly nonverbal signals of mood indicating whether he or she is enthusiastic, depressed, angry, apathetic and so on. Depending on the manager's cause-and-effect beliefs, such signals, if picked up, may lead the manager to depart from the planned or usual way of conducting the interaction.

Having selected a particular approach, structure and component to initiate the interaction, the manager uses the component, and the subordinate then responds. This response provides an important part of the intrinsic feedback (that arising directly from the task itself). In addition, feedback is also available to the manager concerning his or her own behaviour (e.g. the manager's own tone of voice, phrasing of questions, manner, and so on) as it appears to him- or herself. The extent to which such feedback is actually registered will be dependent on his or her observational skills – the ability to recognise such things as signs of acceptance or rejection on the part of the subordinate or the vaguely phrased question on the part of the manager. Another factor will be the manager's skill in using different approaches, structures and components. The more skilled the manager, the more he or she will be able to select and perform them without conscious thought, and the more attention this will leave available for observing intrinsic feedback.

If relevant intrinsic feedback is registered by the manager, this may lead him or her to modify the approach, interaction structure, or type of component used. On the other hand, less sensitive managers, or those who are insufficiently flexible to change their approach mid-interaction, may ignore quite obvious feedback (hence the dotted lines in Figure 8.1). Other sources of inflexibility are the manager's cause-and-effect beliefs and skill in handling different approaches. Thus the manager may register the subordinate's adverse responses, but ignore them because he or she either believes that the approach taken is the only effective way to treat subordinates or does not know how to handle the situation differently.

By the end of the interaction, certain outcomes will have resulted, of which three types may be distinguished and may occur either singly or in combination:

1. *Motivational/emotional* The subordinate – and manager – may feel enthusiastic or apathetic, satisfied or dissatisfied, and so on, with respect to the conduct of the interaction or what it achieved.
2. *Informational* Did the manager and subordinate obtain from each other in a precise form any information which they may have required?
3. *Behavioural* Did the manager agree on a precise set of actions – to be carried out either by manager or subordinate, or both – to rectify any performance problem which has been identified?

Formal training courses in the interpersonal skills of leadership

As we noted earlier, formal training courses which provide an opportunity to practise with feedback and guidance from skilled tutors, represent one of the most effective ways of developing interpersonal skills. They have two main advantages. First, they allow the trainee to practise the skills in a relatively risk-free, supportive environment, away from the manager's daily routine. Typically, such courses use role-playing exercises which allow the individual to practise a skill in a situation which approximates to real life, and receive feedback on his or her performance, without the disruptive effect this might have on real-life relationships. Furthermore, research which has been carried out into interpersonal skills training using role-playing shows that new skills are acquired which do transfer to the workplace.[2] A more detailed description of a typical course using the 'Bradford Approach' to interpersonal skills training is given in Appendix VIII.[3] The second major advantage of formal training courses is that they allow the manager to obtain feedback and guidance from a skilled tutor. Such feedback and guidance is likely to be of a higher quality and more pertinent than that obtained through self-analysis or from fellow managers or other untrained observers. The result is that early learning is likely to take place at a more rapid pace. People who are relatively unskilled, either at the activity in question or in giving feedback, can still provide helpful feedback. Nevertheless, they are unlikely to be able to pinpoint quite so accurately as a skilled tutor, the precise learning point which the manager most needs to work on next.

A number of factors are involved here. First, there is the question of selectivity. Of all the things which happened in the course of the interaction, which had most effect on what was or was not achieved? Similarly, of all the things which the trainee *could* improve, which should be worked on *next*? Secondly, there is the question of interpretation. A recorded playback of an interaction may reveal *what* happened but not *why*. Suppose a manager uses a moderately forceful Tell and Sell approach and merely achieves the reluctant compliance of the subordinate. The manager may assume that this was because he or she did not put his or her ideas forcefully enough and was too lenient. An alternative, and perhaps more valid, interpretation might be that the manager expressed his or her ideas *too* forcefully, and the subordinate might have been more committed had he or she been allowed to contribute more to the discussion.

Finally, there is the question of the action(s) to be taken to improve performance in similar situations in future. Again, differing views are possible. The manager in the previous example may feel that he or she should be less soft in future and immediately stamp on any attempt by the subordinate to take control of the interaction. An alternative view might be that, under certain circumstances, it would be better to allow the subordinate to participate in making decisions rather than simply telling him or her what to do. In other words, the mere availability of feedback does not necessarily mean that a trainee will be able to make good use of it. Indeed, if the trainee draws inappropriate conclusions from the feedback or becomes demoralised because he or she cannot see how to improve an apparently inadequate performance, then detailed feedback may even be counterproductive. It is for this reason that the help of a skilled tutor is invaluable in the early stages of skills acquisition.

We would suggest that the interpersonal skills tutor has two main functions. The first is an immediate function of helping the trainee to decide what should be worked on next to improve performance and what should be done differently in order to achieve this improvement. In part, this will involve giving or eliciting feedback about what happened in the interaction and why, but in moving from this stage to what should be done to improve performance in future, we have moved imperceptibly from feedback to guidance. In our view, this is one of the primary functions of the interpersonal skills tutor. Unless the trainee has a clear idea of what to do next in order to perform better, then he or she is unlikely to improve to any great extent.

The particular aspects of performance selected to work on next will depend not only on their influence on the trainee's performance, but also on the trainee's ability to make significant improvements in these areas at this stage of his or her skill development. It may be better to improve a relatively minor skill than attempt to rectify a major shortcoming and fail. Similarly, the number of improvements attempted needs careful thought. If too many different steps are identified, this may both confuse and demoralise the trainee; two or three things to work on at a time is usually sufficient. The specific points selected for feedback and guidance may relate to any of the processes identified in our model of manager–subordinate interactions. Thus the manager could be given feedback concerning the approach and interaction structure selected, the components used, the way in which the subordinate responded, the extent to which the manager appeared to adapt to these responses, and the outcomes apparently achieved by the end of the interaction. Next, any relationships between these processes could be drawn out. For example, were the subordinate's responses during the interaction the result of the particular approach, structure or components used? Did lack of sensitivity to feedback lead to important information being missed? Did the outcomes achieve the intentions the manager had at the beginning of the interaction? As noted previously, such feedback is likely to be highly selective. Particular aspects of the interaction will be chosen to be discussed, but the tutor needs to be able to understand and monitor all of them in order to make an appropriate choice.

Lastly, the tutor may give guidance on how to conduct a more effective interaction should similar circumstances arise again. Such guidance can be classified in terms of the factors listed in Figure 8.1 that determine the type of interaction the manager chooses to carry out, as follows:

- *Observational skills* Guidance on whether the manager needs to pay more attention to nonverbal cues, which cues to watch out for, what they signify, and so on.
- *Cause-and-effect beliefs* Guidance on which approaches, structures and components are more appropriate for different purposes, people and situations.

- *Intentions* Guidance on whether certain intentions are appropriate in certain circumstances; for example, the purposes of certain kinds of formal interactions such as grievance or performance appraisal interviews.
- *Repertoire of approaches* (i) Expansion of the repertoire of approaches by giving information about an alternative approach not already in the manager's repertoire. (ii) Guidance on how to perform an existing approach more skilfully.
- *Structuring skills* Guidance on how to structure interactions more skilfully by such methods as forward planning, agreeing an agenda within the interaction, using components such as bridges and summaries, and the need for flexibility, and so on.
- *Repertoire of components* (i) Expansion of the repertoire of components by describing other components not already within the manager's repertoire. (ii) Guidance on how to perform an existing component more skilfully.

The tutor will certainly not wish to give guidance on all these topics, but it is necessary to be aware of all of them in order to decide on which to concentrate.

The second, more long-term function of the tutor is to develop the trainee's ability to become his or her own source of feedback, interpretation and guidance, so that the trainee can go on improving his or her skill without the help of a tutor.[4] Even at the early stage of training, the tutor can, in addition to providing the extrinsic feedback so important at this stage, lay the foundations for the later use of intrinsic feedback to continue skill development once the course is over.

Like any skill, the skills of attending to feedback, interpreting it and planning one's own performance improvement are acquired most easily through practice with feedback and guidance. Thus if these skills are to be acquired during a training session, the tutor must give the trainee the opportunity to practise them, and also provide feedback and guidance on the trainee's performance. The Problem Solving approach described in Chapter 7 is ideal for this purpose. The tutor can ask open questions, such as: 'How far do you think you achieved your objectives?', 'What was it that you did in the course of the interaction which had the biggest effect on what was achieved?' and 'What could you have done differently in order to have achieved more from the interaction?'. If necessary, such questions can be followed up by probes, comparisons, hypotheticals to obtain more precise information, and recognition to reinforce insightful comments. The immediate aim is to guide the manager to reach his or her own conclusions that are both appropriate and explicit enough to be acted upon in the manager's next interaction of a similar type. This guidance may take the form of helping the manager to sharpen up vague conclusions or consider alternatives to less appropriate conclusions by the use of skilful questioning technique. The long-term aim is to encourage managers periodically to analyse subsequent interactions in the same way, and give them practice in the skills involved so that they will be able to analyse their own performance in much the same terms as the tutor would if he or she were there. For example:

- How did that interaction go on the whole?
- How far do I think I met my objectives?
- What were the significant things that I did which influenced how much I achieved?
- What could I have done differently that might have enabled me to achieve more?

Of course, even tutors sometimes choose the wrong approach. It may happen that the trainee manager either cannot or will not come up with suggestions for improving his or her interpersonal skills, or the manager may give what the tutor thinks are highly inappropriate solutions and there is simply insufficient time to achieve more appropriate conclusions using a Problem Solving approach. In this case, the tutor may be reduced to using the clear and quick Tell and Sell approach. As a last resort, a told solution is probably better than no solution at all, despite depriving the manager of the opportunity to practise and gain feedback and guidance on his or her skills of self-development.

On courses using the Bradford Approach to interpersonal skills training, a further opportunity to practise self-development skills is provided in the final plenary session of each day (see Appendix VIII). One problem with this kind of training, however, is that it is labour intensive. A skilled tutor is necessary in each syndicate group and the groups will necessarily be small in order to give each member adequate opportunity to practise.

Outside these training groups, the problem is, in effect, one of finding substitutes for the skilled tutor that would enable the manager to take over the various tasks of selection, feedback, interpretation and guidance described earlier in this chapter. This problem is taken up in the next section.

Self-development approaches to the acquisition of interpersonal skills

The role of feedback in skill development

It is worth re-emphasising here that the extent to which feedback is available and registered is dependent upon the manager's knowledge of the important variables which influence an interaction and his or her ability to observe the effects of them on a subordinate in an interaction. This latter ability will improve as the manager becomes more skilful since one of the aspects of skilled performance is that skilled performers do not need to concentrate on their actions. With this reduction in apparent mental effort comes the additional ability to attend selectively to the processes occurring in the interaction. The skilled motorist simply drives somewhere – he or she does not have to concentrate on what the arms or legs are doing. Similarly, the person skilled in the interpersonal skills of leadership does not think about questions and statements, and nonverbal cues, but of objectives. Once the objective of the interaction is clear, the questions and statements, and nonverbal cues automatically occur in the required way to suit the objectives. But where to begin?

There seem to be three overlapping phases in the development of interpersonal skills. The first is the *preparation phase* in which learning the basic material occurs. This includes the basic components – the types of questions and their purpose, nonverbal cues and so on – from which interactions are built. This is the book learning phase.

The second or *structuring phase* is directly related to the development of structuring skills, that is, how to structure an interaction. It often requires the modification of 'unlearning' of existing conceptual structures relating to interpersonal interactions and the development of new ones. For example, old word habits such as asking leading questions and closed questions to gather information may need to be compared with, and modified to incorporate, the alternative approach of asking open questions and probes in order to achieve certain outcomes. Expansion of the repertoire of approaches and their common components – being able to Tell and Sell or Problem Solve when required – is another aspect. Unlike the previous phase, this phase needs both practice and feedback. It also requires a lot of effort, and in terms of achieving skilled performance it is the most important phase.

The consequent improvement in skill leads to the third phase, the *refinement phase*, which is characterised by efficient performance where questions and statements and styles and approaches automatically occur once the objective of the interaction is clear. It involves the application of knowledge and conceptual structures into smooth and efficient performance to suit individual situations. Performance at this level characterises the expert and usually requires long hours of practice with feedback.

These three phases, then, give a guide to how to develop the skills required for successful performance. Initially the most important learning in the preparation phase is that of the question and statement types (the repertoire of components in Figure 8.1) and the repertoire of approaches (these are discussed in Chapters 4, 5 and 7 respectively). However, this is not the only learning in this phase, but it is sufficient to provide a basis for phase two: practising, implementing and structuring the skills. In the first instance, when learning the basic question and statement types it is worth trying to formulate examples of them for different circumstances. Hearing yourself formulating and saying these components will help you to learn them more quickly and to apply them, for example, with a more appropriate tone of voice. You can even imagine answers which will help you to formulate your next question and so on.

The next stage of practice is testing out your learning in an actual conversation. You can do this immediately within your organisation on your subordinates and peers, or, if you wish to check both that you have adequately learned the techniques and that they really do achieve what we claim, then you can use them anywhere. In restaurants (e.g. 'Can you tell me about the dishes?' – open question; 'What are the ingredients of the sauce?' – probe/closed question), in bars (e.g. 'What do you think about the local football team?', 'What difference do you think Jones would make to the team if he replaced Jordan?'), in the home, and so on. Children are frequently good for practising your techniques on reticent individuals. Asking 'How did your day at school go today?' is likely to bring one or two words of response such as 'All right', or 'Not bad' or 'Same as usual'. Where do you go from there? The tendency for people unskilled in this area is immediately to start asking closed or leading questions of the sort 'Did you have history?' or 'You did some English and maths, didn't you?' This limits the information gathering and probably stops the conversation fairly rapidly. Instead one could probe the answer, 'What do you mean by all right?', or try another open, 'Tell me about it'. Trying to keep a conversation going with children can be extremely difficult and is thus excellent practice.

As you practise these conversations, other factors relevant to the overall activity become apparent, for example, nonverbal cues (see Chapter 5). Are you paying enough attention to them? Which cues should you watch out for in each situation? What do they signify? These are phase one learning variables, but they cannot be observed and learned without second phase activity. This is why the phases are described as overlapping.

Once you have implemented some form of practice, you need consciously to use the techniques and extend their use to as many appropriate situations as possible. In this way your structures, techniques, strategies and tactics will become more naturally suited to your intentions and purposes in the situation. This may prove difficult at first due to the need to 'unlearn' various word habits, beliefs about people and behaviour and approaches to people which have gradually developed over many years. It takes a lot of effort and time, but will eventually be rewarded by achievement of that stage in development where questions, statements, nonverbal behaviour, approaches and structure automatically flow in response to the objectives of the situation.

Self-development checklists

To help in this process of self-development, we have drawn up two checklists. The first, which is presented in Appendix IX, is intended to help in the preparation for an interaction. It asks what objectives the interaction is intended to achieve and what approach, structure and question and statement types are most likely to achieve these objectives. This checklist can be used not only for purposes of self-development, but also as a means of preparing for any interaction which is both important and likely to be 'difficult'. For both purposes, it may be useful to write down at the end the actual questions and statements those which you believe would be most likely to produce the outcomes you wish to achieve. Dillon suggests that the best way to find out whether we have formulated the right question is to compose a dummy answer.[5] By sketching out all the possible answers we can imagine and comparing these with the information we want, we can reformulate the question until it expresses what we have in mind. The next step, according to Dillon, is to arrange the questions in an order which we judge suitable and rehearse them, preferably out loud in the voice we would use in the real situation. An audio or video recording of such rehearsals would also permit the refinement of the nonverbal cues accompanying the questions. Finally, Dillon suggests that the best way of rehearsing questions is to hold a dress rehearsal by putting the questions to a collaborator and seeing how someone else makes sense of the questions and actually answers them.

The second checklist, presented in Appendix X, is intended to be completed shortly after an interaction. Its aim is to help the manager to identify what he or she should be doing differently to carry out such interactions more skilfully. It may be used periodically as a check on how your interpersonal skills are developing or as a means of analysing a particular interaction that produced less satisfactory outcomes than you would have wished.

Question 1 asks *what were the objectives of the interaction*. In the case of planned interactions, these will be the intentions which you had at the beginning of the interaction. In the case of spontaneous interactions these may be either what you were trying to achieve in the interaction or what you now realise you should have been trying to achieve in the interaction, if these are different. Question 2 asks *what were the outcomes of the interactions*. Obviously, comparison of the first two questions will give an indication of *how successful the interaction was* (Question 3). Question 4 is concerned with *how a successful interaction could be made even better*. Question 5 seeks to identify *the ways in which the outcomes of an unsuccessful interaction were unsatisfactory*. Question 6 asks *in what ways the manager's handling of the interaction contributed to the unsatisfactory outcomes*. To help managers who may be unsure why a particular interaction was unsuccessful, a number of hypotheses concerning the reasons why interactions may fail are suggested in Appendix XI. We are not saying that all these hypotheses will be relevant or that there might not be other reasons for the problem encountered. Interpersonal relations are far too complex to be able to give hard and fast rules, particularly when the exact circumstances are not known. Rather, the hypotheses are extended as suggestions which might help you to consider a wider variety of options in deciding how to improve your interpersonal skills. If none of our suggestions is relevant, then perhaps in thinking why our suggestions do not apply, this will trigger you to think of more relevant ones.

Finally Question 7 asks *what changes you could make in order to carry out a more successful interaction if faced with a similar situation in future*. Firstly, it asks what your main objective(s) should be. These may be general objectives for this type of interaction (e.g. 'Make sure of my facts before criticising subordinates', or 'Ensure that all actions are agreed and summarised before moving on to the next topic'). Alternatively, the form can be used to plan for a specific interaction, in which case you may wish to specify exactly what you wish to achieve (e.g. 'Find out how Bob would feel about a transfer to another location should one arise' or 'Find a way of ensuring that shortage of spare parts does not cause production bottlenecks').

Secondly, question 7 also asks *in what ways you would like to change your actual behaviour in the interaction in order to obtain more satisfactory outcomes.* Again, this can relate to this type of interaction generally or to a specific interaction with a particular subordinate in the near future. If the latter, then it is of course possible to analyse this later interaction using the checklist to assess how successful you were in achieving your objectives and whether any further improvement is called for. In terms of our model of the processes involved in manager–subordinate interactions (Figure 8.1), the checklist covers a variety of factors. These include the approach, structure and components used, the subordinate's response and the outcomes of the interaction. Much depends upon the manager's awareness of feedback. A checklist can only ask the manager to think about his or her behaviour and the way the subordinate responds. If, however, the manager thinks he or she is asking open questions when in fact he or she is using leading or closed questions or thinks that he or she has gained commitment when the subordinate has signalled reluctant compliance at most, then there is no way in which a checklist can tell the manager that he or she is wrong.

A tempting solution to this problem might be for the manager to solicit feedback from his or her own subordinates after a real-life interaction. However, the manager who could most afford to do this is the one with considerable interpersonal skills, and who, therefore, probably is in least need of the feedback. The manager in most need of the feedback is the one with poor interpersonal skills, but this probably means that he or she will solicit the feedback in an unskilled way and will not know how to handle it when he or she receives it. There is a serious danger, therefore, that the manager with relatively poor interpersonal skills, by soliciting feedback ineptly, could permanently damage the relationship with his or her subordinates.

An alternative approach therefore would be to develop your own training programme. If fellow managers, not necessarily in the same organisation, wish to improve their interpersonal skills, then they could get together informally to practise these skills and give each other feedback and guidance. The cases included in Chapter 2 could be used to provide the basis of role-play exercises or these could be drawn from real-life situations. Whilst this form of practice may not reflect the real-life situation perfectly, it does have several advantages. The interaction can be recorded, thus providing an opportunity for more detailed and focused analysis. The person role-playing the subordinate can be asked to play the role in the way which the manager would find most useful to practise on (e.g. aggrieved, angry, over-compliant, taciturn). Furthermore, the manager can use the role play as an opportunity to try out questioning techniques, gambits, approaches, and so on, which he or she would not normally use, without having to live with the results should everything not work out as planned.

This brings us to a final point. Should you decide to change the way you interact with subordinates on the basis of this book, we would recommend that you proceed by small steps. First, this is because a sudden major change would surprise subordinates and give them problems in knowing how to handle it. Secondly, a major change may not produce exactly the results hoped for, and the unwanted repercussions could also be great. Minor changes, such as the use of more open questions or probes, using a somewhat more organised structure or departing somewhat from an over-rigid one, are unlikely to have a dramatic impact, adverse or beneficial. If the effect is beneficial, however, one can continue to experiment and expand the range of one's skills step by step.

Notes and references

1. D. Meister (1976), *Behavioral Foundations of Systems Development*, Wiley.
2. C. W. Allinson (1977), 'Training in performance appraisal interviewing: an evaluation study', *Journal of Management Studies*, **14**, 179–91; P. L. Wright and D. S. Taylor (1990), 'An evaluation package for the small one-off interpersonal skills course', *Training and Management Development Methods*, **4** (3), 2.19–2.30.
3. A full description of the 'Bradford Approach' to interpersonal skills training can be found in D. S. Taylor and P. L. Wright (1988) *Developing Interpersonal Skills Through Tutored Practice*, Prentice Hall.
4. G. A. Randell (1982), 'Management development through self-analysis and self-tutoring', paper presented at the 20th International Congress of Applied Psychology, Edinburgh.
5. J. T. Dillon (1990), *The Practice of Questioning*, Routledge.

APPENDIX I
Critical incidents

A model answer to Exercise 2.1

What is the problem in behavioural terms?

Victor has taken actions – stopping the bonus payments, omitting information from the management information system (MIS), passing on information concerning James Smart's promotion – which have caused other members of the organisation (process workers, Personnel manager, managers on the MIS circulation list, Technical manager) to become angry, dissatisfied or embarrassed. In each case, he apparently did not check out the facts of the situation or take advice from other people before taking action.

Is the problem worth spending time and effort on?

Yes. The organisation will benefit if Victor does not take actions which cause problems for other people. Bill Bean will benefit because there will be fewer complaints to deal with, and ultimately Victor will benefit because further complaints could be detrimental to his career prospects/job security.

Possible reasons for performance problems	Possible solutions
Goal clarity Victor believes that the most important aspects of his job are cost saving and efficiency rather than providing a service which fulfils the needs of his organisational 'customers'.	Draw Victor's attention to the need for a balance between cost saving, efficiency and providing a service.
Ability Victor lacks essential knowledge or skills (e.g. the requirements of the managers on the MIS circulation list, industrial relations, decision-making skills, time management skills, and so on).	Send him on a relevant course, secondment to appropriate departments. Coaching (e.g. talk through recent decisions with him and discuss the potential benefits and drawbacks of alternative actions).

Possible reasons for performance problems	Possible solutions
Task difficulty Victor's workload is such that he does not have time to consult people before taking actions and does not have time to collate all the information required for the MIS when under pressure from other aspects of his job.	Provide extra staff, perhaps temporary support at specific times, or reduce workload or accept a lower standard of performance.
Intrinsic motivation Victor finds the challenge of designing cost-effective systems the most satisfying aspect of his job.	Give him more responsibility for cost-effective systems, with the constraint that they must meet the requirements of his organisational customers.
Extrinsic motivation Victor believes that showing himself to be a cost-effective manager will make him appear a better performer and result in higher merit increases and enhanced career prospects. Victor has received praise in the past for his cost-cutting exercises, but has never received any praise for the quality of service he provides.	Point out that complaints from other managers, if they continue, will have a detrimental effect on merit increases and career prospects. Provide praise for efforts to increase the quality of service or consultation before making decisions, as appropriate. If the problems continue, then disciplinary proceedings may be initiated.
Feedback Victor did not know that managers were dissatisfied with the information they received, how serious the near strike was or how upset the Technical manager had been.	Provide non-evaluative feedback on these issues. Set up a feedback system which will allow the managers to report on their degree of satisfaction with the MIS system. Set up regular meetings with Victor to keep him informed.
Resources Victor has insufficient staff to carry out all his responsibilities effectively, either in general or at certain times.	Provide permanent or temporary staff. Look into ways of organising the work more effectively.
Working conditions Working in an open plan office next to the general office means that Victor is often interrupted and is unable to plan his work effectively.	Check whether partitions might help to reduce this problem.

Possible reasons for performance problems	Possible solutions
Personal problems Victor is having to cope with some family problem, relationship problems or substance abuse, which is affecting his work performance through stress, loss of sleep or loss of concentration.	Carry out a counselling interview to determine the source of the problem. On the basis of this assess whether that is sufficient, or whether a temporary solution is appropriate, or whether specialist help is required.

A perceptual analysis

Answers and guidance to Exercise 3

1. The complaints from managers regarding Victor have influenced Bill's motivational state. Although Bill may have other important business to attend to, his need to sort out the problems created by Victor has given it increased priority. This is not a direct perceptual factor, but it has implications for perception and judgement insofar as high-priority problems focus attention and the selectivity of perception.

2. That Bill was angry when he called Victor in to tackle him on the special bonus issue will influence Bill's perception and judgement in several ways:

    (a) It is worth noting that the situation was ambiguous because Bill had left clear instructions for payment. He had not informed Victor and could not understand how Victor had become involved. Ambiguity should trigger information gathering, as a result of mild anxiety created by the ambiguity. This conscious information gathering would assist a meaningful interpretation of events, lead to a resolution of the problem and thereby reduce any anxiety created.

    (b) Bill, however, was angry, indicating strong emotional arousal. Strong emotional arousal reduces capacity to use information and leads to more simple interpretations of events. Bill already had some information from the Personnel manager, that 'Victor had interfered in matters beyond his remit'. He probably assumed this was correct (information from high-status people is more readily believed). In his 'narrow focus' created by the strong emotion, Bill probably felt no need to gather more information and therefore 'told' Victor rather than asking for more informaton about his involvement. It is also worth noting that in his 'angry state', even had Bill asked for more information, he may have been unable to process it due to reduced capacity to handle it, that is, he would have had an information overload in the strong emotional state he was experiencing.

    (c) The *fundamental attribution bias* – underestimating situational factors and overestimating the individual's responsibility for the event – probably influenced Bill's judgement. This will have been exacerbated by *hedonic relevance* (the payment was authorised by Bill), *personalism* (Victor's action directly affected Bill as the person responsible for the payment) and the *seriousness of the outcome* (a near-strike occurred).

(d) It is also worth noting that Bill was possibly unlikely to process Victor's emotional state (suppressed anger) indicated by the nonverbal cues (e.g. tight lipped) because of his own emotional state reducing his capacity to process information and think of future implications for his working relationship with Victor. In a calmer state, Bill would be more likely to recognise the cues and tackle any problems which might arise as a result of Victor's anger.

3. Bill's categorisation of Victor, in terms of suitability for the position of office manager, had begun with his reading of Victor's references. Presumably, prior to the selection process, Bill would have determined criteria within which to assess applicants for the job. (There is no indication of this, nor the validity of criteria for the job if he had determined them.) Whatever the situation, and whichever criteria Bill was using to assess applicants, Victor's references indicated fulfilment of them at high levels.

Bill's rating of Victor as 'impressive' on the basis of his references has begun the development of a possible *halo effect*. Certainly an example of *selective perception* is apparent in the interview itself. Bill seems to have attended to and remembered more information which supports his high rating of Victor than information which questions that rating. (The references tend to indicate Victor as a relative 'high-flyer', in the context of his work level, in comparison with his peers, and gives apparently no negative information to cause Bill to reconsider this.) It is possible that in the interview Bill asked questions which sought to confirm his impression of Victor rather than information which may have checked its validity.

There is also the interesting point that, in order to maintain his positive impression of Victor, he 'blamed' the situation for the 'less than ideal' answers which other panel members had noted, rather than Victor. This is a commonly occurring approach to rationalising events to maintain one's first impressions. It may be consciously done or even unconsciously done in that people may go through the process without realising they are doing it to protect a possible false impression. To have to admit to forming an incorrect impression would temporarily, at least, lower self-esteem.

4. A second pointer to Bill's apparent 'halo' regarding Victor occurred earlier insofar as Bill 'believed Victor had performed exceptionally well in his role as office manager'. A third pointer is that Bill believed Victor's excuse for 'cutting corners' (managers overstating their need for information) rather than the managers' complaints, without apparently checking it out.

5. Bill's halo effect for Victor has begun to be questioned as a result of the number and seriousness of recent negative comments, indicating a move to recategorising Victor from that determined by first impressions, sustained previously through selective perception. This is an example of the *recency effect* – more recent information affecting an earlier judgement.

6. Although not specifically mentioned in the chapter, an interesting phenomenon tends to occur with the process of recategorisation relating to memory and recall. The recategorisation tends to 'unblock' previously 'forgotten' information which links in with and supports the new impression. Thus whereas under the halo effect Bill recalled the long hours worked and so on (i.e. positive cues supporting the halo – these can also be seen as *salience* factors or the *illusory causation effect* which influences the attribution process), memories are now released, as a result of the recategorisation process which support the newly reformed impression, such as staff being too familiar, idle gossip and so on. It is also worth noting that Bill interprets these in an evaluative way which assists the reinterpretation. For example, how did Bill know it was 'idle gossip' and not discussion about work problems? Perhaps Bill is 'going beyond the information given' to justify the reinterpretation!

7. Although Bill's consideration of his role in streamlining the paperwork system is another example of reinterpretation of existing information to fit the new impression, it could also be interpreted in terms of egocentric attributions – more readily recalling one's own contribution than those of others.

8. Bill is using the three variables of *consistency, consensus* and *distinctiveness* in the mode of a 'naïve scientist' to assess Victor in terms of personal competence in influencing outcomes which relate to his work record. This indicates a move to a more rational attempt to assess Victor's overall work record and how well he has performed. As a result, Bill decides to use a more appropriate 'information gathering' approach to assist this.

Question-and-statement types

Answers to Exercise 4.1

Recognising question-and-statement types

A	Open	K	Comparison
B	Feedback	L	Closed
C	Leading	M	Self-disclosure
D	Criticism	N	Order
E	Reflective	O	Probe
F	Warning	P	Factual statement
G	Multiple	Q	Advice
H	Summary	R	Hypothetical
I	Explanation	S	Lubricators
J	Evaluative statement	T	Promise
		U	Bridge

Answers to Exercise 4.2

Appropriate use of question-and-statement types

1.	A	6.	J
2.	I	7.	B
3.	U	8.	Q
4.	K	9.	S
5.	L	10.	E

11.	C	16.	O
12.	N	17.	M
13.	F	18.	H
14.	R	19.	P
15.	T	20.	D

Dealing with emotion and frustration

Answers to Exercise 4.3

1. 'I feel just like a slave round here. I was employed as a shorthand-typist and yet I'm expected to make tea and coffee, do the shopping and stay around during lunchtime and at hometime in case something needs doing at short notice. Last night I didn't get home until nearly 7 o'clock.'

   (a) 'I'm sorry about last night. Did you have something special on?' (Poor response – inappropriate sympathy – closed question irrelevant to frustration being expressed.)

   (b) 'I understand how you feel but often it's not anyone's fault, especially if there's an urgent order to be completed.' (Poor response – placating, excusing and inappropriate sympathy.)

   (c) 'I'm sorry, but the person before you really liked getting involved and I assumed you would too.' (Poor response – inappropriate sympathy, excusing or premature confrontation depending on tone of voice and so on.)

   (d) 'You resent being expected to do things which you don't think are part of your job.' (Positive response which attempts to reflect back an understanding of the person's expressed feeling.)

2. 'I don't know if it's me or not. Over the last two years we've hired a lot of young people. They're all polite to me, but that's about it. I can't seem to find out what makes them "tick". I don't understand them and I find it hard to establish any kind of relationship with them.'

   (a) 'You don't seem to know where the fault lies.' (Inappropriate reflective, judgemental in choice of word 'fault'.)

   (b) 'You're having difficulty handling your subordinates.' (Poor response – judgemental/interpretive; it may be true but it has not been expressed.)

   (c) 'You feel somewhat isolated from them and it's puzzling you.' (Good response – attempts to reflect back the stated problem.)

   (d) 'What do you think I can do to help?' (Poor response – either scathing or premature problem solving depending on tone of voice and so on.)

3. 'If it keeps on like this we'll go under. The shop stewards in my department are giving me hell. If I try to move people around there's an uproar. With the

company the way it is and pressure on me to improve productivity, I've just got to have more leeway to run the department more efficiently.'

(a) 'You're feeling under pressure from both management and shop stewards and it's affecting your efforts to organise the work.' (Good reflective insofar as it attempts to show understanding of the person's expressed feeling.)

(b) 'Could you elaborate on that a little more?' (Poor response – depending on how it is said, it could indicate lack of listening, premature confrontation or premature problem solving.)

(c) 'You've got to use more discipline. Take away their privileges if they don't do as you want them to.' (Poor response – premature advice, rejection of complaint and no attempt to understand the frustration being expressed.)

(d) 'OK, it's hard on you but if we keep our heads we can work something out. Let's see if we can sort it out.' (Poor response – inappropriate sympathy, placating and premature problem-solving attempt regarding actions.)

4. 'I really find it hard to work for him. He's so inconsistent. I seem to be getting along fine then for no apparent reason he blows up. I just don't know where I am with him.'

A positive statement should contain something like: 'You feel puzzled by his behaviour' or 'You feel uncertain about how to behave with him'.

5. 'Do you know, I've really enjoyed working here for the past three months. The work's really interested me and I get a lot of satisfaction out of doing it.'

A positive statement should contain something like: 'You seem to have got a lot of pleasure out of doing the job lately' or 'You seem very satisfied with the job and have got a lot of pleasure out of it lately'.

Identification of nonverbal cues

Answers to Exercise 5.1

Interview 1

(a) Liking, friendliness, warmth

(b) Interest

(c) Boredom

(d) False happiness, masking negative emotion such as anxiety

(e) Sadness

(f) Surprise

(g) Confidence

(h) Desire to retain speaking role

(i) Attention

(j) Desire to relinquish speaking role

(k) Happiness

Interview 2

(a) Status, power, dominance

(b) Low/moderate anxiety

(c) Contempt

(d) High anxiety

(e) Disgust

(f) Shame

(g) Overt anger

(h) Difficulty in expressing verbal message

(i) Desire to take over speaking role

(j) Deception (insincerity)

(k) Masked anger

Note that if you have obtained a high score on this exercise – well done! But remember that nonverbal cues often occur at a low level. We have had to make them explicit for this exercise, but they could be very fleeting in real life.

Structuring interactions

Answers to Exercise 6.1

1. The funnel technique consists of an open question followed by a narrowing sequence of probes or other more precise questions and ending with a closed question or summary.

2. (a) Gathering specific information when the manager initially lacks sufficient background information to ask the precise question required.
   (b) Helping the other person in an interaction to identify the precise causes of a problem.
   (c) Helping the other person in an interaction to arrive at his or her own solution or solutions to a problem.

3. Using the funnel technique first to identify the causes of a problem and then to identify a potential solution or solutions to it.

4. When using the funnel technique to identify either the causes of, or potential solutions to, a problem, it may be necessary for the manager to give information (e.g. factual statements, feedback) in order to ensure that the subordinate has all the necessary information required to reach effective conclusions.

5. An initial closed question, followed by progressively more open ones.

6. Quickly establishing whether an issue is worth pursuing and, if so, what direction further questioning should take.

7. A series of questions with the same degree of openness.

8. (a) Eliciting a large amount of information in a relatively short time.
   (b) Pinning someone down to specific factual information when he or she is attempting to evade the issue by talking generalities.

9. The unvarying question style, when using relatively narrow questions, may not give the other person an opportunity to elaborate, with the result that important additional information may be lost.

10. It typically consists of a series of orders, requests, pieces of advice or explanations, interspersed with leading questions.

11. If the manager stops too early, the subordinate may not have 'got the message', but if he or she goes on too long there is the risk that the subordinate will become irritated and resentful.

12. (a) If 'successful', it is likely to cause resentment and may also be damaging to the subordinate's self-esteem, neither of which are particularly effective ways of improving performance.
    (b) Having fallen into the trap once, subordinates are likely to become very wary of being caught in the same way again and refuse to give the expected answers.
13. (a) The use of brief, general praise followed by long, detailed criticism.
    (b) Using the gambit in a mechanistic manner, so that the subordinate comes to expect blame every time he or she hears praise.
14. (a) The subordinate may become so angry or demoralised by the initial criticism that the manager either does not have the opportunity to get round to the praise or the subordinate does not respond to it positively if it is used.
    (b) The lavish praise at the end of the interaction may help the subordinate to feel better, but may also wrongly give the impression that his or her poor performance was not such a serious problem after all.
15. (a) By avoiding criticism or blame, it is less likely to arouse negative reactions.
    (b) It provides subordinates with an opportunity to practise their problem-solving skills.
    (c) Subordinates are more likely to be committed to solutions which they have identified for themselves than to those which have been imposed on them.
    (d) Even if the subordinate does not come up with a solution, it provides the manager with a way of introducing his or her own suggestions.
16. When the manager attempts to lead a subordinate towards a solution that he or she has already identified in a manner which is perceived as condescending or patronising.
17. (a) It denies the subordinate time to give a reasoned, relevant reply.
    (b) It denies the manager time to understand the implications of what the subordinate is saying.
    (c) It denies the manager time to phrase the right question or statement that will produce the response which he or she wants.
18. (a) Allowing silence.
    (b) Labelling silence – saying why the manager is remaining silent.
    (c) Using restatements.
19. (a) Try to avoid the adverse effects of preconceived ideas (see Chapter 7).
    (b) Instead of planning one's next contribution to the discussion whilst the other person is talking, think about how one might briefly restate what the other person is saying.
20. (a) It draws together the main points of the discussion.
    (b) It allows the manager to compare what is summarised with what he or she intended to achieve in the interaction.
    (c) It provides an opportunity, if the manager is willing to allow it, for the

subordinate to disagree with the content of the summary, provide additional information or make further suggestions.

21. If the manager gives a summary, the subordinate may simply passively agree even though he or she is not paying attention. If the subordinate makes the summary, it:
    (a) provides a check on how much of the discussion he or she actually remembers; and
    (b) increases the probability that the subordinate will remember what has been discussed or decided.

22. (a) Ask the other person whether he or she has anything to add to the discussion (e.g. additional information, further suggestions).
    (b) Check how the subordinate feels at the end of the interaction; for example, how satisfied is the subordinate with any decision which has been made or to what extent negative emotions have been dissipated in a counselling interview?

23. (a) It avoids going over the same ground several times.
    (b) This makes it easier to summarise the conclusions reached in each section of the discussion.
    (c) This in turn should make the final summary easier to do, because it is simply a recapitulation of the previously agreed summaries of each section.

24. If the structure is too rigid, important issues may not be discussed and the subordinate may be dissatisfied because topics he or she wishes to discuss are either not discussed when the subordinate thinks they should be or not discussed at all.

25. (a) Asking the subordinate at the beginning of the meeting whether there are any particular issues which he or she would like to raise.
    (b) Asking the subordinate whether there are any issues which he or she would like to discuss first.
    (c) Using issue planning rather than sequence planning, so that the manager is able to change the order in which issues are discussed whilst still maintaining an organised structure for the interaction.

Note that we are not saying that the manager should invariably do all these things. There may be times (e.g. in a disciplinary interview) when it would be appropriate for the manager to set a rigid agenda and stick to it. Like most of the techniques we describe, the above suggestions are ways of increasing the likelihood that certain objectives can be achieved. Whether they are appropriate or not will depend on whether the manager has other, conflicting objectives which may be more important in that particular interaction.

26. When the manager is attempting to defuse a highly charged emotional situation by allowing the subordinate to talk him- or herself out.

Analysis of an interaction

A model answer to Exercise 7.1

1. Classification of questions and statements used by Manager. (2. Brief notes of significant events which may have influenced the course of the interaction are given in brackets.)

001–003	Explanation (including assumption)
005-010	Explanation
012	(Interruption), open question (perhaps *too* open and introduced too abruptly)
014–017	Multiple question
018–020	(subordinate answered last question and ignored the rest)
021–023	Lubricator followed by open question (although expressed in a closed form)
027–028	Reflective
032–033	Restatement
035–036	Factual statement
037	Self-disclosure
038–040	Advice
040–042	Closed question or narrow probe
044	Open question
046-048	Hypothetical question
050–052	Promise
053–054	Suggestion
054–056	Promise

056	Open question
058–060	Bridge plus threat
064–066	(Interruption), open question
073–074	(did not probe for details)
074–075	Evaluative statement
075–077	Explanation
079	Probing question
082–083	(Interruption), probing question
085–086	Evaluative statement
086–088	(Introduces another issue before dealing with the current one.) Difficult to classify. Could be explanation of previous evaluative statement or factual statement with evaluative overtones
095	Reflective
099	Open question
104	Probing question
108	Probing question
117	Probing question
123	Probing question
127–128	Comparison question
135–136	Closed question or narrow probe
139–140	(Got Victor to do a summary)
140–141	Hypothetical question
143–144	Praise
144	Open question (in closed form) (also a useful check)
148	Praise
149–150	Bridge
149–152	Restatement
151–152	Leading question
154–157	Leading question
158	(compliance)

161–162   Order

162–165   Order

166–167   Order

167–168   Order

168–170   Order

170–171   Evaluative statement?

171   Closed question

172   (compliance)

176–179   Evaluative statements, (taking the form of praise before blame)

179–184   Summary in the form of suggestions

185   Promise

186–188   Promise

188   Closed question

190–191   Evaluative statement

3(a). Structure of the interaction

Bill did not explain the purpose of the meeting. He assumed that Victor would know what it was and only gave an explanation when Victor asked for one.

There were two examples of the funnel sequence. First, Bill used the funnel sequence to obtain informaton about Victor's career aspirations (021–056). Secondly, he used a double funnel sequence to identify both the causes of and potential solutions to the bonus problem (099–148). Within this there was a short tunnel sequence of precise behavioural probes (104–123). However, the attempt to solve the missing information problem (148–171) was probably nearer to trap setting, consisting as it did of leading questions followed by orders.

In the main, Bill used a relatively organised structure in the interaction. However, there were two examples of recycling issues which in places made the structure more diffuse. First, Bill introduced the purpose of the meeting, then broke off to ask how things were going generally (012) and then came back to the main purpose of the meeting rather clumsily later (058). Secondly, he raised the bonus issue whilst dealing with the missing information from the management information system (086), dropping the latter topic whilst the bonus issue was dealt with and then returning to it later (149).

The main points relating to each issue were summarised as the interview progressed and in one case the manager got the subordinate to do a summary (141–142). There was also a final summary, but the item concerning 'hasty decision making' (184) was vague and Bill did not include in the summary the 'good idea' of keeping Victor informed about anything unusual which was likely to come up when he was going to be away (148).

3(b). Approach to the interaction

Bill's approach to the interaction varied considerably. He used a considerate problem-solving approach with respect to Victor's career aspirations and the bonus issue, but a somewhat patronising Ask and Tell approach with respect to the missing information from the management information system. We cannot know what the intended approach to the confidentiality issue was going to be because Victor managed to curtail further discussion of the subject by means of an apology. However, Bill's acceptance of the apology was again somewhat patronising.

Whilst having the flexibility to change one's approach during an interaction can be a useful skill, it seems to be done here too abruptly and with too little justification and probably had an adverse effect on what was achieved. There were signs of compliance rather than commitment concerning the solution to the missing information problem and Victor may also have left the interaction confused as to why he was listened to on some issues but not on others. One possible explanation, of little consolation to Victor, is that one of Bill Bean's main problems was preconceived ideas. He did not feel the need to probe or check when he thought that he already knew the answer (confidentiality, missing information), but did probe and probe effectively when he realised that he did not have all the necessary information (career prospects, bonus issue).

3(c). Main learning points

(i) Things which the manager did well

- Bill showed that he could use open questions, probing questions and other information-gathering components well, when the need for them was recognised.
- The questions were integrated into well-structured funnel sequences on two occasions (021–056, 099–148), the second a 'double funnel'.
- Reflective questions were used appropriately on two occasions (027–028, 095).
- Good listening skills were shown when Bill picked up that Victor had reinstated only some of the missing information from the management information system (079).
- Bill responded well to Victor's concerns about his career prospects.
- The main conclusions were summarised throughout and (with one exception) at the end.

(ii) Things which the manager needs to work on in order to improve his performance

- Bill interrupted quite often and may have lost useful information as a result.

- Evaluative statements, containing such words as 'failing' (075) and 'lapses' (178), may have unnecessarily irritated Victor.
- Multiple questions (014–017) should be avoided.
- The start could have been more constructive, setting out an agreed agenda.
- Once having started discussing an issue, Bill should take care not to get side-tracked into other issues unless there is a compelling reason for doing so.
- The conclusions need to be more precise and care needs to be taken to summarise all important conclusions.
- Praise was relatively rarely used with respect to Victor's work performance and when used was weak and general, and immediately followed with blame (176–179).
- Bill needs to watch out for assumptions and preconceived ideas. It is worth checking these out even when he thinks that he already knows the answer (but *not* by means of leading questions!).
- Related to this is the fact that Bill needed to probe further on one occasion even though he thought that Victor had given the answer which he wanted. Apologising profusely and with apparent sincerity (067–072) is a gambit sometimes used by subordinates as a means of avoiding a detailed discussion of an indefensible mistake. It is all too easy to accept the apology as genuine and move on to something else. Bill needed to probe more to find out about the circumstances, the reasons why Victor behaved as he did, what he might have done differently to avoid the problem and so on. Giving away confidential information about the impending promotion could have been an isolated example of thoughtless gossiping, but equally it could have been a symptom of a more significant underlying problem which was never uncovered.

A training course for the development of the interpersonal skills of leadership

Introduction

The precise content of the course would depend to some extent upon the needs of the managers and therefore the particular skills being developed. For example, there might be a need to develop skills for handling disciplinary or grievance interviews, fact finding, negotiations, day-to-day interaction with subordinates, and so on, and thus the emphasis of the course would change accordingly. For purposes of illustration, however, let us consider a course on performance improvement, because these can be designed to cover not only influencing behaviour but also gathering information and handling emotion.

Typically, courses using the 'Bradford Approach' to interpersonal skills training have 12 participants and last 2 days, although we have run longer courses and those with 3, 6 and 15 participants. The course outline is given in Figure A8.1, and follows closely the structure developed by Randell et al.[1] for training in performance appraisal interviewing. For the sake of simplicity, coffee, tea and lunch breaks are not shown.

Day 1

The first morning is mainly taken up with a lecture/discussion session on the interpersonal skills of leadership. It covers, although more briefly, the material dealt with in Chapters 2–7 of this book. Its aim is to give a basic grounding in the need for and nature of the interpersonal skills of leadership.

This is followed by a short briefing session concerning the afternoon's role-play exercises. The role plays are based on a performance-improvement case of the type included in Chapter 2. For role-playing purposes, however, the case has two sides – the same events as seen from the manager's viewpoint and that of the subordinate. The course members receive the manager's side of the case before coming on the course, and should be familiar with its contents. The aim of the briefing session is therefore to describe the format for the role plays, share ideas on how the case might be handled and clarify any points of detail. The subordinates are role-played by non-course members on the first day, often postgraduate students, but sometimes other members of the same organisation as the course members, if the course is run in-house.

Day One

Morning

Plenary lecture/discussion (2½ hours)
The interpersonal skills of leadership
- the role of the individual manager and the need for skill
- analysing work performance
- observational skills
- performance skills

Briefing and preparation for role-played interactions (45 minutes)

Afternoon

Role-played interactions (3 hours)

Review of role plays in plenary (1¼ hours)

Briefing for second day (15 minutes)

Day Two

Morning

Plenary lecture/discussion
Handling motivation and emotion in manager–subordinate interactions (1½ hours)

Briefing and preparation for day two role plays (45 minutes)

Role played interactions (1 hour)

Afternoon

Role played interaction (2 hours)

Review of role plays in plenary (1¼ hours)

Course review (open-ended)

Figure A8.1   *A leadership skills development course*

In the afternoon, course members split into syndicate groups of three, each led by a tutor. Each member of the syndicate group then carries out one interview on the same case but with the subordinate role played by a different person. The format for each role play is as follows.

Role-played interaction (approximately 30 minutes)
The 'subordinates' are briefed not to act the part, but to respond naturally to the manager as they would respond in real life if being treated in the same way. Thus, if the 'subordinate' is playing his or her role properly, the manager should receive his or her 'just deserts' in terms of the skill with which the subordinate is handled.

Analysis (approximately 30 minutes)
The tutor then leads and participates in a discussion on the role-played interaction, eliciting the views of the manager who has just carried out the role

play, the other two course members who observed it, and the person who role-played the subordinate. By the end of this discussion, the manager should have a clear idea of:

1. The effect of the interaction on the 'subordinate':
   (a) emotionally – how the 'subordinate' felt at the end of the interaction; and
   (b) behaviourally – what, if anything, the 'subordinate' intends to do differently in the way he or she carried out his or her job.
2. What the manager did, or did not, do during the interation which produced these results.
3. What the manager is going to do differently next time, if faced with a similar situation, to produce even better results.

In the final session of the day, which is held in plenary, the 'head tutor' goes round each course member in turn eliciting from them information about what they achieved in their interaction, what they learned from it and, again, what precisely they are going to do differently in their next interaction to improve their performance. This is partly to check whether the learning points from the analysis sessions have been absorbed and to gain public commitment to them. More importantly, as Randell argues, it provides another opportunity to practise self-analytic skills.

Day 2

As shown in Figure A8.1, Day 2 begins with a more detailed discussion of motivation, and the Day 2 cases typically involve a heavier emphasis on motivational problems than Day 1. This reflects the complexity of the subject and, in our view, its importance in achieving performance improvements. However, this could be changed for course members with different priorities and other aspects of performance improvement could be emphasised on the second day. The remainder of the course repeats much the same format as the first day. One exception is that we use two different cases on Day 2 and the course members act as manager and subordinate in different role-played interactions. This has two advantages. First, it provides the 'manager' with feedback from a 'subordinate' who is by now familiar with the course contents and concepts. Secondly, it gives the 'subordinate' the opportunity to analyse what it feels like to be handled skilfully (or not, as the case may be), which may have important lessons concerning the way he or she handles his or her own staff.

Summary

The course described above represents a typical two-day course using the Bradford Approach to interpersonal skills training. However, the format can be modified to suit different purposes. If the main aim was to provide training for short day-to-day interactions between managers and subordinates, then shorter role plays would be used and the number of course members per syndicate group increased. Similarly, the course can be extended to three or more days.

The extra time can then be used to set up practice sessions to suit the needs of individual course members. Some may wish to have another attempt at the standard type of case because they are not satisfied with their overall performance so far. Others may wish to practise particular types of interactions, such as grievance or disciplinary interviews and cases are available or can be improvised for this purpose.

Reference

1. G. A. Randell, P. M. A. Packard, R. L. Shaw and A. J. Slater (1972), *Staff Appraisal*, London: Institute of Personnel Management; G. A. Randell, P. M. A. Packard and A. J. Slater (1984), *Staff Appraisal: A first step to effective leadership*, London: Institute of Personnel Management.

Preparing for an interaction

Self-development checklist I

1. What objectives do I wish to achieve in the interaction?
   (a) *Handling emotion* How do I want the subordinate to feel at the end of the interaction?
   (b) *Gathering information* What information do I wish to elicit from the subordinate?
   (c) *Giving information* What information do I wish to impart during the interaction?
   (d) *Influencing behaviour* What do I want the subordinate to do as a result of the interaction? (Try to phrase this as precisely as possible; for example, if you want the subordinate to stop doing something, what would you like him or her to do instead?)
   (e) Others.
2. What approach do I wish to employ, either for the interaction as a whole or for specific parts of it?
3. How do I wish to structure the interaction?
   (a) *Diffuse structure* Responding spontaneously to what the subordinate says.
   (b) *Organised structure* (i) Am I going to impose my own structure on the entire interaction or invite the other person to contribute to the agenda? (ii) What topics do I wish to cover during the interaction? (iii) What outcomes would constitute a successful outcome to the discussion of each topic?
4. What questions and statements would be most likely to help me to fulfil my objectives?
   (a) What *types* of questions and statements are most appropriate for the approach and structure I have chosen?
   (b) (where appropriate) What *specific* questions and statements could be used to help me to achieve my objectives during the interaction?
   List both (a) and (b), practise and refine if necessary.

Analysing an interaction and identifying learning points

Self-development checklist II

To be completed after a recent interaction with a subordinate.

1. **What were the objectives of the interaction?**
   (a) *Handling emotion* How did I want the subordinate to feel at the end of the interaction?
   (b) *Gathering information* What information did I wish to elicit?
   (c) *Giving information* What information did I want the subordinate to have by the end of the interaction?
   (d) *Influencing behaviour* What did I want the subordinate to do as a result of the interaction?
   (e) Others.
2. **Outcomes of the interaction**
   (a) How did the subordinate appear to feel at the end of the interaction?
   (b) What new information did I have at the end of the interaction?
   (c) What new information did the subordinate have at the end of the interaction?
   (d) What actions have been agreed at the end of the interaction (i) by the subordinate; and (ii) by me?
   (e) What other outcomes were there?
3. **Did I achieve *all* my objectives?**
   (a) Yes – go to Q.4.
   (b) No – go to Q.5.
4. **Well done! Now, what can I do to maintain this level of performance or make it even better next time?**
   (a) Why was the interaction so successful?
      (i) *Appropriate question-and-statement types* If so, which did I use and why did they appear effective?
      (ii) *Appropriate use of nonverbal cues* If so, which did I use or observe the subordinate use, and how did this affect the interaction?
      (iii) *Appropriate structure* If so, precisely how did I achieve the structure I used?

(iv) *Appropriate approach* If so, what approach did I use and why was it appropriate?

(b) In what situations and with which subordinates would similar question-and-statement types, nonverbal cues, structure and approach also be likely to produce favourable outcomes?

(c) In what situations and with what subordinates would similar question-and-statement types, nonverbal cues, structure and approach be likely to produce *un*favourable results?

(d) Could anything be done to improve my performance; for example, make it more elegant, achieve the same results in a shorter time?

Now go to Q.7.

5. **In what way(s) were the outcomes of the interaction unsatisfactory? Give details under the appropriate heading(s).**

(a) Handling emotion
(b) Gathering information
(c) Giving information
(d) Influencing behaviour
(e) Others

6. **In what ways did my handling of the interaction contribute to the unsatisfactory outcome(s)? Give details under the appropriate heading(s). If you are unsure why the interaction produced unsatisfactory outcomes, a number of hypotheses concerning the reasons why interactions may fail to achieve their objectives are suggested in Appendix XI.**

(a) Handling emotion
(b) Gathering information
(c) Giving information
(d) Influencing behaviour
(e) Other

7. **Having analysed the interaction, what could I do differently next time I am faced with a similar situation, in order to achieve a more successful outcome?**

(a) What should my main objective(s) be?
   (i) Handling emotions better.
   (ii) Gaining more precise information.
   (iii) Giving information in such a way that it is both clearly understood and accepted.
   (iv) Gaining commitment to a specific action plan.
   (iv) Other.

Specify as clearly as possible under each heading, where relevant, what you would like to achieve differently from the last interaction.

(b) In what ways would I like to carry out the interaction differently?
    (i) Verbal components used. If so, which?
   (ii) Nonverbal components used. If so, which?
  (iii) More effective or appropriate structure. If so, which?
  (iv) More appropriate approach to interaction. If so, which?

Some hypotheses concerning reasons why interactions may produce unsatisfactory outcomes

Handling emotion

Objective
To reduce the subordinate's sense of grievance, frustration or anger.

Outcome
Subordinate still left with feeling of dissatisfaction.

Hypotheses

- Insufficient use of reflectives, restatements, lubricators, apologies; over-use of closed and leading questions.
- Inappropriate nonverbal cues (e.g. leaning back, lack of eye contact, fidgeting).
- Insufficient attention to subordinate's nonverbal cues (e.g. signs of rejection, doubt).
- Structure too rigid, insufficient listening or appearance of listening.
- Inappropriate approach; for example, Tell and Sell, attempting to solve the problem, rather than Ask and Listen until the subordinate has had a chance fully to express the emotion.

Objective
To enhance the subordinate's sense of satisfaction, self-esteem, sense of achievement.

Outcome
Subordinate seems dissatisfied, lacking in enthusiasm, responsiveness.

Hypotheses

- Insufficient use of reflectives, restatements, lubricators whilst subordinate wishes to talk; insufficient praise, praise not well done (e.g. too general).
- Structure too rigid, insufficient listening or appearance of listening.
- Inappropriate approach for this particular individual.

Note that in both cases, the subordinate may wish both to express some emotion *and* to see some action as a result of the interaction (e.g. a grievance redressed or a reward for good performance). Usually, it is more effective to allow expression of the emotion first and then move on to action. However, if this is delayed too long, or not reached at all, then the subordinate may be dissatisfied because there have been no concrete outcomes from the interaction. If the subordinate's aspirations seem justified, therefore, then a move to problem solving or a discussion of rewards may be called for.

Objective

To make the subordinate aware that there are shortcomings in his or her performance about which he or she should be seriously concerned.

Outcome

The subordinate does not show concern, but is instead flippant, dismissive, angry or resentful.

Hypotheses

- Lack of information gathering prior to or in the early stages of the interaction allowed the subordinate to produce mitigating circumstances to excuse his or her poor performance. An Ask and Tell approach using searching probes during the Ask phase might have produced the additional information which would have made the subsequent Tell – if still necessary – more relevant.
- Inappropriate technique during the interaction:
  (a) Lack of information *giving*. Subordinate not told the gravity of the situation. Adverse organisational and personal consequences of poor performance not spelled out precisely enough. Verbal and nonverbal signals that situation is not really serious; for example, 'There's just one small matter we have to discuss' said with a smile and dismissive manner.
  (b) Diffusely structured interaction, allowed to go off main, serious topic into less tense side issues before the message is precisely stated.
  (c) Inappropriate approach; for example, problem solving with a subordinate who comes up with unacceptable solutions. Try Tell and Sell if sure of facts, Ask and Tell if not.

Gathering information

Objective

To gather the information necessary to make a decision, either during the interaction or subsequently.

Outcome(s)

- The issue is left undecided during the interaction because insufficient information was gathered to make it with confidence. – *or*
- A poor decision is made during the interaction because the information on which it was based was incomplete or erroneous. – *or*

- The subsequent decision cannot be made because there is insufficient evidence to make it with confidence. – *or*
- The subsequent decision is made, but turns out to be incorrect because it was based on erroneous information.

Hypotheses

- Lack of information-gathering components (e.g. open, probes, comparisons), particularly probes to follow up initial general information and nail down the precise fact(s) needed. Too many leading questions.
- Diffuse structures, wandering off the point before the precise information required is nailed down. No summary.
- Inappropriate approach, i.e. anything other than Ask and Listen.

Giving information

Objective
To let the subordinate know information which will be useful in the performance of his or her job.

Outcome
The subordinate does not remember the information and may even claim never to have received it.

Hypotheses

- Information not clearly expressed in the first place. It may have been 'buried' amongst a great deal of other information, approached too cautiously in order to avoid arousing adverse emotional reactions, or simply expressed incoherently due to haste or lack of preparation.
- Information not summarised at the end of the discussion by either the manager or subordinate.

Influencing behaviour

Objective
To gain the subordinate's commitment to a plan of action which is intended to improve his/her performance.

Outcomes
Either (i) the subordinate is not committed to the plan, or (ii) the plan is not as precise as you would like.

Hypotheses
Subordinate not committed to plan:

- Lack of information-gathering components. The plan does not seem workable to the subordinate or he/she thinks there is a better solution. More information gathering might have revealed the source of the subordinate's dissatisfaction or additional facts which would have enabled a better plan to be drawn up.

- Over-use of criticism and under-use of praise of past performance, causing resentment on the part of the subordinate.
- Lack of explanations of why the improvement in performance is organisationally desirable.
- Lack of inducements to persuade the subordinate that the improvement is personally desirable. If Figure 2.4 (p. 54) were filled in for this subordinate, would the benefits from good performance significantly outweigh the benefits from poor performance, and were the benefits from good performance spelled out in sufficient detail (promises and threats)?
  Note 1: Threats are more likely to bring about compliance than commitment.
  Note 2: If insufficient is known about the inducements which would influence this subordinate, then information gathering on this subject may be called for.
- A diffuse structure, leading to no firm conclusions leaving the subordinate with the impression that the interaction was a 'non-event'.
- Inappropriate approach to the interaction; for example, Tell and Sell with an experienced subordinate with useful ideas of his or her own, or Problem Solving with an inexperienced subordinate or one whose solutions are organisationally unacceptable.

Plan not sufficiently specific:

- Insufficient use of information-gathering components; for example, open questions and probes, to gather the precise information needed, and summaries to crystallise solutions.
- Diffuse structure leading to no firm conclusions or over-rigid structure preventing relevant information gathering.
- Inappropriate approach to interaction (as above).

Other

If none of above hypotheses applies in your case, the following questions may help you to pinpoint why the interaction produced less satisfactory outcomes than you would have liked:

1. (a) What verbal and nonverbal components did you tend to use most during the interaction?
   (b) Were there any components in particular which appeared to have an adverse effect on the subordinate's responses or the outcomes of the interaction?
2. (a) How was the interaction structured?
   (b) Did this appear to have an adverse effect on the subordinate's responses or the outcomes of the interaction?
3. (a) What approach did you use for the interaction?
   (b) Did the approach selected appear to have an adverse effect on the interaction?

Now return to Question 6, Appendix X.

Index